smthdem

# A Christian Response to the New Genetics

# A Christian Response to the New Genetics

## Religious, Ethical, and Social Issues

Edited by
David H. Smith
and
Cynthia B. Cohen

ROWMAN & LITTLEFIELD PUBLISHERS, INC.
*Lanham* • *Boulder* • *New York* • *Oxford*

ROWMAN & LITTLEFIELD PUBLISHERS, INC.

Published in the United States of America
by Rowman & Littlefield Publishers, Inc.
A Member of the Rowman & Littlefield Publishing Group
4501 Forbes Boulevard, Suite 200, Lanham, Maryland 20706
www.rowmanlittlefield.com

PO Box 317
Oxford
OX2 9RU, UK

British Library Cataloguing in Publication Information Available

**Library of Congress Cataloging-in-Publication Data**

A Christian response to the new genetics : religious, ethical, and
social issues / edited by David H. Smith and Cynthia B. Cohen
    p. cm.
Includes bibliographical references and index.
    ISBN 0-7425-1498-6 (cloth : alk. paper) — ISBN 0-7425-1499-4 (pbk. :
alk. paper)
    1. Human genetics—Religious aspects—Christianity. 2. Genetic
engineering—Religious aspects—Christianity. I. Smith, David H., 1939–
II. Cohen, Cynthia B.

QH438.7.C48 2003
174' .28—dc21

                                                          2003005328

Printed in the United States of America

∞™ The paper used in this publication meets the minimum requirements of
American National Standard for Information Sciences—Permanence of Paper
for Printed Library Materials, ANSI/NISO Z39.48-1992.

# Contents

# Introduction

*David H. Smith and Cynthia B. Cohen*

As our understanding of human genetics has increased at an explosive rate over the last half century, genetic knowledge has become more relevant to us and to those we love. In the 1990s and early 2000s, scientists mapped the human genome and began to understand the ways in which a variety of different genes function in human beings. Their initial goal was to gain information and insight into how the genes we are born with might affect our lives and the lives of our children. The knowledge scientists uncovered is revolutionizing our understanding of human development and enlarging our power to predict what we might become. In addition, it is raising a host of challenging ethical questions that have personal import for many of us. For example:

- Embryos and fetuses may be tested for the presence of genes. Some of these genes may be linked to serious diseases that might bring suffering and even early death to a future child. Others may be associated with desired traits, as when couples seek a child of one gender, rather than the other. Should this sort of testing be banned or controlled? Or should it be mandatory? What are the responsibilities of parents, professionals, government, and the church when genetic testing is considered?
- Diagnostic genetic testing of adults or children may reveal surprising information not only about the individuals tested but about others as well. This information may be medical, as when a woman learns that she carries a gene indicating an increased possibility of developing breast cancer and realizes that her sisters might also have this gene. Or it may be social, as when testing incidentally reveals that a man is not the biological father of the child. Should genetic testing be carried out in instances

where it will provide uncertain or troubling information that will have an impact on others? How can we help people cope with the early warnings and unsought information that genetic testing may produce?

- Genetic information may be used as a basis for denying employment or health insurance to a person who has tested positive for a condition that might appear in the future. Even if the information is accurate, the fairness of these decisions is problematic, for no one controls her or his own genetic makeup. The "genetic lottery" allocates genes by chance. Should we revamp our employment and insurance systems to prevent unfair discrimination on the basis of genetic knowledge?

Genetic discoveries of the past half century have not only raised daunting ethical questions about what sort of information about our genes we should seek and what we should do with that information, but they have also set the stage for investigators of the twenty-first century to attempt to move, replace, or alter our genes in remarkable ways. For example:

- Gene transfer promises to add to or alter genes in order to treat or prevent disease; it offers revolutionary possibilities for enhancing or improving some of the traits of our children and ourselves. Moreover, genetic interventions into embryos may affect future generations, enabling us to control the sorts of children our descendants will bring into the world in ways we can scarcely imagine today. Would it be morally acceptable for us to exercise that power? How should we understand our responsibilities for the well-being of those already living and those who will come after us?
- Couples concerned about passing deleterious genes to their children have set before them an increasing range of new reproductive technologies. They might seek a sperm or egg donor who is free of the unwanted gene so that they can produce a disease-free child. Or, should reproductive cloning become available, they might elect to clone the spouse who does not carry the gene at issue. Are there limits to the lengths to which prospective parents should go to create healthy children? Are we in danger of converting procreation into a process of manufacturing children by engaging in the use of such technologies?

These powers and possibilities raise ethical, personal, and social issues of concern to all thoughtful persons. This book sets out a Christian response to those issues—a response nurtured within the Anglican tradition.

Contributors to this volume do not agree on every detail of what the Christian response to our new genetic powers should be; we don't all agree about every sentence in each chapter of this book. That is not surprising, as the Christian heritage in moral, pastoral, and ascetical theology on which we draw does not—and could not—speak with one voice on the issues we confront here. Yet the Anglican tradition is known for its efforts to strike a via media among diverse and even conflicting theological and ethical views. As John Donne, the seventeenth-century Anglican poet and priest, put it: "From extreme to extreme, from east to west, the angels themselves cannot come, but by passing the middle way between. . . ." The Anglican tradition has taken this way while retaining a distinct identity and aiming for reasonableness and consistency in its teachings.

We have followed this Anglican approach by facing up to the fact of moral dissonance and taking into account voices or perspectives that do not easily fit with our own. We are aware of a family resemblance among our views, and we believe that the disagreements among us appear on the margin rather than at the heart of the matter. We think it is helpful to imagine our work as a polyphonic chorus, rather than a solo or an attempt to sing in unison. We are not all singing the same notes, but we are all on the same page of the score.

Some may object that those within various religious traditions have no business participating in public debate about these issues in a pluralistic secular society. Their argument must be taken seriously. Religions are always particular and more or less specific. The Anglican tradition, indeed Christianity in general, is obviously a tradition that many do not share. Moreover, religious passion can be intense and many religions, including Christianity (and of course Anglicanism), have at times been overcome by zeal. As a result, they have been sources of cruelty, intolerance, and disrespect. Better, critics say, to learn from that history and to keep moral debate and religious particularity and zeal apart. Religion can only prove divisive: it has seldom been a reconciling force, they insist.

There is more truth in these claims than we would like to admit. Yet we recognize that secular traditions such as the liberal tradition of the rights of man that informed the French Revolution and the communist tradition that overtook Stalinist Russia also led to cruel and intolerant programs that violated human dignity. We hold no brief for the view that a religious perspective should simply dictate public policy. But many options exist between theocracy and total exclusion of religious tradition, image, and metaphor from public life and politics. Religious voices have been part of public debate in the United States since its founding. Visions of the good life and a civil community are often connected to religious belief. When religious leaders effectively share their views with those outside their traditions, that can help others to understand the rationale and context for their views and the views of others who respond.

Moreover, truth may come in unexpected forms and formulations; it is the height of prejudice to assume that one can learn nothing from traditions that have sustained persons and groups for millennia. Thus, if we are to sustain the democratic practices and respect for individuals that are at the foundation of our lives together, books like this one are an essential part of the conversation.

A primary set of issues that we address concerns the power and importance of moral teaching and ethics. The authors resist the idea that all imaginable choices are morally equivalent. Thoughtful persons will reflect on the new questions they face and recognize that some answers are morally better than others, that some possible answers can be ruled out on ethical grounds, and that sometimes we are in doubt or perplexed. At such times, no choice clearly commands assent as the best moral option.

The new genetics opens some perennial theological questions in powerful ways. For example, the comparative roles of fate and choice in life seem to be changing, as phenomena we once deemed beyond human control turn out to be within our power. We wonder not only how much of that power we should exercise, but, indeed, whether we are free to make any choices at all or are simply the products of our genes. As we see the influence of our genetic heritage in what we do, is there room left for us to take responsibility for our lives, or to hold other persons responsible for what they do with theirs?

Furthermore, a genetic misfortune that once seemed to be just bad luck may now come to be seen as someone's fault—perhaps that of a parent who knowingly chose to proceed with the birth of a child with a serious inherited disease, perhaps that of a physician who failed to perform a test that would have warned a family of future illness. Ultimately, the logic of blame pushes us to consider the possibility of God's own responsibility for the suffering caused by genetic disorders. Engagement with these questions is now unavoidable.

Discussions of genetics sometimes raise strong emotions because it is impossible not to identify with one's own body. Whereas bad luck in education, love, or employment seems to be something that happens to me, my genetic makeup seems to *be* me. I am the person born with that hair, nervous tic, bad teeth, and "wrong" stature. The power of genetics is as obvious to each of us as our own bodies, and genetic knowledge can be either empowering or threatening.

Questions of identity, of ethics, and of coping with misfortune are challenges that have always been central in the lives of Christians, but modern genetics raises them with special force. We think that these questions deserve more attention and discussion than they have received, and we believe that informed Christians, as well as those of other religious traditions, should be involved in the conversation. Genetic knowledge makes the work of vital and well-informed religious communities all the more necessary.

People need assistance and reconciliation as they cope with genetic knowledge. Of course, they also need the ability to rejoice. The discoveries of modern genetics can only inspire awe and reverence at the wonders of creation. Our increasing knowledge of the biochemistry of life promises help for people in misery. We may hope to see significant clinical advance in our lifetimes, thanks to research in genetics. This increase in human understanding and power is cause for celebration, and it is also a fitting occasion for some reflection.

The discussion of these matters proceeds as follows: In chapter 1, David H. Smith and Timothy Sedgwick set out the basic theological affirmations that inform our reflections and conclusions, stressing the centrality of community in our tradition and the importance of ritual and reasonableness in sustaining that community. They argue that Christians should see themselves as participating in the accomplishment of God's purposes through the use of certain genetic interventions and deny that all uses of the new genetics entail "playing God." Yet they acknowledge that it is wrong to gloss over possible abuses of our growing genetic powers. They address the problem of reconciling suffering due to our genetic legacies with the love and justice of God and the increasingly complex role of families in a world with increased genetic knowledge. They conclude with an affirmation of the importance of social justice in decisions about the use and distribution of genetic tests and possible future treatments.

In chapter 2, Ellen Wright Clayton, Cynthia B. Cohen, and Lindon Eaves explore and synthesize the genetic research and knowledge that has evolved since Gregor Mendel first set hand to the seeds of peas. They explain how our growing reproductive capabilities can be merged with our growing genetic powers to open the door to the possibility of creating children with certain selected genes. They present a picture of genetics that offers contours of exciting intellectual achievement and emerging power, even as it paints in dark shadows of uncertainties and unknown probabilities. The authors urge humility in the face of the limits of our genetic knowledge.

Chapter 3 by Mary T. White takes up the question of genetic testing of adults, children, and fetuses, explaining how this testing differs from other sorts of medical tests. Prenatal testing, newborn screening, diagnostic testing of children, and adult testing for late-onset disease raise unique ethical, social, and theological concerns. She explores the disability critique, the abortion debate, whether there is a duty to be tested, and the use of genetic information in discriminatory ways. Defense of human dignity in the face of social pressures and increased attention to the importance of informed counsel and community support are at the core of this chapter.

In chapter 4, Cynthia B. Cohen and LeRoy Walters turn to questions related to the impact of genetic interventions on our lives and those of our descendants. They present two sorts of interventions made possible by our new genetic powers—somatic cell and germline interventions—emphasizing their exploratory and experimental nature. The potential of these measures to enable us to overcome disease and to select and enhance our traits and those of our descendants is moderated by their eugenic implications. In responding to the question whether such interventions overstep human limitations and defy God, they bring to bear both stewardship and cocreationist responses. They accept somatic cell interventions as morally sound, if they are rendered safe and effective. However, they are reluctant to sanction germline interventions, which they view as morally acceptable in principle, without major safety precautions and without public discussion of their ethical and social import and public oversight of their uses.

The merger of genetic and reproductive interventions promises to enable us to test the genes in embryos and create children of our choice. In chapter 5, Cynthia B. Cohen and Mary R. Anderlik explore possible uses and misuses of such contemporary and futuristic measures as preimplantation genetic testing, gamete donation, genetic modification of gametes and embryos, and reproductive cloning. They explore the meaning of procreation and parenthood in the Christian and secular traditions, asking whether the network of relationships and responsibilities that has heretofore framed our lives is in danger of dissolving, leaving no guides for decision making save the desires of would-be parents. Use of our new genetic powers to avert genetic disease in children should instead be guided by a commitment to the good of those children, even when this focus may restrict adult choices in nontrivial ways.

Chapter 6 by Cynthia B. Cohen grapples with the mystery of our own genesis and the question of when an individual human life begins. These questions are raised by two interventions into the procreative process affecting embryos: preimplantation genetic diagnosis and germline interventions. She traces views about the moral status of the human embryo through Scripture, Christian tradition, and contemporary religious, secular, and scientific thought, making clear the differences between questions about uses of early embryos and those raised by elective abortion. She reviews several leading theories about when nascent human life gains moral status and addresses conflicting views raised by recent embryological findings that suggest that an individual organized and biologically stable embryonic entity with the moral status of a potential human being is not formed until fourteen days after fertilization. She then explores the implications of these views for the use of preimplantation genetic diagnosis and germline interventions.

Chapter 7 by Bruce Jennings and Elizabeth Heitman begins a shift to a greater emphasis on policy by setting the social context of the contemporary discussion. Instead of concerns about eugenics of the form that prevailed in the early twentieth century, the focus in our day shifts to an emphasis on social pressure, the problematics of the definition of disease, and the bewitching power that may be exercised by biomedical technology. All these factors complicate the quest for justice in a world of genetic knowledge.

Chapter 8 by Mary R. Anderlik and Jan C. Heller continues the shift begun in the previous chapter to focus on some relevant questions about money and power. Although federal funding for research in genetics has been instrumental in the knowledge explosion of recent decades, the benefits of that knowledge are inequitably distributed. Society is in the midst of a legal and political debate over ownership of genetic information, as is revealed in questions concerning the patenting of human genes; the authors suggest the importance of the metaphor of stewardship in dealing with these issues. They argue for a national health policy that will guarantee at least a minimal level of health care to all and attend to the need to avert genetic discrimination.

Chapter 9 by David A. Ames provides an example of how a religious community—in this case the Episcopal Church—can meet its responsibilities to its members and to the wider community in light of our growing genetic powers. He proposes that the church should both celebrate the new knowledge at our disposal and provide support and counsel to persons as they face bad news, hard decisions, and misunderstanding. Churches face a major educational effort, and they have an increased responsibility to provide worship forms and practices that vitally inform the minds and hearts of Christians. The church cannot possibly provide the right answers to all genetics-related questions, but it can contribute to efforts to address them. It can be prepared to offer informed and caring conversation partners and counselors, offer some guidance, and, through effective liturgy, provide food for the soul.

We started on the path that led to this book in July 2001, when the Executive Council of the Episcopal Church confirmed the appointment of a Task Force on Ethics and the New Genetics. We met over a two-year period and proposed a set of resolutions to the triennial General Convention of the Episcopal Church in 2003. *We wish to make clear, however, that the conclusions that we draw in this book do not provide an official position of the Episcopal Church.* We are not the first to recognize the importance of the issues addressed here. Various bodies and individual scholars within and outside the Anglican Communion have explored questions in genetics and ethics over the past few decades. For example, the Episcopal Diocese of Washington published an unusually helpful book, *Wrestling with the Future: Our Genes and Our Choices,* and the denomination's General Convention has passed a number of relevant resolutions on genetic testing and genetic engineering. The thinking of many Anglican theologians and ethicists is reflected in our work. Contemporary theologians and moralists from within the Roman Catholic, Methodist, Evangelical Lutheran, United Church of Christ, Presbyterian, and Jewish and Reformed traditions are among those whose writing we have turned to for assistance. We are also indebted to the work of many secularist thinkers who represent various ethical traditions. We have tried to build on their work, and that of many other scholars, and we are proud to be part of a religious tradition that encourages this catholic range of sources of insight.

We are particularly grateful to the Right Reverend Theodore Daniels for his willingness to join our group and to the Very Reverend James Lemler, whose absence on the list of names of chapter authors has the effect of greatly misrepresenting his extensive involvement in our work. Judith Granbois early on shifted her role from task force member to editor, and all readers of this book will be grateful for her rigorous hand with our prose. The Reverend Rosemari Sullivan, executive officer and secretary of the General Convention of the Episcopal Church, and the Right Reverend Robert Johnson, bishop of western North Carolina, provided us with invaluable support and counsel. We are also grateful to Summer Johnson for her prompt and efficient work on the index.

Despite all this assistance, we are under no illusion that the book that follows offers definitive and final answers to the questions we raise. We hope that we have helped to identify issues that must be addressed, for a large part of the problem for humankind and genetics is locating the moral tension or uncertainty in the right place. We try to specify points at which Christians should draw the line and say "No," others where we must offer unequivocal support, and still others where we should have the courage to admit that we don't know the answers. We mean to offer food for thought, and we volunteer our work as a statement in an ongoing public conversation—a conversation from which we have already learned and from which we will continue to learn.

# 1

# Theological Perspectives

*David H. Smith and Timothy Sedgwick*

We approach our task in this book from a distinctive angle of vision, and our goal in this chapter is to explain something of what we understand that angle of vision to be. The core of our perspective is that we see ourselves reconciled to God in Christ. We confess that in the work of Christ, life and love have triumphed over death and estrangement, and we work to make that reality more visible and accessible. Those commitments inform the life of the church, and our task here is to suggest their implications for issues raised by genetics at the beginning of the twenty-first century.

In the Anglican tradition, worship is the first response to the saving act of God in Christ. We celebrate and renew our reconciliation in the Eucharist; we acknowledge its reality in baptisms, weddings, and funerals. These rituals of incorporation and transition form us as the people of God, shaping our identity as a community and our individual identities as persons. Our reasoning about ethics and the new genetics should cohere with our ritual practices, and our ethics should fit our understanding of ourselves.

Our ethics should also be scriptural, as the liturgy is. For us, that does not mean proof texting, as if a major moral controversy could be settled by pointing to one sentence in Scripture. The scriptural record is diverse, as any document written over several hundred years must be, and it requires interpretation. Some theological and moral ideas are difficult to reconcile with Scripture, and on some topics a fairly clear general direction can be extrapolated. Christians over the centuries have attempted to do so, and the tradition of conversation about theology and ethics that has been passed along should be taken very seriously. Of course this tradition is diverse. Augustine and Aquinas, Luther and Calvin, Hooker and Butler, Temple and Kirk did not agree on everything, but we hope to draw on their thinking in what follows.

We also mean to be reasonable—using that term in a very broad sense. We reject the idea that one must choose between being rational and being Christian, between faith and reason. We hope that we write as reasonable women and men whose attitudes, hopes, and views of the world have been deeply influenced by Christian worship, life, and belief. We will challenge some aspects of the modern world, and we regret some components of historic Christianity. We seek coherence in our thought and life; we mean to be clear, logical, and comprehensible.

## THE WONDER OF CREATION AND THE POWER OF GENETICS

Our first response to modern genetics is a sense of awe. Increased understanding of the world in which we live is cause for celebration. The extraordinary power of the genetic code, its commonality among persons and across species, and the diversity it enables among humankind are nothing short of wondrous. There is nothing distinctively Christian in appreciation of this amazing new knowledge, but Christians share and rejoice in it. Our Eucharist begins with a song of praise, often the "Gloria" beginning with "Glory be to God on high," and that is just the response inspired by the new genetics.

We are further awestruck by the promise of this new knowledge to help people in trouble. Our Lord's ministry was a ministry of healing and the relief of suffering. For us, healing and the medical arts are a consistent and coherent response to Christ's ministry, a sacred vocation. The work of the Creator is good, and our ability to understand and use it is further cause for celebration.

Theology enters the picture because difficult issues surround the significance of this knowledge for our lives, because the benefits it yields may be unfairly distributed, and because it may be used for ends not in accord with God's purposes. Genetic knowledge raises questions of meaning and power—questions with which thoughtful Christians must wrestle.

## WAYS OF UNDERSTANDING OURSELVES

Scripture and tradition use several metaphors to suggest the appropriate way for human beings to understand themselves. We are particularly interested in three metaphors.

## The Image of God

Christians have often sought to clarify their responsibilities by explaining what it means to say that human beings are created in the image of God. The idea is drawn from the creation account that begins Holy Scripture. Following the creation of the land and sky from the water, after all other living beings were created, God created human beings. "Then God said, 'Let us make humankind in our image, according to our likeness;[1] and let them have dominion over the fish of the sea, and over the birds of the air, and over the cattle, and over all the wild animals of the earth, and over every creeping thing that creeps upon the earth.' So God created humankind in his image, in the image of God, he created them" (Gen. 1:26–27).

The early church drew upon this analogy in specifying the value and responsibility of humankind, as is revealed by the use of the *imago dei* in the Eucharistic Prayer in the Liturgy of Saint Basil, believed to have originated in the fourth century. As translated into English for the *Book of Common Prayer (BCP)*, the Eucharistic text reads, "We acclaim you, holy Lord, glorious in power. Your mighty works reveal your wisdom and love. You formed us in your own image, giving the whole world into our care, so that, in obedience to you, our Creator, we might rule and serve all your creatures."[2]

The basic idea is that humans are like God in that they have the capacity to act in order to preserve or bring about "the good." Exactly what responsibility requires depends upon more specific claims about how humans are created in the image of God and how they share in God's work in creation. Thus, many Roman Catholic scholars have identified the image with our power to reason, suggesting that some form of rationality is the defining attribute of human beings. Orthodox theologians have suggested that we are like God in our ability to love. Many Protestant thinkers have been highly skeptical of these endeavors, holding that whatever image of God we may have received at Creation was lost in the Fall.

Emphasis on the purposes of God and on human participation in those purposes gives our understanding of the nature of the *imago dei* features that are broadly Catholic and Orthodox. The image of God is revealed in human persons' rational and loving aspects. The knowledge of God is found in our participation in the purposes of God as they are seen in the natural order of life, lived in our life together in community, and celebrated in worship. Jesus Christ reveals the truth of creation and in that sense was from the beginning of time. As expressed in the Gospel of John, "In the beginning was the Word . . . and the Word was made flesh and dwelt among us" (1:1, 14).

Sometimes users of the concept of the "image of God" assume that if we can specify just what the "image of God" is, we will have a criterion for determining which aspects of our lives are most distinctively or essentially human. Difficulties arise for this notion when it is used as a criterion for exclusion—if we were to say that someone who is unable to reason or love lacked the characteristics that make human life valuable. Something very much like that reasoning is common in bioethics. Some writers focus attention on the concept of personhood, and persons are understood to be morally competent adults. Nonpersons are then devalued. This devaluing or exclusion is problematical on moral grounds, as it defines the human person too narrowly and calls in question the moral status of infants, the developmentally disabled and the demented.

Attempting to provide a religious rationale for such exclusions through use of the "image of God" metaphor is even worse because it mistakes the intent of the scriptural metaphor. Humans are like God in the sense that they are God's agents as they share in responsibility for God's creation by knowing it and caring for it. The metaphor of "the image of God" does not in itself define the nature of the human person and so cannot provide a litmus test of who counts as human.

Still, the metaphor of "the image of God" suggests that human beings are to be treated with something like the reverence that properly belongs only to God. The natural word to use is "respect." Our lives are worthy of respect— self-respect and the respect of others. The image of God is not something to be treated carelessly or frivolously. Developing habits of self-respect and respect for others is particularly important in the face of new genetic knowledge and possibilities. It provides a guard against overt or covert eugenics policies; it serves as one basis for a right to privacy; and it is a bulwark against research on human subjects without their consent.

## Life as a Gift

A second metaphor that powerfully reverberates in Christian consciousness is the notion of life as a gift. There is something gratuitous about the fact that we exist. The world itself, even our very lives, are not exactly our own; rather, they are gifts from a giver who is other than and prior to ourselves. The effect is to challenge any idea that we are our own creators. Our lives and the creation are good, but they are not our possessions. Instead, we are stewards or trustees of life, which is to be "tilled and kept," not exploited.[3] The images of gift and stewardship suggest both our distance from and our responsibility to God. They push us to an ethic that celebrates the diversity of life and resists treating the world or ourselves as pure raw material.

Like all the metaphors we discuss, the notion of life as a gift can be misused. In this case the misuse is rationalization of uncritical acceptance. If all life is a gift from God, and all gifts must be respected, then it might seem to follow that all misfortunes—including genetic problems—are gifts from God and crosses to bear. We resist this interpretation as carrying a valid point too far. The valid point is that the gifts of God can be seen in all things; the mistake is suggesting that everything that happens is designed for our flourishing and that acceptance is the only correct response. To the contrary, the task of stewardship is attempting to discern what is gift to be cultivated and what must be pruned, when to preserve and when to let go. A gift should not be idolatrously venerated or carelessly destroyed.

### Metaphors of Family Life

A third cluster of metaphors are domestic, referring to family life. Sometimes the church is spoken of as the "household of God." A related term is "children of God." God is referred to repeatedly as "Father." The Greek word for "household" (*oikos*), moreover, is the same word from which our word "economy" (in Greek, *eikonomia*) derives. In our exchanges with one another, we enter into the divine economy, the household of God, marked by close and loving relationships. At the heart of these relationships are the virtues of compassion, kindness, humility, meekness, patience, and above all love as a matter of bearing each others' burdens (Col. 3:12–14). A life lived in the household of God is above all a life of gratitude and thankfulness (Col. 3:16–17).

Again, these metaphors taken from family life may be misused if they suggest an inflexible and hierarchical set of domestic relations or more certainty about controversial relationship issues than we in fact possess. We are concerned with their broader connotations: that at the heart of the holy there are relations—within God, between God and God's creation, and among the members of the household of God. These domestic metaphors suggest the depth of our responsibilities for each other and our partnership with God in discerning our responsibilities.

These ways of seeing our lives—as created in the image of God, as gifts from God, and as children of God—all suggest how we should structure our relationships to each other. Christians are to care for others, especially those in need. They should be compassionate. They should seek to relieve suffering and to do good. Love is grounded in a sense of grace and gratitude, and motivated by reverence and thanksgiving for the life that is given us. Loss of these attitudes of love, hope, reverence, and thankfulness can result in a superficial preoccupation with the self and what it is "permitted" to do. Our self-worth or self-respect is then narrowly caught up in what we do. This error is what Paul described as works righteousness in contrast to justification by grace. When it occurs, the significance of our relationship with God has been lost from view. When trust in God can be sustained the central question shifts from what is fulfilling for me? Or what do I need? The question becomes what do my neighbors need? What kind of community and world do I live in? How may I honor and sustain rather than destroy other people and this creation of which I am a member?

## PLAYING GOD?

These ways of understanding our lives set the stage for our reflections on three general topics that we will pursue in the rest of this book. The first is the issue that the Greeks called *hubris* or pride: whether it is possible to assume too much power over human life. "Letting nature take its course" was once the only option, but that is no longer so. Increasingly, the genetic world is plastic to our touch. According to some critics, we are beginning to "play God" and forget our role as God's creatures and children.

As God's agents, stewards, in creation, we cannot best care for one another by rejecting in principle the development and use of genetic technologies as a matter of "playing God," which would as easily be applied against any biomedical innovation whatsoever—not only genetics but antisepsis, anesthetics, or antibiotics. Theologically this primitivism reflects a failure to recognize that God works through us, as well as on us. Reason, wisdom, and skill are not weapons against God but may be God's weapons against ignorance, self-absorption, and injustice.

At the same time, we live in a world too broken and misdirected simply to assume that everything will automatically come out right. Human history is a story of power used for bad ends as well as good ones and of the misuse of people and the rest of creation in the name of certainly good ends. Individuals are distracted from works of love by anxiety, jealousy, and the quest for security, fame, and fortune. As Christians confess in the Eucharist, "Have mercy, Lord, for we are sinners in your sight" (*BCP,* 370).

Sin is neither the first nor the last word, but its reality is undeniable. No invisible hand preserves us from walking down a wrong path. Our actions may reach too far in the attempt to secure life from suffering and ultimately death. In pursuing idols, our focus narrows. Obsessive pursuits break the human bonds of community until human persons become only striving individuals ruled by narrow self-interest and motivated by anxiety leading to despair.

Given our possibilities for good and evil, neither uncritical opposition nor blanket endorsements of new genetic possibilities are faithful responses. Instead, we must discern both moral and intellectual limits to our research and the use of subsequent technologies. We wrongly "play God" when we fail to recognize any limitations to our actions. We betray God when we fail to care for those who suffer. The very difficult issue—on which persons of good faith may differ—is where to draw the lines. What practices and procedures go too far? We will show where we think some of those lines should be drawn in the chapters that follow, but we are clear that we cannot avoid making the hard and often controversial choices that blanket permissions and prohibitions are able to avoid. Nuanced line drawing is never popular with everyone.

## SUFFERING AND THE GOODNESS OF GOD

A second important issue that genetics raises for theology arises from our belief in the goodness and power of God. The genetic lottery is unfair, and the human suffering associated with it has been extensive. Parents of a child with cystic fibrosis or Down syndrome; a couple trying to decide if one of them should be tested for Huntington disease; a young woman who discovers she carries the BRCA1 gene for breast cancer; a patient who finds that he is at increased genetic risk for Alzheimer's disease—all these persons may plausibly ask, "Why me? What have I done to deserve this?" Are these genetic predispositions and diseases the work of a just and loving God?

It would be foolish to pretend that we can glibly solve this problem, but some components of our response are clear. First, we reject a retributivist view that lays the blame for genetic problems either on the sufferers themselves or on their parents or family members. We do not dispute that retributivist texts can be found in the scriptures or that some theologians may have defended this view. Perhaps there were no genetic diseases in the Garden of Eden and will be none in Paradise. Genetic disease *may* best be seen as a component of a broken world after the Fall and before the eschaton. In this metaphoric sense, it *may* make sense to describe genetic disease as part of the world crying out for consummation and full redemption. It may be an inescapable part of the lot of humankind after the Fall. Genetic disease and disabilities, however, cannot be said to be the fault of human persons.

Categories of guilt and blame have no place in understanding the natural and often random distribution of genetic abnormalities. The birth of an impaired child is neither the parents' fault nor reflective of a blemish on their character; nor is it sensible to say that the special difficulties the child will have as it grows are somehow its fault. Of course some exceptional cases result from deficient prenatal care or diet. Even then, however, the genetic lottery has an apparently random character that defies attempts at moral domestication. Trying to find someone at fault for genetic disorders is religiously overreaching and morally destructive.

We find it equally wrong to regard genetic abnormalities as given to us for our well-being, as necessary obstacles in life understood as a school for character. On this account, we grow as we learn to cope with difficult situations in life. In the process, our characters mature and more closely approximate a kind of moral perfection. If life were too easy, true depth of character would be impossible. Thus genetic and other problems appear as necessary components in the good life, perhaps as occasions for discipleship and redemptive suffering.

We think it right to suggest that there are reaches of character that can't be found apart from disappointment, pain, and loss, and it may be impossible really to appreciate life and love without having tasted death and abandonment.

Still, attempts to use this notion of the teaching value of suffering as a way to explain or "justify" genetic disease fall far short for two reasons. First, the moral instruction of the genetic lottery is remarkably inequitable, with some persons experiencing a very hard course while others have what seems to be an easy ride. Why should these opportunities for moral growth be so unevenly distributed? Second, not everyone can respond constructively to impairment and limit. Some souls grow and shine, but others are crushed, and it is not clear that this spiritual defeat is entirely their fault.

In fact, these two attempts to hold together God's love and genetic impairment both fail because they try to explain something inexplicable.[4] We do not think God's will is so easily encompassed in the categories of human morality. Attempts to make moral sense of the theologically inexplicable create greater problems than they solve.

Two lines of thought, however, seem to us more promising. First, Christians may take comfort in their vivid sense of the presence of God in their lives. They have a clear sense of their lives as lived in the presence of God, who can be trusted if not understood. This miracle of trust in God can carry someone a long way in the face of disappointment and grief. Renewal of that trust is a central task of the church's worship and particularly its funeral liturgies. As expressed in Psalm 139 from the burial service, "If I say, 'Surely the darkness will cover me, and the light around me turn to night,' Darkness is not dark to you; the night is as bright as the day; darkness and light to you are both alike" (Ps. 139:10–11; *BCP,* 475). Although many things are inexplicable, all will somehow be well because of God's almighty power.

Second, as a related but distinct line of thought, human suffering is not explained away by the Christ's crucifixion, but the cross offers consolation. A central event in our confession of faith is God's identification with us in Christ, including Christ on the cross. God suffers with us. Those words are easy to write and read but difficult to internalize. Recognition of their significance may require a miracle; certainly explanations of why some suffer and others escape exceed our powers. Everyone knows doubt and despair. But to the extent that someone recognizes the work of God in Christ, the isolation of doubt and despair is broken. The disappointment and difficulties and heartache of suffering do not go away, but the experience of them is transformed by the fact that they are not borne alone.[5] Indeed, they are shared by the Lord of Heaven and Earth.

Neither of these responses to suffering offers an explanation of how or why genetic disorders occur in the reign of God. They involve no attempt to justify God's action or inaction. They are less speculative and more concrete. Rather, what is central to the church's confession is God's reconciling presence. The Eucharist is the church's central means of celebrating, renewing, and reminding us of God's reality and action. Christian worship keeps alive and deepens the knowledge of God's presence in our lives and so helps us to cope with worries and misfortunes, including those caused by genetics.

As the celebration of Christian faith, the Eucharist also celebrates and deepens Christian identity. Central to this identity is the idea of being the household or people of God. The Eucharist is a communal rite in which individuals come together and offer themselves to God so that they may become "members incorporate . . . in the blessed company of all faithful people" (*BCP*, 339). The celebration and renewal of community between humankind and God and among persons is not an accidental spin-off of the Eucharist; it is what the Eucharist is all about. The community of faith constituted in worship can provide support that can matter profoundly to people as they deal with genetically related knowledge and genetic disorders. Being part of the family or household of God creates obligations to others and provides consolation for all who suffer.

Two dimensions of this sense of self as a member of the people of God call for comment. One has to do with our families; the other relates to our economic and political life.

## FAMILIES

Genetic issues must always involve whole families in addition to the patients themselves. Genetic connection is a matter of biology rather than of choice. We do not choose our biological parents, grandparents, aunts, uncles, cousins, or siblings. Even with the most radical futuristic scenarios, one can exercise only limited choice over one's genetic offspring, and for the vast majority of persons those choices will always be limited. We may like some of our relatives more than others. We may tolerate some, cherish some, and keep our distance from others. There are some for whom we might be willing to give our lives and others to whom we would rather not give the time of day.

All of these feelings and affections may be oblivious to the fact of genetic connection until we begin to address some hereditary disorder. Will I donate my kidney to Uncle Bill, who needs it now, or will I hold it in reserve for my sister, who may need it in a decade? Will I tell my nieces, or my grandchildren, of the frightening results of my test? What will I do when Aunt Sarah refuses to give a blood sample that might help with a genetic diagnosis of my son? The fact of genetic connection gives us power over each other. It reveals our interdependence in ways that may be very uncomfortable, and it vividly forces the question of what, if any, special responsibilities we may owe to our biological relatives.

Given our genetic links, we have information that others may need in order to make decisions. Relatives—others with genetic links to ourselves—may ask us to undergo genetic testing in order to reveal particularities of their genetic legacy. By agreeing to such testing we can serve others in ways that no one else can. This request, however, may conflict with our own interests or the interests of third parties.

As well as our inherited genetic lineage, human beings create genetic links. Sexual desire is "hardwired" genetically. In Judaism and Christianity, this desire has been shaped and integrated into the context of the family household by making the norm for sexual intercourse that of sexual exclusivity between husband and wife. This standard is explicable, at least in part, by children's relatively long period of dependence during the process of development to maturity. In turn, children contribute to the success of the household, including care for their parents in older age. The mutual dependence of parents and children is a major reason the family has been a major value in human society in general. Judaism identified the prosperity of the family with the very promise of God. As God says to Abraham, "I will indeed bless you, and I will make your offspring as numerous as the stars of heaven and as the sand that is on the seashore" (Gen. 22:17).

The natural desires and needs that lead to the formation of families with children raise significant moral questions. For example, should persons seek to conceive children of their own when they could adopt, provide foster care for children in need, or otherwise serve others? Should persons seek the benefit of their children when that may conflict with the well-being of others? These general questions are raised in particular fashion by reproductive and genetic technologies. Should parents seek to conceive their own children when they know that they are carriers of a genetic disease that places possible future children at risk? Should they use preimplantation genetic diagnosis (PGD) to select healthy embryos to implant through in vitro fertilization (IVF), often at considerable cost? Should PGD be used to select embryos that are "above average" in order to give an advantage to future persons in their possible life pursuits? And if the use of PGD is morally appropriate, should parents use other genetic interventions in order to enhance human possibilities for the possible benefit of their children, even if such benefit gives them an unfair advantage over others? These questions will be addressed in the following chapters, but what they all share is that they raise the troubling question, "Why should parents bear children and give preference to those children?"

While children and specifically our own children are understood as gifts from God, the Christian tradition has refused to identify God's purposes and human fulfillment with any particular family. To do so would be a form of idolatry, to narrowly consecrate, worship, and serve one's own at the expense of others. God's purposes are larger than any one family. We are called into the human family and called to live out our lives as the household of God.

That has meant that Christians do not acknowledge an obligation or responsibility to marry. Marriage is an "honorable estate," but so is singleness. This idea is not revolutionary. It is based on the example of the Christ, formulated in his own distinctive way by St. Paul, and illustrated by the prominent role played by celibate religious communities in the church through the ages. Moreover, Christians do not acknowledge an obligation to have children. Christians believe that having children is optional, not a necessity for a fulfilled life or marriage. As the Prayer Book says, "if it be God's will," marriage may include the procreation of children. The conception and birth of children are to be celebrated, but parenting is not a necessary part of Christian marriage.

Christians understand parenthood as part of the broader vocation to care for and serve beyond oneself, for Christians are the procreators and not the creators of children. God is the child's creator, and the role of parent is a form—perhaps the quintessential form—of stewardship. Parents are then responsible for protecting, nurturing, and educating the child, but their authority is limited by the fact that children are gifts from God. Parental love always has two components. One side is instructing, leading, and pointing, but the other, and prior, side is listening, discovering, and liberating. Children need guidance, but they are separate and novel individuals and must be recognized as such. They should never be made to fit narrow parental expectation. This belief is reflected in baptism, where children are claimed as "Christ's own forever" (*BCP*, 308).

Procreation is much less important in the Christian view of marriage than is often supposed. Wonderful as the experience of parenting may be, in its biological forms it is unnecessary for a fulfilled or meaningful life. On the other hand, we do have a stewardship responsibility for children, as support for the practice of adoption makes clear. In a world with many children whose parents are unavailable or unable to provide care, adoption is an invaluable practice. The existence of children needing parents provides a wonderful opportunity for persons who wish to play a parental role, but the moral driving force in adoption is the needs of children, not of prospective adoptive parents. Adoption properly begins with parental love and strength at least as much as from a "need" to parent. These components are widely accepted in theologies of marriage today. They suggest that childlessness is not a horrendous evil and that children are to be accepted and loved for who they are and not for what parents might wish they were.

The development and use of genetic technologies offer more powerful means of intervention in the forming of children, and these interventions will affect future generations. Given a Christian view of family and children, care for children is the highest of obligations, but genetic intervention in human life is limited by the fact that children are not our own. We will explore the implications of these claims in chapters 6 and 7.

## SOCIAL JUSTICE

Given the understanding that humans are created in the image of God, that each life and person is a gift from God, and that we are all children of God sharing in the household of God, Anglicans have characteristically defended a concept of justice in which fairly meeting the needs of all is crucially important. This conception of justice is central to Christian scripture and tradition. It is reflected in the Hebrew Bible's concept of covenant and people of God, in the proclamation and understanding of the Kingdom of God that is so central to Jesus' proclamation, and in the words and actions of the prophets. Justice is at the heart of the household of God celebrated in Holy Communion as reflected in the apostle Paul's concept of the body of Christ. A just society would be one in which all acknowledge their responsibilities for others, in which the conscience of each person is honored, and where the basic needs of all are met.

Reasonable, faithful persons have disagreed and will continue to disagree about the implications of a commitment to justice. We believe that it is fair to say, however, that any Christian vision of justice carries with it the claim that the basic needs of all persons should be met. These needs include everyone's ability to participate fully in human society, as required by the fact that all persons are children of God sharing a common household.

Roman Catholics have claimed that this requirement is the most basic moral demand of Christian faith and so have spoken of meeting basic human needs as basic justice.[6] Basic justice is basic in that it is more fundamental than claims about the rights of property. While property rights are important components in a just society, they are not absolute. Life and the world are gifts; we are their stewards, and God is their owner, if anyone is. Human community is more fundamental than economic or property rights.

We call this view radical, and in a sense it is, but it is the radicalism of the Bible, of Augustine and Aquinas, Luther and Calvin, Richard Hooker, F. D. Maurice, and William Temple. This view does not require "socialism" or the denial of a right of private property in land, money, or things. There are compelling reasons for individuals to hold jurisdiction over property, as Christianity has insisted at least since the time of Thomas Aquinas. We proudly support the basic structure of liberal democracy, of American democratic institutions. But in novel situations, for example the issue of property rights in genetic sequences, the legitimacy of a property right by the inventor or discoverer cannot simply be assumed but must be argued for. We will return to this issue in chapter 9.

A final component of justice concerns the locus of decision-making authority. Justice concerns not only what should be done, but who should decide. In addressing this question, we find a helpful resource in the so-called principle of subsidiarity, first clearly enunciated in the Roman Catholic tradition.[7] The core idea is that the ideal decision makers are the persons closest to the issues and facts. Individual persons are honored and respected only when the power to make decisions affecting their own lives is honored. The burden of proof is, therefore, on someone who wants to argue that the most concerned persons ought *not* decide. Whenever possible, decisions should be made at the local level rather than in some centralized location. There are times when centralized authority should intervene—if local decisions are patently unjust or biased, for example, or if local resources are inadequate to resolve a problem. This view does not rule out government action, but it is an argument for limited government and for maximum local autonomy consistent with basic demands of justice.

When applied to the issues with which we are concerned here, the implication of the principle of subsidiarity is that decisions about genetic information or responses to genetic disease ought to be made by the persons most directly affected. This conclusion is rooted in the notion of basic respect for persons that we discussed earlier, but it is not simply a matter of *individual* rights, for several persons are often directly involved. Perhaps an individual's or family's choices should be overridden by health professionals or the state in come circumstances, but those circumstances are rare and require rigorous justification.

With these general considerations in place we turn to explore the issues in more detail. We begin with a brief summary of the biology of genetics.

## NOTES

1. Image (*tselm*) and likeness (*demut*) are nearly synonymous. In Hebrew they convey the notion of representation: humankind is a "representation of God who is like God in certain respects." Anthony A. Hoekama, *Created in God's Image* (Grand Rapids, Mich.: Eerdmans, 1986), 13.

2. *The Book of Common Prayer* (New York: Church Hymnal, 1979), 373. For history of the text see Marion J. Hatchett, *Commentary on the American Prayer Book* (Minneapolis: Seabury, 1980), 377.

3. For a philosophical analysis of gift as central to human responsibility and self-understanding see Jacques Derrida, *The Gift of Death* (Chicago: University of Chicago Press, 1995), 40–41.

4. For a somewhat larger discussion of these approaches in the tradition, see David H. Smith, "Suffering, Medicine, and Christian Theology" in Stephen E. Lammers and Allen Verhey, *On Moral Medicine* (Grand Rapids, Mich.: Eerdmans, 1987), 255–261.

5. See Bradley Hanson, "School of Suffering," in Lammers and Verhey, *On Moral Medicine*, 249–255.

6. The National Conference of Catholic Bishops, *Economic Justice for All* (Washington, D.C.: Office of Publishing and Promotion Services, United States Catholic Conference, 1986), para. 39, 68, 77.

7. See Pope Pius XI, *Quadragesimo anno* (1931), para. 79.

# 2

## Basic Biological Concepts

*Ellen Wright Clayton, Cynthia B. Cohen,*
*and Lindon Eaves*

It is not unusual to open a newspaper and read of yet another discovery about our genes. Most of us have been taken by surprise by the pace of these discoveries. The structure of DNA was first described less than fifty years ago, and now we know the location of many genes. We are even beginning to understand the sometimes tight and sometimes loose connections between genes and disease.

The shifting landscape of genetic discovery has led some of us to believe that we can never understand this complex field. Genetics, however, is not that difficult to understand if presented in ordinary language and explained by analogy with things that are familiar to us. Because ethical and theological analysis depends on an accurate understanding of the biology involved, that is what we plan to do here.

In the chapters that follow, we address a wide array of topics: genetic testing, genetic modification, new reproductive technologies, and "cloning." It is our purpose to describe some of the basic concepts in these areas, as well to provide a framework for understanding how these topics, which may seem unrelated, fit together. We begin with an extended discussion of genetic variation and gene-environment interactions and their implications for humanity. We then turn to the ways in which increasing understanding of genetics affects and will affect health care.

### STARTING WITH THE SEQUENCE

The genetic information that is passed from one generation to the next is found in DNA, an enormously long molecule that contains the basic roadmap for biological development spelled out in four chemical compounds called *bases* (adenine, cytosine, thymine, and guanine, usually abbreviated as A, C, T, and G). Humans actually share 99.9 percent of this sequence. Put another way, 999 out of 1,000 of the letters in the sequence appear in the same order in all people. The remaining 0.1 percent of the sequence is where variation among individuals comes in.

The main actor in the long DNA molecule is the *gene*. A gene is a segment of DNA that "codes" and represents the blueprint for a product, usually a protein. It currently appears that humans have approximately 30,000 genes. Genes in turn are contained on very long pieces of DNA that are organized as chromosomes. Humans typically have twenty-three pairs of *chromosomes*. In twenty-two of these pairs, the two parts are always similar to each other, so that a person has two versions, or *alleles*, of each gene. The last pair, the sex chromosomes, can differ, depending on whether you are a man or a woman. Females have two X chromosomes and so have two versions of these genes as well as of all the others. Males, by contrast, have one X and one Y chromosome; these chromosomes are completely different from each other, so that males have only one copy of the genes found on each of these chromosomes.

What happens when genes contain variations? Sometimes, the variations are silent, appearing to make no difference to biological function. Sometimes, variations simply make us look different from each other. Differences in hair and eye color, for example, are caused by genetic variation. Certain genetic variants make people ill or increase the chance that they will get sick. Particular changes in certain genes, such as BRCA1 and BRCA2, for example, make some women more likely to develop breast cancer even though any woman can still get this disease without these changes. The word *mutation* is often used to describe those variations that adversely affect function.

## HOW CAN GENETIC CHANGES BE DETECTED?

The most common approach to learning whether a person has a genetic variant associated with a disorder is to look for the effect of the mutation on the person, or what we call *phenotypic* manifestations. For instance, a boy will be diagnosed with hemophilia A if he bleeds far too easily and if testing shows that he has abnormally low levels of Factor VIII, a blood clotting factor. Children with cystic fibrosis typically do not grow as well as other children and have respiratory problems; the diagnosis of this condition is usually confirmed by finding an abnormally high amount of salt on their skin, which is the result, we now know, of an abnormal salt or chloride channel in the body.

When a disorder is caused by having too many or too few chromosomes or where large parts of chromosomes have been lost or moved, looking at the chromosomes through the microscope can assist in diagnosis. For example, a person with Down syndrome has an extra chromosome 21, for a total of three. This sort of microscopic examination is useful only for fairly large changes in the chromosomes and typically cannot detect small additions or deletions.

Sometimes it is necessary to test the DNA itself. Perhaps the results of phenotypic test are modestly, but not definitively, abnormal, as sometimes happens with children who appear to have cystic fibrosis. Perhaps the person is not yet symptomatic, or it is not yet known what phenotypic or clinical manifestation to look for. People with the mutation for Huntington disease, for example, have the genetic change from the moment of conception. They may not develop symptoms for decades, but the mutation can be detected at any time by direct DNA testing. The same is true for mutations in BRCA1 and BRCA2. Numerous methods now exist to test DNA directly, and more are being developed all the time.

## WHAT DOES KNOWING THE RESULTS OF GENETIC TESTING TELL US ABOUT WHO WE ARE?

Is human life simply the inexorable playing out of the genes that are found in the fertilized egg? The success of materialism, reductionism, and determinism as foundations for scientific insight and technological progress has encouraged many to believe that humans ultimately are "nothing but" sophisticated machines constructed from and determined by elementary laws of physics and chemistry. Striving for change is pointless; fate was settled long before birth. The result of this orientation is moral skepticism or cynicism.

A full analysis of these issues is outside the scope of this book, but the outline of our answer is clear enough. We can accept the notion that everything we do is affected and shaped by our genetic makeup, but we reject genetic reductionism, the view that genes determine everything. That claim is incredible on its face. First, it ignores the reality that from its first instants of existence, the human zygote is interacting with its environment, beginning with the uterus and continuing on after birth through the natural and social environment in which a baby lives. From childhood through old age, biological and psychological development is shaped by the particulars of the surrounding world. Genes continue to matter throughout life, but they are not the only determinants of thought and action.

Many large genetic epidemiological studies have shown that genetic differences do indeed influence a wide variety of human traits—not only physical and physiological traits such as stature, body weight, blood pressure, or heart function, but a wide range of behavioral traits including personality, abilities, and even socioeconomic success and social or religious values. However, it is a grave mistake to assume that genes are the only, or even the greatest, part of the story of human differences. One example will suffice to make the point. Developed countries in the world are currently experiencing an "epidemic" of adult-onset diabetes, obesity, and high blood pressure. All these traits are influenced in important ways by genetic variation, but the dramatic increase in their prevalence has occurred not because of changes in our genes—genes don't change that quickly—but because of changes in our environment and levels of physical activity.

Moreover, it is one thing to demonstrate that genes and/or environmental effects contribute to particular human differences, but it is quite another to identify the specific genes or environments that create such phenotypic differences. This identification is difficult for several reasons. The number of genes and environmental factors may be very large. Complex traits are affected by large numbers of individual genetic and environmental factors whose individual effects are usually too small to stand out against the noise created by all the others. Understanding where characteristics come from does not get much easier even if one looks solely at the genes. The number of possible combinations among the 30,000 genes humans are thought to have exceeds the number of humans who have ever lived. These genetic differences interact, making it difficult to predict how combinations of genes behave simply from knowing what each gene does in isolation. Thus merely reading the genetic code of an individual may not allow us to predict much about how the person's genes work with any degree of certainty. And of course, genes do not act in isolation from the environment in which the person lives.

Most importantly, the organism is not simply the sum of its genetic and environmental influences. Humans are not passive recipients of their genetic code. Humans act. Their genes affect their interactions with the physical and social world around them, and those worlds are changed as a result of their actions. The result is a changed environment that affects genetics over time. Science itself is but one of the astonishing ways in which humans interact with one another and the world around them. Human actions are limited or empowered by biological, social, and economic forces. They are actions of response given meaning by the way humans interpret them to themselves and each other. Sorting out the relative power of the various determinants of human action, and the reach of human initiative, is a difficult task; although science has made some progress, the wealth of possible modes of analysis reflects a human person who is richly textured in ways that we are only now beginning to analyze from a scientific perspective. Scientists are reluctant to speak of "mystery," but there is no better word to summarize the complexity of human persons and their actions.

Genetic reductionism, therefore, is wrong because it oversimplifies genetics, ignores the power of environmental factors, and fails to take account of the human power to interpret, initiate, and explain. Everything we do is shaped in some way by our genetic makeup; very few things we do are entirely so determined. We have some choice about how we respond to the genetic features that we and other persons have received. Thus, far from absolving us of responsibility, modern genetics extends the scope of responsibility by expanding the possible terrain of choice.

## HOW CAN GENETIC INFORMATION BE USED TO IMPROVE HEALTH?

The most obvious use for genetic information at present is to influence treatment and health-promoting behavior, particularly when the evidence for the efficacy of intervention is strong. It is known, for example, that a child with cystic fibrosis is more likely than other children to need a special diet or pancreatic enzymes to gain weight. A young child with sickle cell anemia and a fever is at much greater risk of overwhelming bacterial infection and therefore needs closer evaluation and follow-up and often powerful antibiotics. A child with phenylketonuria needs a diet low in phenylalanine and high in tyrosine to avoid severe mental retardation and to achieve intelligence in the normal range. Genetic risk information can alter intervention even for multifactorial traits or incompletely penetrant traits. Adults with a strong family history of early onset serious cardiovascular disease clearly should pay closer attention to control of weight, cholesterol, and hypertension because they may have inherited mutations associated with this disorder.

The desirability of testing is not as clear when there is no strong evidence for the efficacy of intervention, an issue discussed in more detail in later chapters. When it first became possible to test for mutations in BRCA1, there was no evidence to prove that early intervention—such as early mammography or prophylactic mastectomy or anything else—affected long-term outcome.[1] Why then did some women, and men, want to be tested? Some simply wanted to resolve uncertainty or to receive reassurance. Both men and women often wanted to know their genetic status for their children's sake, to let them know whether they were or were not at risk. In later chapters, we will attempt to understand why people seek this sort of knowledge and will ask whether some reasons for being tested are better than others. Genetic information can also be used outside the clinical context, for example, to limit access to insurance and employment and to challenge notions of personal responsibility. Here, as well, we will ask whether theologically informed ethical principles can shed any light on the appropriateness of such social responses to genetic information.

## GENETICS AND CREATING CHILDREN

Genetic information is often used to inform decisions about having children. Some people reject any use of genetic information in reproductive decision making, seeing the idea of attempting to alter the natural course of events as unacceptable because they believe that acting would alter God's plan. Others may be willing to use this information to decide not to have any more children or any children at all once they understand their risk of having a child with a certain genetic trait. Increasingly, however, couples consider other options.

### Methods of *Selecting* Embryos and Fetuses

Many opportunities to use genetic information to aid in decisions about procreation arise as a result of technologies that were developed to assess the health of the developing fetus. Techniques such as amniocentesis and chorionic villus sampling make it possible to obtain fetal cells, which can then be examined for genetic abnormalities, using whichever phenotypic, chromosome, and direct DNA tests are required. Ultrasound can detect a host of problems that can occur in the way fetuses develop, such as neural tube defects and kidney abnormalities, many of which have a significant genetic component. If a problem is detected, the only choices usually available to the pregnant woman and her partner are to continue the pregnancy, perhaps altering the time or manner of delivery or preparing for postpartum care, or to have an abortion.[2]

People vary widely in defining which conditions are sufficiently severe to warrant testing and possible termination of pregnancy. In the United States, amniocentesis is most often performed when the pregnant woman is more than thirty-four years old because older women are more likely to have a child with an extra chromosome, such as chromosome 21, which causes Down syndrome. Others seek prenatal diagnosis to determine whether the fetus they carry is affected with a single-gene disorder, such as Tay-Sachs disease, a disease characterized by progessive neurologic decline and death by the age of four to five years of age. Still other people seek prenatal diagnosis of mutations that cause or predispose to late-onset disease, such as Huntington disease or BRCA1, or even diagnosis of gender where there is no risk of an X-linked disorder that could affect male offspring. Most clinicians, however, refuse to fulfill such requests for sex selection.

The possibility of creating embryos outside the uterus, while technically and physiologically burdensome as well as expensive, provides further opportunities for using genetic information to avoid having children with certain traits. The development of in vitro fertilization (IVF) provided us with a novel power to observe and manipulate the human embryo as it develops in a laboratory dish. The advent of genetic testing gave us the additional ability to learn about genes present in embryos and to select or reject embryos for transfer to a woman's uterus on the basis of this information. To understand how these methods of embryo selection work, it is first necessary to grasp the main details of the IVF procedure.

In vitro fertilization gets its name from the fact that fertilization occurs outside the body in a glass dish (in vitro), instead of in a woman's fallopian tube. In almost all IVF procedures, the woman gives herself daily injections of a sequence of powerful hormones that cause her to ovulate and produce about a dozen eggs. Just before ovulation, her eggs are removed in a minor surgical procedure known as transvaginal aspiration. Meanwhile, semen has been obtained from the man and is now introduced into individual culture dishes into which an egg has been inserted. Any embryos that result are usually transferred to the woman on the second or third day after egg retrieval, when they comprise four to eight cells.

IVF success rates, meaning that the procedure has resulted in the birth of a baby, are about 20 percent for each initiated cycle, although the numbers reported vary widely. In any event, the rate of success is highly dependent on the causes of infertility. Younger women tend to have greater success than older ones.

IVF has been widely embraced as a new way to create babies for those who are infertile. In recent years, its uses have been extended beyond infertility to avoiding passing deleterious genes to one's children and to giving children certain specific traits.

## Preimplantation Genetic Diagnosis

Preimplantation genetic diagnosis (PGD) provides a way to identify the genes in embryos created through IVF and to select those that their creators wish to implant. PGD entails creating several embryos in laboratory dishes. At an early stage, a single cell is removed from each embryo, and its genetic makeup is analyzed. Since an embryo's cells at this point are still exact duplicates of each other, the results tell geneticists whether the remaining cells in each embryo have the gene at issue. If the embryo is found to be suitable, it can be transferred to the woman's uterus and, if things go well, a child without the gene of concern will be born. This method is confined to use on whatever genes happen to have been imparted to the embryo by egg and sperm. It does not change the genetic components of those embryos.

The primary use of PGD has been to avoid the birth of children with major illnesses such as Huntington disease, sickle cell anemia, or cystic fibrosis. Couples can elect to discard affected embryos and transfer other embryos free of the genes connected with a serious condition. Some couples choose this method to avoid an agonizing decision about abortion, since PGD does not require becoming pregnant and then learning that a fetus is affected.

The use of PGD has gradually extended beyond disease prevention to se-lection of characteristics. For instance, it was initially used to detect whether an embryo had a gene connected with a serious disease that affected only male offspring. To avoid having a child with this condition, a couple uses PGD to screen multiple embryos created in vitro and then selects only fe-male embryos for transfer. This use of PGD assures the couple that their baby girl will not have the disease of concern.

However, at some fertility clinics, the use of PGD for sex selection has been extended beyond therapy to enhancement. Couples who want to have a child of one gender—perhaps they want a boy first—may use PGD to se-lect only male embryos. In the future, many predict that PGD will be used more directly to enhance children by allowing couples to select embryos with genes linked with tall stature or a certain hair or eye color. Another use of PGD that extends beyond its original purpose of disease prevention is the creation of a child with a certain genetic and immunological makeup to serve as a tissue donor to a family member with a serious medical condition.

## DNA Chip Analysis

In the future, DNA chips may be used to provide more accurate analyses of genes in embryos. These chips carry DNA fragments in a pattern of microscopic blocks. Each block can determine whether or not a particular gene is present in an embryo. DNA chips will enable us to produce computer-generated profiles of the attributes of embryos within a few hours. This technology might then be used to identify embryos with genes associated with serious disease or traits the parents consider desirable and to select or discard them on that basis. It there-fore promises a more accurate and wide-ranging way to analyze the genes in embryos created in vitro than does PGD.

## Methods of Creating Embryos without Certain Genetic Variations

Rather than create embryos in vitro and then discard those with unwanted genes, some elect to create embryos that will be free of the genes of concern from the start. They can do so by using sperm and eggs from donors who do not have the genes at issue to create an embryo by means of IVF. In theory, they could also clone a single cell that is free of the unwanted gene to cre-ate an embryo without that gene.

## Sperm and Egg Donation

Sperm and egg donation can be used not only to bypass infertility for those who cannot produce their own gametes, but also to create embryos that are free of genes associated with inherited disease. Although sperm donation does not necessarily call for the use of IVF, since a pregnancy can be achieved with donated sperm using simple household instruments, using donated sperm does sometimes proceed by means of IVF. Egg donation, in contrast, requires the use of IVF. Some couples have chosen to substitute the gametes of donors who are free of the disease-related mutation at issue during IVF. In this way, they can avoid passing the deleterious genes they bear on to their children.

Other couples have used sperm and egg donation to create children with certain specific traits. Sperm banks and egg donation clinics (at the time of this writing, eggs cannot be frozen for later use) often keep records indicating the genetic history, features, and interests of would-be donors. Those seeking to create a child of a certain sort can select a donor likely to help them produce a child who falls into the categories they are seeking. Couples have been known to advertise for egg donors of a certain height, athletic ability, IQ, and type of education in the hope of having a child with related characteristics. When IVF is used in combination with gamete donation, the resulting child is a genetic descendant of one biological parent and of the donor.

## GENETICS AND FUTURE INTERVENTIONS

It is not possible to anticipate all the possible ways in which genetic information and technology might be used in the future, but certain technologies are sufficiently likely to become effective to warrant consideration now. Two of those are cloning and genetic modification.

Cloning, which is more accurately characterized as somatic cell nuclear transfer (SCNT), involves taking an egg, destroying its nucleus, which contains the chromosomes, and inserting the nucleus of another cell. The resulting cell, which contains almost all the DNA of the donor,[3] can develop in two different ways. One path is to permit the cell to divide, form an embryo, and implant it in a woman's uterus to be gestated to develop a new child. There is no proof that this feat has been accomplished in human beings, although one group has claimed success, and a number of groups have announced plans to try. Such so-called *reproductive cloning* has been highly controversial, leading to numerous calls for regulation and outright bans. The reasons for concern are many, including the emerging evidence that all the mammals that have been cloned to date have developed abnormally, raising the fear that any child created by cloning would also be irreparably harmed.

Creating a new child, however, is not the only potential use for this technology. The process of SCNT may also be useful in creating cells and tissues that can be used to repair damaged body parts. The first steps would take place as described above to create an embryo; instead of implanting the embryo, however, certain cells would be removed from it and used to create stem cells, which could then be coaxed to develop into any cells or tissues that are needed. This proposed use has been referred to as *therapeutic cloning* or *cloning for research or treatment*. Using cloned cells for treatment, rather than stem cells that were derived from other sources, would reduce the risk of rejection in much the same way as using matched organs for transplantation. Much needs to be learned about how to create these cells and how to direct them to develop in the desired fashion, but questions will still remain about the ethical and theological appropriateness of creating and using such cells.

*Genetic modification* or *gene transfer*[4] seems, to many, the logical goal of genetic technologies: If a gene has a mutation that makes it malfunction, why not fix it? This goal has turned out to be difficult to achieve. It is hard to get a new gene to the right place and to coax it to work appropriately. To date the successes have been very limited and the failures sometimes disastrous. Here as well, we can anticipate that some of these technical problems will be resolved, leaving us to consider the appropriateness of using genetic modification, which can be accomplished in two different ways.

One kind entails modifying body cells in the already existing person— so-called *somatic genetic modification*. The other—*germline genetic modification*—involves altering cells in the embryo, which could permit more genetic disorders to be fixed but which also alters the eggs or sperm so the changes will be passed on to future generations. This potential to affect future generations has made germline genetic modification far more controversial. Eventually, couples and individuals will no longer be limited to using only those embryos that they happen to produce in vitro. Instead, they will be able to combine IVF with new methods of gene transfer to create embryos of their own design. Some will use these technologies to create embryos that are free of disease-related genes while others will employ them to shape features of their future children. In some instances, they will do so for therapeutic purposes and in others for purposes of enhancement. A combination of cloning and genetic modification of the resulting embryos could also be used to enhance future children. In such a case, those cloning themselves would not merely duplicate their own genes in embryos but would replace some genes with new ones that they consider superior to create a new, improved version of themselves!

Clearly, Christian understandings of the significance of procreation and parenthood are challenged by our developing abilities to fashion embryos in a laboratory dish into children who are free of disease or who have selected features. Deciding to use such forms of procreation seems a far cry from the decisions we used to make to try to have children in the old-fashioned ways in the privacy of our homes. Yet procreation, especially that carried out in a glass dish, is not exclusively a private matter. Bringing children into the world involves a shared, intimate relationship between those who would be parents and a second close relationship between parents and children. Consequently, evaluating which, if any, are right uses of these reproductive and genetic technologies requires careful consideration of the personal and social meaning of procreation, the obligations of parents, the good of the resulting children, and the integrity of family bonds. Procreation is inseparable from broader social relations and goods in that it brings new members into the community who are owed care and protection. Hence, it also calls for reaffirmation of core social values such as recognizing the equal dignity and worth of each person and refraining from treating individuals only as a means to the ends of others.

## CONCLUSION

The structure of DNA was first described in 1953.[5] Looking back on the fifty years that have passed since the publication of that historic paper, the amount that has been learned about genetics, about how genes affect human well-being, and about how we as humans are related to all creation, is simply staggering. Certainly, this perspective of mastery and promise is the one that pervades the media and hence the public imagination. Some of this new knowledge indeed has already led to improvements in clinical diagnosis and care. For most people, these achievements are just cause for celebration.

It is important, however, to remember also how much is *not* known. We must realize that understanding these biological processes is always more complicated than it first appears and that each new discovery opens up new areas of biology that are not understood. To select just one example, the "central dogma" of genetics for many years was that each gene "coded" for one and only one product or protein. Partly as a result of this tenet, it was predicted that humans had over 100,000 genes since we are such complex organisms. When the "rough draft" of the human genome sequence—the order in which the bases appear—was completed in 2001, however, it was discovered that humans have only about 30,000–40,000 genes. The reality of this small number of genes doomed the central dogma because genes must have more than one product. Some progress is already being made in understanding how one gene can have more than one product, but much remains to be learned. Consequently, as a prelude to the discussions in the rest of this book, we wish to urge the importance of humility as we think about humankind's ability to understand all there is to know about our genes. It seems to us fair to say that, at least in the foreseeable future, no matter how rapid scientific progress may be, we will not know everything about how genes affect human health and disease.

## NOTES

1. For a debate about some of the newer evidence about interventions, see, e.g., H. jers-Heijboer, B. van Geel, W. L. van Putten et al., "Breast Cancer after Prophylactic Bilateral Mastectomy in Women with a BRCA1 or BRCA2 Mutation," *New England Journal of Medicine* 345, no. 3 (July 19, 2001): 159–164; A. Eisen and B. L. Weber, "Prophylactic Mastectomy for Women with BRCA1 and BRCA2 Mutations—Facts and Controversy," *New England Journal of Medicine* 345, no. 3 (July 19, 2001): 207–208.

2. In a few cases, the child's outcome can be improved by starting treatment during the pregnancy. The best example of prenatal therapy is giving blood transfusions to babies with profound anemia who are developing heart failure, but other prenatal treatments are likely to be developed.

3. DNA is also found in the mitochondria, the primary energy-producing parts of the cell, which are located in the cytoplasm or outside the nucleus. Thus, a cell created by SCNT contains the mitochondrial DNA of the egg and the nuclear DNA of the donor cell.

4. We use the terms "genetic modification" and "gene transfer" rather than the more commonly used term "gene therapy" for two reasons. The latter term implies efficacy, and these interventions to date have only rarely been successful. The techniques theoretically could be used to improve characteristics as well as to treat illness, raising questions about the proper role of therapy.

5. J. D. Watson and F. H. C. Crick, "Molecular Structure of Nucleic Acids—A Structure for Deoxyribose Nucleic Acid," *Nature* 171 (1953): 737–738.

# 3

# The Many Facets of Genetic Testing

*Mary T. White*

## IDENTITY AND CONTROL THROUGH GENETIC TECHNOLOGY

A variety of diagnostic technologies can be used to identify the genetic basis of human similarities and differences, in terms of our physical attributes and certain aspects of our behavior and personality. Today, genetic testing is primarily used to diagnose disease or predispositions to disease. The most common form of genetic testing, *prenatal testing*, is used to diagnose chromosomal disorders in developing fetuses considered at high risk of disease or disability. *Newborn screening* programs are mandated by states as a public health measure. They are targeted at certain conditions at birth that can be prevented or treated if diagnosed early. *Carrier screening* is performed to determine whether individuals carry recessive genes that they may pass on to their offspring even though they are not affected themselves. Genetic tests can also be used *diagnostically*, to identify or confirm hundreds of genetic conditions in children and adults, or to determine the likely course of a disease. Finally, *presymptomatic genetic testing* is increasingly used to identify people who are at risk of developing diseases for which they have no symptoms at the time of testing (See chapter 2).

Genetic testing offers new opportunities for choice and control. For example, today, through prenatal testing, we may choose the kinds of children we *don't* want to bring into the world. In the next generation, we may be able to choose the kinds of children we *do* want to bring into the world. The choices we make reveal which kinds of similarities and differences we most value and disvalue. Our choices may also lead to prediction of our disease risks, which may offer opportunities for planning ahead or taking preventive action. But powers of genetic prediction can be burdensome. Do we really want to know our fate—that we will likely suffer the ravages of cancer or Alzheimer's disease? If no preventive intervention exists, is genetic information empowering or incapacitating? How much responsibility do we want to take for our health or the health of our children? How much of our fate or future would we rather leave to powers beyond our control?

This chapter will discuss the types of genetic tests that are currently available, exploring some of the medical, ethical, and theological questions they raise for clergy and laypersons. This discussion is intended to serve only as an overview of some of the primary concerns that have been identified to date; for further or more detailed exploration of these issues please consult the bibliography at the end of the book.

## WHAT GENETIC TESTING TELLS US

Genetic tests are perhaps most commonly thought of as tests that examine the structure of an individual's chromosomes, analyze specific gene sequences in the DNA molecule, or determine the presence or absence of particular genes. Tests for defects in chromosomal structure use a small sample of cells to produce a karyotype, which is a picture of all the chromosomes contained in one human cell. All normal human cells have twenty-three pairs of chromosomes, which are revealed on a karyotype lined up by size. When they are arranged in this way, it is easy to spot chromosomal abnormalities, which typically take the form of extra or missing chromosomes, chromosomal translocations (in which portions of one chromosome are broken and reattached to another) or deletions or insertions of parts of chromosomes.

Testing the DNA molecule for errors in gene sequences involves identifying the order of the nucleotide bases (AGGCTA . . . , etc.) in a particular stretch of DNA, and looking for unusual patterns, additions, or deletions of nucleotides in comparison with what is thought to be the normal pattern. Other types of genetic tests look for the presence of particular gene products—proteins or metabolites—that indicate the presence (or absence) of particular genes (see chapter 2).

Although the correlation between genotype and phenotype (visible bodily characteristics) is still largely a mystery, the notion that our genes determine our identity has been widely promulgated by the media and popular science writers. The idea that "genes make protein which makes us" has been called the "Central Dogma," and it dominates much of popular and professional discussions of genetics. Frequent reference to genes as "the instructions for life," the "master molecule," the "program" or "code" for human development, reinforces the notion that who we are and what we become is largely determined by our genes. However, this view is highly misleading. The process of becoming a human being requires innumerable other biological processes within cells, tissues, organs, and the whole organism that are constantly responding to external stimuli throughout the life of the individual. Thus while our new diagnostic capabilities offer exciting opportunities to learn something about our genetic endowment, it is important to realize that genetic testing provides a very limited kind of information about our health.

## GENETIC COUNSELING

Because genetic testing is so value-laden, and test results so fraught with psychological and social ramifications for individuals and their families, physicians are urged, and in some cases legally required, to provide comprehensive information about the risks and benefits of testing to patients before testing is performed. The scope and use of genetic testing have grown exponentially over the past generation, however, and many physicians have been unable to keep pace with advancing knowledge. Moreover, most are not able to spare the time for the lengthy discussion their patients may need. Instead, when possible, they refer patients to a genetic counselor.

Genetic counseling emerged in the late 1960s as a multidisciplinary profession dedicated to helping patients use genetic testing to achieve the greatest possible health benefits. The responsibilities of genetic counselors include assessing patients' genetic risks, educating them about the benefits and burdens of testing and their alternatives, providing accurate interpretation of test results, and supporting individuals in their decision making following testing. Professionally trained genetic counselors have an average of two years of graduate education that involves intensive study of genetics, genetic diseases, ethics, and personal and family counseling. Because there are still relatively few training programs, there are currently fewer than two thousand formally educated genetic counselors in the United States. Many other health care professionals, including nurses and some physicians, may also provide genetic counseling, although not all have trained specifically for this purpose.

Genetic counseling has evolved as a practice that is best described as "patient-centered," in which the focus of counseling is driven by the needs and values of the particular individual(s) seeking testing. The aim of counseling is to enable people to make decisions about testing that are consistent with their own goals and beliefs. To this end, counselors are trained to communicate in value-neutral terms and to express empathy and unconditional respect for their patients'[1] feelings, values, and decisions, but to counsel "nondirectively," refraining from offering guidance. Although many have argued convincingly that value-neutral communication is not possible, maintaining that ideal helps to ensure that counselors stay alert to their own biases and make every effort to avoid manipulating others' decisions. A typical counseling session thus begins with risk assessment and a certain amount of education. Then counselors invite their patients to voice their concerns and provide information and support as patients explore their alternatives. Counselors offer specific recommendations only when circumstances indicate that testing offers clear opportunity for medical benefit. As tests are developed to diagnose diseases for which preventive or therapeutic interventions are available, it is likely that genetic counselors will increasingly find themselves departing from the nondirective stance.[2]

Individuals are usually referred for genetic counseling by a physician who is concerned about their genetic risks. However, some genetic testing is also commercially available, and contacting a laboratory directly may seem attractive to individuals who are concerned about confidentiality. Commercial laboratories often promote the benefits of their confidential reporting, but they do not always provide professional guidance on the benefits and burdens of testing or the meaning of test results. Ideally, genetic testing should be accompanied by genetic counseling, in order to ensure that testing is performed appropriately and that test results are interpreted accurately. Individuals who pursue genetic testing independently should be aware that laboratory quality may vary and that genetic counseling may not be provided or required prior to testing.

One notable dimension usually missing from genetic counseling is the theological perspective. Research on health care and spirituality suggests that many people are grateful for health care professionals who can address their religious and spiritual concerns. Although genetic counselors may inquire about how their patients' religious beliefs and values influence their responses to genetic illness, few counselors have formal education in religion or pastoral care. Thus genetic counselors may not be able to address their patients' questions about religious teachings or to discuss patients' concerns about the theological ramifications of the decisions they may be considering. Parish clergy and clinically based chaplains who are willing to learn about genetics and genetic testing are needed to provide pastoral counseling about these concerns.[3] Those who offer counseling should be aware that the Episcopal Church and most religious communities embrace a variety of theological perspectives and that no single approach or doctrinal stance will adequately address the range of questions and concerns raised by genetic testing. Counselors should also become informed about the genetics services and professionals in their areas and refer their parishioners appropriately. Episcopalians should urge that such services be available in their denominational health care institutions and in hospitals with active clinical pastoral education programs.

## NEGOTIATING UNCERTAINTY IN GENETIC DECISION MAKING

### Risk Perception

Persons who seek genetic testing usually do so because they are thought to be at risk of a heritable disease. Risk assessments and genetic test results are typically given in terms of numerical probabilities. Such assessments are often the most important factor contributing to genetic decisions; however, how individuals interpret their risks varies greatly, depending on each person's knowledge, experience, circumstances, and general outlook on life. Studies have shown that people often use a number of mental strategies to make judgments in the face of uncertain information. One such strategy, known as "representativeness," refers to the extent to which a person may assume that one person's experience of an illness is representative of the way all people experience the illness. For example, an expectant parent who only knows one child with Down syndrome may assume that all children with Down syndrome share the same or similar characteristics. A second strategy, called "availability," refers to how easily ideas about disease are imagined or recalled. For example, a woman whose sister just died of breast cancer is likely to be much more concerned about her genetic risks for cancer than someone with equivalent genetic risks who has had no such experience. Finally, a person's knowledge base, even if it is grounded in misinformation or superstition, often "anchors" the perception of risk, overwhelming or blocking out new information. For this reason, even detailed and personalized educational efforts may have little or no effect on individuals' beliefs about their own risks.

Other factors contributing to risk perception include the priorities and stresses that dominate a person's life. For example, a thirty-five-year-old woman pursuing a challenging career or worried about feeding her children may not be concerned about her cancer risks, as opposed to a woman of the same age whose sister was just diagnosed with the disease. General outlook on life—whether anxious and pessimistic or calm and optimistic—can also make a difference in how individuals respond to risks. Finally, individual perceptions of control—whether individuals believe that there is anything they can do to reduce risks through medical intervention, increased surveillance, or changes in behavior—have been shown to play a large role in the ability to cope with uncertainty. In short, the perception of risks is highly subjective, dependent on a host of psychological, experiential, cognitive, and circumstantial factors. As a result, different people may perceive similar risks very differently, including genetic risks revealed by testing.

### Ambiguity

In addition to the subjectivity of risk perception, genetic tests rarely provide definitive diagnostic information. A test may reveal the presence of a

chromosomal abnormality, but if the particular configuration is rare or its effects unknown, it may be impossible to determine the meaning of the finding. Some chromosomal disorders can result in significant and even lethal
physical abnormalities, while others may not: Some make no difference at
all. Even if the abnormality is relatively common, a positive diagnosis often
reveals nothing about the severity of the disorder, which may be expressed
very differently in different individuals. Above all, it is important to realize
that a normal karyotype means only that the chromosomes are structurally
normal; it does not rule out the possibility of genetic disorders caused by
mutations in gene sequences.

Diagnoses of specific mutations in gene sequences also may be ambigu-
ous. The presence of a particular mutation may provide a strong indication
that a person has or will develop a disease, but again, the way in which the
disease will manifest in a particular person is rarely evident from the diagnosis alone. For example, over 800 mutations are known in the gene that accounts for cystic fibrosis. Some of these mutations cause more serious symptoms than others, and some cause no symptoms at all. The type and severity
of symptoms may also be affected by other genetic or environmental factors.
Because the test for cystic fibrosis only identifies the presence of a few of the
most common mutations, a positive or negative diagnosis provides only a
strong indication—not certainty—that a person will or will not develop the
disease. In the case of a few diseases, such as Huntington disease, a positive
diagnosis is a definitive predictor, but the age of onset and severity of the
symptoms will vary with individuals.

The problem deepens with multifactorial diseases—those caused by a
combination of genetic, environmental, and behavioral factors. Because
we do not understand how all these factors interact, the significance of
most mutations for multifactorial disease is poorly understood. Typically, if
an individual is found to carry a disease-bearing gene, say, a BRCA mutation that is known to increase the risk for breast cancer, a numerical risk
can be calculated for the patient's likelihood of developing the disease
based on the family history and other environmental and behavioral factors. While risk statistics can be important signals, however, the calculations may also be suspect. This uncertainty is due to the fact that the research that discovers links between specific genes and disease is usually
carried out using high-risk populations, which makes it easier to find the
links between genes and disease. The same mutation may carry a much
lower risk in the general population. Because it is difficult to conduct genetic research on large populations, we do not know the significance of
most of these mutations for a person who has no other risk factors. And because our knowledge of the relationship between genes and disease is rapidly changing, a risk we think is conferred by the presence of a particular
mutation may be shown to be higher or lower in the future. For this rea-

son, caution is advised in predicting risk in multifactorial diseases, especially for potentially life-threatening conditions such as cancer.

To compound these difficulties, the genetic test results may not be reliable. At present, only limited standards govern the expertise of laboratory technicians and the quality of the materials used in testing, with the result that the quality of test results may vary. Third-party payers may require physicians to use low-cost laboratories to process their genetic tests. Moreover, few physicians are adequately trained to interpret genetic test results.[4] Until comprehensive regulations are developed to govern genetic testing procedures and health care professionals are trained to use available tests, physicians and the public should be cautious about making clinical decisions based on a single set of test results.

## Implications for Families

Regardless of the kind of genetic testing, one of the counselor's first tasks is to take a detailed family history from which to develop a pedigree, which is a kind of diagrammatic map of a person's extended family that illustrates how blood relatives are related and whether any family members are afflicted with or carriers of genetic disease. The pedigree provides the basis for genetic risk assessment for the individual seeking testing. It also illustrates the extent to which genetic testing has implications for relatives of the person tested and whether future children may be at risk.

In addition to developing the pedigree, depending on the condition for which the person is tested, the counselor may ask about other factors or behavior that may affect the patient's risk of disease. Behavioral and environmental factors known to affect late-onset diseases such as cancer or heart disease include diet, alcohol consumption, obesity, occupational hazards, and smoking. If the patient is seeking prenatal testing, the counselor may ask about the health risks of the parents, substance abuse, exposure to toxins, incest, and previous pregnancies. While such questions may seem intrusive, they are nonetheless necessary in order for the counselor to assess accurately whether testing is likely to be worthwhile and informative.

Genetic testing also raises the possibility that a test will reveal unanticipated information in addition to the knowledge that is sought. The classic example is finding that the tested individual is not biologically related to his or her presumed parents or other family members. If the full range of information that might be made available by testing is not disclosed beforehand, the individual tested may be faced with unsought and possibly unwanted genetic information. Patients and clinicians should be aware of this possibility.

Finally, because genetic test results may have implications for the blood relatives of the person tested as well as for the person's insurability and employability, privacy and confidentiality are primary ethical concerns

surrounding genetic testing. Confidentiality is a particularly sensitive issue. People who seek testing need to know how their tests results will be
recorded and who will have access to them. Given the increasing use of
electronic data management, coupled with requirements for insurance au-
thorization and chart review in managed care, it is becoming increasingly
difficult to assure patients that their medical information will remain confidential. Those who seek testing should understand that while efforts will
be made to maintain confidentiality, third parties may gain access to the
information, with potentially discriminatory consequences. More immediately, individuals should be assured that family members do not have a
right to their test results, although ethical considerations may suggest that
the person tested should make the results available.

## GENETIC TESTING AT LIFE'S STAGES

### Prenatal Genetic Testing

The most widely available and frequently used type of genetic testing in
the United States is prenatal testing, performed to diagnose a range of genetic conditions and physical anomalies in fetuses considered at high risk for
a genetic disorder. On average, 3–5 percent of live births are affected with
some kind of disability. Prior to genetic testing, two common nongenetic
tests are typically performed as indicators of possible genetic risks. (1) Maternal serum testing, using a blood sample from the pregnant woman, provides a preliminary indication of an increased risk for a neural tube defect or
Down syndrome. Because the test carries a high rate of false-positive and
false-negative results, additional testing is usually recommended if results are
abnormal or other risk factors are present. (2) Ultrasound imaging produces
a crude picture of the developing fetus that skilled observers can use to detect physical abnormalities. If physical features detected on the ultrasound
suggest a possible genetic abnormality, confirmation by genetic testing is
usually recommended.

The most common prenatal genetic tests are amniocentesis and chorionic
villus sampling (CVS). Amniocentesis, which is performed twelve to sixteen
weeks into a pregnancy, samples fetal cells from the amniotic fluid surrounding the fetus in the uterus, which are subsequently examined for chromosomal defects. This procedure carries a slight risk of spontaneous abortion. The newer procedure, CVS, obtains cells from the chorionic villi, which
are tiny projections on the fetal membrane that eventually becomes the placenta. These cells are also karyotyped and examined for chromosomal defects. This test can be performed at about nine weeks. Because CVS is

thought to carry an increased risk of malformations and spontaneous abortion, amniocentesis is the more common of the two tests.

Most of the time, testing reassures expectant parents that their fetus is developing normally. Rarely, the test diagnoses a chromosomal defect or other anomaly. The most common chromosomal abnormality that is compatible with life is Down syndrome, or trisomy 21, an extra twenty-first chromosome. Other common abnormalities include translocations, in which portions of one chromosome are broken and reattached to another chromosome; deletions and insertions of parts of chromosomes; and sex chromosome disorders, in which a person has an abnormal number of X or Y chromosomes. Many individuals with either an extra X or Y chromosome are never diagnosed, as these chromosomal abnormalities do not manifest in abnormal behavior or appearance. Again, it is important to understand that a normal karyotype does not necessarily mean that a child will be free of genetic disease, only that the chromosomes are structurally normal.

### Who Should Be Tested?

Typically, pregnant women age thirty-five or older are encouraged to have amniocentesis to detect trisomy 21, with or without maternal serum screening. Although more children with Down syndrome are born to women under age thirty-five (because most children are born to younger women), the probability of chromosomal defects increases with the age of the mother and her eggs. The increase occurs because aging is accompanied by an increasing risk of error in cell division during meiosis, the process that produces an egg prior to ovulation. Age thirty-five has been chosen as a dividing line as it is the age at which the risk of having a child with Down syndrome is thought to be roughly equivalent to the risk of a spontaneous miscarriage following the procedure. Amniocentesis is generally not recommended for women under age thirty-five, as younger women's risk of a subsequent miscarriage exceeds the risk of having a child with Down syndrome. Additional indications for amniocentesis include having had previous children with chromosomal abnormalities, a history of frequent miscarriages or infertility, substance abuse, incest, and exposure to toxins.

Errors in gene sequences are known to increase when the father is of "advanced paternal age" because the opportunities for errors in sperm cell division increase over a lifetime of DNA replication. Errors may also occur as a result of exposure to toxins or substance abuse. Errors in gene sequences may be detected prenatally, if it is known where to look, using cells obtained through amniocentesis or CVS. Prenatal gene sequencing is most often performed if a parent has a serious genetic disorder that could be transmitted to a child, or if an existing child has been diagnosed with a genetic disease.

## Making Decisions and Selective Termination

The primary benefit of prenatal testing is reassurance. For over 95 percent of pregnancies, amniocentesis reveals that a fetus is developing normally. However, if an abnormality is found, opportunities for medical intervention are limited; almost always, the expectant couple must decide whether to continue or terminate the pregnancy. If they choose to continue, they may be able to plan for medical interventions at delivery or to educate themselves about the special needs of the child-to-be. But most often, most of those who choose to test decide to terminate the pregnancy if an abnormality is found.[5] For this reason, many expectant parents do not announce their pregnancy until the amniocentesis milestone has been passed, preferring to keep their decisions private.[6]

Prospective parents who learn that their child-to-be is genetically abnormal face an agonizing choice. Following amniocentesis, the pregnancy will usually be well into the second trimester, and the expectant parents will have long anticipated a happy delivery. Terminating a pregnancy at this stage is both physically arduous and emotionally wrenching. For this reason, some prefer the slightly more risky CVS test, which permits a first-trimester termination if an anomaly is found. These decisions are always difficult. The expectant parents' first reactions may be shock, grief, guilt, and confusion. Their faith may be challenged as they struggle to understand why they and their child have been affected. Fear that disease is a form of punishment from God may compete with hopes for God's help as they attempt to answer the universal questions: Why me? Why us? What did we do wrong? Why is God doing this to us? What does God want us to do? Pastoral clergy who are conversant with the issues accompanying genetic testing can be of great help to parishioners coping with these decisions by exploring with them what parenting, children, and testing mean to them in the context of their faith.

Without knowing how severely the child may be affected, expectant parents must make their decision in a context of great uncertainty. Faced with a choice between continuing or terminating the pregnancy, they may wish to find out all they can about what the disability would mean for their future child and for their family. They may want to meet children with the same diagnosis and speak with their parents. They may need to evaluate their resources—financial, social, and spiritual—and whether they feel they have the strength, support, and faith to raise such a child. They may find they will reconsider their feelings about abortion, and in doing so explore what the act of choosing to terminate a pregnancy on the basis of a diagnosis means to them. They may worry about what their friends and acquaintances may think or say, whether or not they choose to continue the pregnancy. They will undoubtedly worry about what the future might bring for the child, knowing that life is at some level always a struggle, but that the struggle may be harder for those who are different or disabled.

Whether they choose to terminate or continue the pregnancy, when a child is longed for, planned for, and perhaps worked for in the sense of requiring infertility treatment to be conceived, it is a major loss for them to relinquish their hopes and expectations. This loss is always accompanied by grief. Clergy and others in a counseling role have an opportunity to help them through this process, to recognize what the loss means for them, and try to help them come to terms with what may seem like a terrible injustice. For people of faith, one of the most intractable questions is why an omnipotent and loving God would permit the illness and suffering of an innocent infant. While there are no simple answers to this question, counselors may want to explore how the expectant parents interpret their loss, dispelling destructive interpretations—such as those that would assign guilt and responsibility—and providing reassurance that God is with them. It may be helpful to explore how faith in God can provide hope in times of crisis and loss, or to ask what they feel their faith requires of them in terms of a response. It may also be worthwhile to know enough biology to be confident in discussing notions of natural error, nature's mistakes. There is a long path between conception and a live, healthy baby, and up to 70 percent of conceptions do not result in the birth of a child.[7] This high rate of loss is nature's way of correcting mistakes. Many people, stricken with grief and remorse, may fail to appreciate that mistakes are a natural occurrence.

## Motivations

Expectant parents who are faced with a diagnosed genetic disorder must not only cope with their own suffering; they must also be prepared to deal with public opinion. Prenatal testing has received a great deal of attention in the popular press and the ethics literature in part because it suggests a form of eugenics and in part because it is difficult to talk about prenatal testing without addressing the morality of abortion. Abortion opponents and disability rights advocates have criticized selective termination of abnormal pregnancies as playing God and commodifying children. Many of these criticisms are based on concern that such decisions reflect a general disvaluing of people with disabilities. People who make these decisions have been charged with selfishness, narcissism, and irresponsibility. To be sure, many parents speak of the rewards of caring for children with disabilities, and people of all ages with disabilities have greatly enriched their communities. The experiences of these individuals offer a powerful argument against selective termination following diagnosis of a genetic disorder. Less frequently discussed are the expectant parents' concerns about the well-being of the future child, their fears about the burden of care imposed by a child with a disability, or the financial, emotional, and social costs of such a child for them, their other children, their extended families, and their communities.

Disability advocates' efforts to dispel the fears and misperceptions associated with disabilities are not always convincing to families faced with a diagnosis of unknown severity. Without professional guidance, they may not be aware of the many services, resources, or financial aid programs that are available to assist them and their children with special needs.[8] Ultimately, decisions to terminate reflect the expectant parents' confidence, their experience with individuals with similar disabilities, and competing demands for their attention, love, resources, and energy.

Genetic counselors can provide enormous help in the decision-making process, chiefly by providing accurate and complete information about the diagnosis, putting families in touch with others who have had similar experiences, and informing them about existing supports. However, although they will help them explore any questions they may have, counselors are unlikely to offer their own recommendations. The factors impacting these difficult decisions are highly subjective and variable, reflecting individual families' unique interpretations of the facts, their particular circumstances, and a diversity of moral and religious beliefs. For this reason, genetic counseling for reproductive planning has steadfastly maintained the profession's tradition of nondirectiveness. This approach has drawn criticism, for while it respects parental autonomy and reproductive freedom, it permits what could be considered poorly informed or frivolous decisions. But despite the criticism, counselors' commitment to nondirectiveness in the prenatal context has not wavered.

People who seek counseling from clergy or pastoral counselors on genetic matters may be interested in the teachings of the church, about which clergy should feel free to inform their parishioners. But counselors should be aware that they may have personal values and judgments about their parishioners' choices. Rather than attempt to impose their own beliefs or persuade their parishioners to their way of thinking, they would do well to heed the nondirective style of genetic counselors, for several reasons. First, the balance of power in their relationship with their parishioners may be unequal, which creates opportunities for manipulation or coercion. Second, although reproductive decisions may be based in part on religious beliefs, they usually involve numerous factors, some of which may be beyond the counselor's knowledge. Third, the people facing the decision are the ones who will have to live with the consequences of their choice. While clergy have a responsibility to ensure that decisions are thoroughly informed and well considered, their parishioners should be strongly encouraged to make their own decisions.

### The Abortion Controversy

In part, what is at issue in genetic testing and counseling is whether abortion is ever morally acceptable. Whether abortion is morally acceptable for any reason is hotly debated, largely due to differences of opinion regarding the moral value of embryonic and fetal life. For centuries, traditions of religious and secular ethics have explored the question of when human life acquires moral value, without achieving consensus.[9] Today, some people believe that human embryos deserve full legal protection, based on their potential for becoming persons. For others, moral value depends on the fetus's gestational age. Still others believe that no matter what value is placed on the fetus, the mother's wishes always take precedence over duties to the fetus. In *Roe v. Wade* (1973), the U.S. Supreme Court attempted to balance these competing views by concluding that for the first twenty-four weeks of pregnancy, women have a legal right to abortion, but because third trimester fetuses are considered viable—able to breathe on their own—states may prohibit abortion after this point. In the absence of moral agreement, the law thus requires that individual choices be respected until the third trimester.

The Episcopal Church has adopted a number of resolutions addressing abortion. The church does not hold that abortion is never justified, but it emphatically claims that human life is sacred, a gift from God, and therefore decisions to abort must be undertaken with gravity and seriousness. The church does not condone abortion for purposes of birth control but encourages responsible family planning and contraception; nor does it accept abortion on the basis of gender selection or other trivial grounds. But it leaves open the possibility that a diagnosed disability may be so debilitating and burdensome for the child and family that termination may be the best alternative. The Episcopal Church also permits abortion in cases of rape or incest.[10]

## The Disability Critique

One of the most important ethical concerns raised by prenatal diagnosis is that the technology can be used to *selectively* abort fetuses that are diagnosed with undesired traits, even traits that are not particularly disabling. It is one thing to terminate a pregnancy when a fetus is seriously compromised, but to abort a fetus on the basis of nonlethal but undesired characteristics suggests a different kind of reasoning. Now the child becomes subject to a kind of quality control that suggests that some children are more (or less) desirable than others. This perspective in itself poses a challenge to recent Western notions of parenting in which the expectation is that all children will be loved equally, as individuals, regardless of their genetic make-up (see chapter 6). Critics argue that once some kinds of children begin to be regarded as preferable to others, either for reasons of health, intelligence, or physical attributes, children will come to be seen not as unique individuals, but as commodities. Futurists claim that social institutions will follow suit, eventually producing a genetically stratified society of the extreme sort

depicted in science fiction literature and films. Whether opportunities for
genetic selection or enhancement would significantly change parenting
practices from those of today, in which parents naturally treat children differently in response to their abilities and needs, remains to be seen. Moreover, it is important to recognize that even if genetic testing and selective
abortion were available to all, disabilities would still be with us. Unless we
can eliminate accidents and injuries, society will always include people with
differing levels of ability and disability who have correspondingly different
needs.

Numerous efforts have been made to try to circumscribe the kinds of
conditions for which selective pregnancy termination might be morally acceptable. Intuitively, such a determination would appear to rest on perceptions of the severity of the condition diagnosed or the fetus's anticipated quality of life after birth. Factors contributing to perceptions of
severity include whether a disorder involves severe physical suffering or
mental impairment, whether it restricts self-awareness and interpersonal
interaction, and whether it is treatable. Arguments have been made for limiting termination to conditions incompatible with life or those known to
cause profound suffering. Agreement over what counts as a sufficiently serious condition or sufficiently poor quality of life to warrant termination is
unlikely to be attained, however.[11]

The difficulty of achieving consensus is due in part to the fact that none of
us is ever really capable of judging when the life of another is no longer
worth living. As Paul Ramsey and others have persuasively argued, we cannot know what life is really like for a person who is mentally handicapped
or in pain. We cannot be sure that no life is ever better than the only life a
person has. We cannot know if a person in a coma will ever recover, or
whether some degree of consciousness is still functioning. Consequently, we
are reluctant to judge when another's life is not worth living. Conversely,
while some conditions are clearly more serious than others, perceptions of
disability also depend on whether the affected persons and their parents,
families, and communities feel confident of their ability to handle it. This
evaluation, in turn, depends on a host of other factors such as financial resources, community support, the needs of existing children, the availability
of caregivers, the existence of medical interventions, and the values and beliefs of the parents. In short, since many of the questions and values that influence possible judgments of severity are either unfathomable or subjective,
severity of symptoms is unlikely to serve as a clear moral guideline for the
permissibility of selective termination.

Decisions to terminate a pregnancy also raise profound social questions
having to do with the value we place on human life in comparison with other
goals. The claim of Christian Scripture and tradition is that all human life is
in some sense sacred, a gift from God, and that all living people are of equal

value in the eyes of God. But our practices do not always reflect what we profess. Here in the United States, the most affluent country in the world, many children do not have adequate food, housing, and education. Many people with disabilities do not have access to needed services and employment opportunities. Their families often lack support in their upbringing, and many continue to perceive people with disabilities as victims, people to be pitied, perhaps intellectually inferior, and socially burdensome.

Some critics of prenatal testing claim that it would be far more valuable for us as a society to support adequate services for people with disabilities, than fund eliminating fetuses with genetic disorders. To that end, the Americans with Disabilities Act (ADA, 1990),[12] perhaps the world's most powerful and progressive legislation on behalf of people with disabilities, mandates extensive entitlements for people with disabilities. These entitlements include accommodations in employment to protect the rights and interests of employees and potential employees, equal access to public services and programs, and mandated accessibility to public buildings. Despite this legislation, our social institutions—schools, employers, insurers, public service organizations—are still engaged in subtle and not so subtle forms of discrimination against people who are different. While some families and individuals find existing resources sufficient to help them provide high-quality care and to help their disabled children to lead fulfilling lives, for others, concern that support services may not be adequate or affordable for a handicapped child may contribute to decisions to abort a fetus with a disability.

In short, people may base their decisions on a variety of factors—medical, social, economic, ethical, or religious. Given that there is no formula for the "right" decision, individuals need to be free to make their own decisions—and their own mistakes. As a people of faith, we take it on faith that most people want to make the decision that is best for them and their families. Although some decisions may appear to be ethically suspect, clear boundaries for right and wrong genetic choices are not easily drawn.

Today, most women and couples who choose to undergo prenatal testing do so because they are attempting child bearing later in life, after establishing their careers. They are often people who value knowledge, who have worked hard for their achievements and delayed having children, and who are ambitious in the sense of having certain hopes and aspirations for themselves and for their children.

Not all people see the world or their options in the same way, however. We know less about those who refuse prenatal testing than about those who accept it, but we know that many people refuse testing essentially because they do not perceive the world or their responsibilities in the same way. Some may refuse testing because they do not wish to expose the fetus to any increased risk or because they would not consider abortion for any reason. They may base their choices on their religious beliefs, their confidence as parents, the place of children in their worldview, or their sense of family and community support. Alternatively, refusals of testing may reflect women's negative experiences with medicine, suspicion of technology, limited financial resources, or lack of access to prenatal care. While a case may be made for increasing access to prenatal testing, it is important to recognize that at present, the demand for testing comes primarily from a particular subset of the population—those who are educated, Caucasian, and relatively affluent, perhaps those whose perspective on life is predominantly secular. Although large and loosely defined, this group reflects an orientation toward the world and responsible parenthood that is not shared by all.

## POSTNATAL TESTING:
## NEWBORNS, CHILDREN, AND ADOLESCENTS

Postnatal genetic testing may be performed for a variety of purposes, including newborn screening for preventive interventions, diagnosis of suspected genetic conditions or disease risks, to ascertain familial relationships (most commonly paternity), for forensic purposes, and increasingly, for research. Each type of testing is accompanied by psychological and social considerations that pose novel ethical questions and dilemmas for those seeking testing. The following section offers a brief overview of the major concerns accompanying each type of testing.

### Newborn Screening

Newborn screening is a type of testing performed immediately or soon after birth. Whereas genetic testing is almost always voluntary, most states mandate one or more specific tests, such as screening for phenylketonuria (PKU), for all newborns. These tests look for certain proteins or metabolites in blood samples, the presence or absence of which indicates whether a gene is present and functioning normally. Newborn screening offers the benefit of early detection of some genetic abnormalities in which interventions are most effective if begun immediately after birth. Phenylketonuria, for example, is a metabolic disorder caused by the absence of an enzyme responsible for converting the amino acid phenylalanine to tyrosine. Untreated PKU can lead to mental impairment, but this outcome can be avoided by placing the child on a special diet from birth. PKU testing is required across the United States because the diet can prevent serious harm to the child and spare society from the costs of special education and support when the child becomes mentally handicapped. Parents often are not aware that these tests are being administered and usually do not object when they are told.

In most states, parents who would prefer their children not be tested have the right to refuse testing, regardless of the reason. This situation again raises the question of parental responsibility: Do parents have a responsibility to screen their children for preventable genetic diseases?

## Diagnostic Testing of Children and Adolescents

Many genetic disorders do not become evident until a child is a few years old. At this point, a child's growth, size, physical appearance, or behavior may suggest some kind of abnormality. Thousands of possible genetic disorders (most of them very rare) may affect children. When parents become concerned that their child is not developing as they expect, they may be referred to a medical geneticist if a cause is not readily apparent. A genetic diagnosis, while painful to accept, often comes as a relief if it provides an explanation for a problem that had previously been dismissed or misunderstood.

When a genetic condition is diagnosed in a child, the first priority is to determine what caused the problem. Was it the result of a spontaneous mutation, a chromosomal error during cell division, recessive traits carried by both parents, or an autosomal dominant trait that was carried by one parent and perhaps only mildly expressed? The answer may have implications for the genetic status of existing and future children in the family, as well as parents, cousins, uncles, and aunts. In order to determine what kind of genetic disorder is involved, the parents are usually tested as well as the child. For parents, testing can be an emotionally charged process. Many parents learn that they are carriers of a recessive trait at the same time that they are informed that they have passed the trait to their affected child. In cases where only one parent is affected, he or she may feel guilty for passing on this legacy to the child, and tensions may arise between the parents as they struggle to accept what they may feel is biological responsibility for their child's condition. Even more problematically, pediatric testing sometimes reveals unexpected information, such as that the presumed father is not biologically related to the child or that a child has an abnormal number of sex chromosomes. Thus while genetic testing sometimes offers the benefit of an explanation for a child's condition, this information may come at an emotional cost to the entire family.

Testing may also confirm diagnoses of genetic conditions that are often fatal in late childhood, adolescence, or early adulthood, such as cystic fibrosis or muscular dystrophy. Only a few years ago children with cystic fibrosis were expected to die before reaching adulthood, but improved understanding of the genetic origins of the disease has prompted many patients and their families to seek aggressive treatment, including invasive procedures such as lung transplantation, in the expectation of increased survival. While medical research has increased the lifespan of many of these individuals, it raises two important questions that have broad relevance across all fields of medicine. First, when is it appropriate for either children or adults to participate in research, and what benefits ought to be anticipated from participation? Second, at what point is treatment futile? People with serious genetic disorders face these decisions no less than people with other kinds of life-threatening illnesses. These questions are very difficult, and pastoral care may be helpful for patients and their families. Perhaps the only significant difference is that the media hype surrounding genetics suggests that genetically based cures are imminent. This perception may encourage people to participate as subjects more than is reasonable, and to press for further treatment well past the point when interventions offer any realistic hope of benefit.

Some parents may prefer not to have their children tested, which may be perceived as an ethical issue. In health care today, every effort is made to respect the religious and spiritual beliefs of patients, even refusals of treatment without which the patient will die. In the case of children, there are precedents for overriding parental decisions—most often refusals of treatment on religious grounds—if the parental decision threatens the health or life of a child. Genetic testing is not a life-saving intervention, however. At present, there is no requirement for testing in the absence of symptoms, nor are there likely to be reasons for such testing in the future. If a child exhibits symptoms for a disorder for which there is no treatment, the grounds for testing over parents' refusal are slim.

## GENETIC TESTING IN ADULTS

### Testing for Late-Onset Disease and Disease Susceptibility

Testing can also be performed for diseases that develop later in life, even before the person tested has symptoms of the disease. Tests of this sort exist for autosomal dominant diseases, like Huntington disease, or for multifactorial diseases, like breast cancer, both of which typically manifest after a person reaches adulthood. People who pursue these kinds of tests usually do so because their family history suggests they are at increased risk for developing disease. For some in this situation, anxiety about their disease risks can be overwhelming. Testing may offer the benefit of reassurance that one does not carry a particular mutation, or opportunities to plan ahead if one does. Because the predictive nature of this type of testing carries potential for serious psychological burdens as well as benefits, genetic counselors have developed protocols for late-onset disease testing that attempt to ensure that individuals who undergo testing fully understand its psychological and social ramifications.

Consider Huntington disease. For individuals who know they are at risk, testing offers a 50 percent chance of relief from anxiety and an equal likelihood of learning that at some point in mid-life they are destined to experience a profound loss of mental capacities and motor control and eventually die from the disease. It is a harsh gamble, and people who take it need to be prepared for the worst. Moreover, the two outcomes are more complex than they may first appear. For someone who has lived his life in the shadow of risk, learning that he does not carry the defective sequence may prove disorienting, disrupting his sense of identity and perhaps provoking "survivor guilt," especially if siblings or other relatives are less fortunate. For this individual, one anxiety may be replaced by another. But for the person who tests positive for the mutation, each passing day without symptoms may either take on new meaning or be occasion for despair. Testing thus provides an opportunity to prepare for the future onset of illness; however, the benefit is limited because the age at which any person will develop symptoms cannot be known in advance.

Multifactorial diseases are caused by a combination of genetic, environmental, and behavioral factors. Unlike autosomal dominant disorders, for which a positive diagnosis means a person will definitely develop disease, for multifactorial diseases, a positive result indicates only an increased risk of developing the disease over a person's lifetime. *It is essential to recognize that some percentage of those diagnosed with a disease susceptibility mutation will never develop disease.* The strength of the risk, including the age of onset and severity of symptoms, varies with the mutation identified, the individual's family history, background genetic factors, and a range of personal and behavioral factors. Given all these variables, the tests have limited predictive value. For all but a few mutations, we know very little about the genetic risks associated with multifactorial diseases, and what we know is constantly changing. It is unlikely that we will ever fully understand the contribution of each gene to these diseases or how genes interact with each other and the environment. Test results must not be taken as conclusive indications of one's disease risks; rather, they best serve as warning signals of varying strength.

In some cases, because some genes may contribute to a number of diseases, genetic testing for one disease may reveal unexpected health risks for another disease. The classic example is a test for genetic predisposition for heart disease that may also indicate an increased risk for Alzheimer's disease. Patients should be informed of this possibility, if it exists, and should be given the option not to be informed about information they did not seek.

When considering whether to be tested for a multifactorial disease, a central question is whether a genetic diagnosis would make any difference in one's health-related behaviors. If the significance of an inherited mutation or

other contributing factors is not understood, or if there is no effective preventive intervention or therapy, testing may have little value. Disease susceptibility testing is of greatest clinical value when the role of the mutation(s)
sought is well known and when measures can be taken to reduce disease
risks.

Testing for breast cancer is perhaps the best example of this kind of testing. In the general U.S. population, it is estimated that women have a 10–12
percent risk of developing breast cancer over a lifetime. In 5–10 percent of
those who develop breast cancer, the disease is thought to be largely attributable to inherited mutations in genes known as BRCA1 and BRCA2. Women
who inherit either of these mutations are thought to have up to a 90 percent
lifetime risk of developing breast cancer, and up to a 60 percent risk of developing ovarian cancer. Women, and occasionally men, who are diagnosed
with one of the known breast cancer susceptibility mutations have the opportunity to be more vigilant about their breast examinations and mammo-
grams, or they may substantially lower their risks by electing prophylactic
mastectomy, or they may join a clinical trial of one of several drugs thought
to delay or reduce the risk of developing disease. For these individuals, the
primary value of testing lies either in relief from anxiety or, if one tests positive, in opportunities for preventive interventions and behavioral change.

In addition to the few mutations in the BRCA1 and BRCA2 genes known
to increase disease risks for breast cancer, hundreds of additional mutations
of unknown significance have been found in these genes. Because most of
these mutations are relatively rare, it is hard to know what they mean, or if
they have any bearing on health at all. If a woman tests positive for a mutation about which little or nothing is known, although her anxiety level may
increase, she may not have useful information on which to base her health
care decisions.

Whether it is appropriate to terminate a pregnancy based on the diagnosis of a late-onset condition is morally problematic. Since these diseases arise
only in later life, if at all, and our day-to-day existence is full of risks and uncertainty, such decisions would appear to elevate genetic concerns above
other, perhaps far more significant, risks. The question also raises the matter
of what it means to be sick. Is one sick if one is diagnosed as a carrier of a
recessive mutation even though such people will never have symptoms? Is
one sick if one is a carrier of a dominant mutation that is not yet expressed
as symptoms? No "normal" or "healthy" human genome exists—countless
genetic variants contribute to our individual uniqueness, and we all carry recessive genes that would be lethal if they had no normal counterpart. Moreover, each of us will eventually die, a death caused in part by some kind of
failure in gene function. In other words, we all carry disease susceptibility
genes; they simply are not yet identified as such, or expressed symptomati-
cally. So what does it mean to be healthy or sick?

## FAMILY ETHICS

Genetic testing raises new questions of rights and responsibilities within families. In the case of testing for genetic predisposition, if an individual is concerned about the risk of developing a genetically linked disease due to its prevalence in the family history, it may be helpful to test a member of the family who has the disease in order to determine whether a mutation is involved. However, the affected family member may not wish to be tested. The reverse is also possible: A person with a genetic disease may wish to inform other family members of their risk, but some relatives may not want to know about them. These situations raise a number of ethical questions. Does an affected individual have any kind of moral obligation to inform relatives of their own risk of disease? Can a person seeking testing claim a right to a relative's genetic information? Does anyone have a right *not* to know his or her risks, even if ignorance will affect the welfare of others? Does a physician have a responsibility to inform relatives of their risks if the patient refuses to tell them?[13] These questions are only just beginning to be asked in clinics and the courts. Conventional wisdom would suggest that all patients have a right to the confidentiality of their medical records, but the familial nature of genetic testing is starting to challenge this view. It may be worthwhile to explore how family relationships in a Christian context provide guidance for family responsibilities in the genetics arena.

One area where some consensus seems to have been established is in the testing of children. Sometimes parents who know they are at risk of developing a disease want to have their children tested for the disease. A father who learns he is a carrier for Huntington disease may want to know whether his children have inherited the gene. A mother who has suffered from breast cancer may want herself and her daughters to be tested for the BRCA mutations. But while parents may desire this information, whether testing should be pursued is debatable. Most genetics professionals agree that because the knowledge of one's risks may be psychologically or socially burdensome, perhaps leading to discrimination by the child's parents, teachers, or future insurers or employers, testing of children for late-onset disease should not be performed until children are old enough to make the decision for themselves. The primary exception to this rule is when it appears that the information would provide immediate medical benefit to the child.

Critics of this position argue that children who have seen their parents suffer may be preoccupied with anxiety about their own risks. Rather than burdening the child, the opportunity to be tested may instead enhance the child's autonomy by providing some degree of empowerment and resolving anxiety. Those who support testing of children for late-onset disease also agree that if testing is pursued, these decisions ought to be made jointly by the children, their parents, and the children's health care providers. Moreover, in all such decisions there must be clear evidence that the child is a mature minor who understands the psychological and social implications of testing.[14]

## THEOLOGICAL IMPLICATIONS OF GENETIC TESTING

Genetic testing forcefully raises some of the theological issues discussed in chapter 2. Perhaps the most common criticism of genetic testing is that it permits us to "play God." This claim is particularly common in the case of prenatal testing, in that it allows the selection of which children to have or not to have. The harshest critics of prenatal testing view it as a medically sanctioned form of discrimination against people with disabilities or undesired traits. Taken to an extreme, these critics argue, prenatal testing could lead to the creation of societies in which children are tailored to parental specifications, no longer gifts from God but "commodified" to conform to particular tastes, just like any other material possession. Certainly this scenario is chilling and, as such, has been given a lot of play in the critical literature. At present, however, such scenarios remain in the realm of science fiction. The cost of testing, limited access to testing world wide, and most of all, limited interest in testing ensure that at least in the foreseeable future, the impact of genetic testing on the gene pool will be slight.

While genetic testing has enabled some parents at risk of having a child with a genetic disorder to bear healthy children, it has also inserted a new element of anxiety, caution, and responsibility into the experience of procreation. At its root, the issue of how much one can or should control the body, health, and disease is a moral question having to do with how we perceive ourselves in relation to the world and to God. We may see ourselves as part of the natural world, as interdependent members of a complex ecosystem, subject to many of the same physical and behavioral laws as all other living things, which we violate at our peril. Or we may feel that by virtue of our intelligence and self-awareness, we stand outside nature, empowered to control and manipulate our environment and ourselves. Similarly, we may perceive God as our creator, through whom we acquired the ability to manipulate nature and whom we join as "cocreators," being made in the image of God. Or we may think of God as one who is omniscient and omnipotent, whose limitless powers remind us of our fallibility and the dangers of overreaching ambition. Or we may think of God as someone like an ideal parent, our beneficent protector and loyal companion in all that life delivers, whose infinite love calls us to love others, especially the vulnerable, and who would not require of us more than we are capable. Although our understanding of ourselves in relation to God and nature may vary with time and circumstances, we often appeal to these relationships for moral guidance.

One moral distinction we often speak of is that between what we consider to be "natural" or "unnatural."[15] This dichotomy is typically used in medicine to delineate arenas in which it is thought we should and should not interfere. Christian views of nature and humans' place in nature as part of God's plan are complicated, seeming to take different forms depending on our needs. In Genesis, we are commanded both to be "stewards" of the earth and to have dominion over nature. These are two very different messages, one of conservation and the other of exploitation, which have been used to justify both approaches to the earth's natural resources. Scripture describes us as created beings, just like all other animals, yet also made "in God's image," suggesting that we are in some categorical way different or separate from the rest of the natural world. We sometimes speak of nature as comprising those living things that are not human, or those geographical places where the landscape has not been transformed by human activity. Yet nature is not so evenly divided. Even in inner cities, airports, and toxic waste dumps, nonhuman life abounds, and no place is left on earth that does not contain evidence of human activity.

The line is equally hard to draw in health care. Medical treatments are often described as unnatural, but most function by harnessing existing biological systems. Vaccines, for example, work by stimulating the body's immune system to create resistance to infectious disease. Assisted reproduction technologies may seem extremely "unnatural" due to their complexity and the hospital environment in which they are provided, but they work by manipulating biological systems that are largely intact. In short, all medical interventions are grounded in natural mechanisms and biological processes. The primary purpose of the natural-unnatural distinction today seems to be as a means of categorizing those technologies of which we approve and disapprove.

The charge of "playing God" is more serious, although is not unique to genetic testing. It refers to human interference in areas that traditionally have been considered the province of God. If God is our creator, and if we are made in God's image, we are both subject to God's will and empowered to take responsibility as creators ourselves. This dual nature poses a problem as we become ever more technologically adept. Centuries ago, God was credited with responsibility for the creation, sustaining, and taking of life, and many natural phenomena whose mechanisms were not then understood. As science and medicine have unmasked the mysteries of physics, chemistry, and biology, that which has been ascribed to God has diminished in scope. Today, we too are capable of creating, prolonging, and manipulating life, and in some cases choosing when life shall end. As a result, it is no longer clear which activities are our human responsibility and which activities are properly reserved for God. For example, some Christians may justify genetic intervention in the name of cocreation; however, this approach fails to impose any boundaries or moral guidelines on human intervention or manipulation of nature. At the extreme, this idea may promote the notion that if something can be done, there is no reason why it should not be done if some benefit can be gained from it. In this and other ways, genetic technologies are posing serious challenges to Christian theology, specifically our understanding of divine and human responsibility, for which our religious tradition and church history provide very little, if any, explicit guidance.

To counter human hubris, God's infinite powers remind us of our limitations. The criticism of playing God is most frequently used with reference to events that some believe *should* be left to God, to chance, or to nature, even if the means for intervention are available to us. These reserved areas are usually life events that are to some extent mysterious and remain beyond our control—typically those involving life and death. We face making end-of-life decisions for others with fear and trepidation, knowing our decisions are irreversible and profound and that they require wisdom that is beyond our grasp. We hesitate to withdraw life-prolonging treatments, knowing that we are incapable of judging the worth of life for another. God's omniscience serves in these times to remind us that as humans, our vision is inevitably limited, our judgment flawed, and that we must act cautiously. Similarly, we may recoil at the thought of "designing" children, knowing that our attempts at control are feeble imitations of the evolutionary process or the wisdom of God's design for us. In an era in which our technological accomplishments would seem to make virtually anything possible, the charge of playing God reminds us that we are prone to error, bias, arrogance, and ignorance. For those who would overreach our human limitations, playing God is a game of high stakes, with consequences for other lives.

One can dismiss charges of playing God as stemming in part from anxiety and fear of change. Often these charges are made when a technology is first introduced and diminish over time, suggesting that the responses may be based more on apprehension about the new, strange, and different than substantial moral grounds. However, this criticism may also reflect what has been described as a "yuk" factor, a gut feeling of distaste or repugnance. Despite the insubstantial nature of this feeling, even a temporary response of this sort may legitimately raise questions of whether an action is or is not acceptable or appropriate. Our gut reactions are significant indicators of our moral identity and should be recognized as worthy of attention, even if only as the first step in an ethical analysis.

If God is perceived as our beneficent parent, protector, and loyal companion, however, we may approach genetic technologies very differently. It is this view that accounts for our personal relationship with God, that assures us that God is always with us, supporting us and providing us with adequate strength for whatever life delivers. If God is beneficent, God is also hoping that we will do our utmost to help ourselves, to reduce suffering, and to act humanely. While the omniscient God reminds us of our limitations, it is this loving God to whom we turn for guidance and who calls us to account for our behavior. Thus it is possible to argue that playing God by controlling our genetic characteristics may be a highly moral thing to do if the intent is to reduce pain and suffering. If God has provided us with the ability to understand and improve our health and that of our offspring, our most loving and humane response might be to use our new diagnostic capacities to ensure that every child enters the world with an optimal genetic endowment. In this view, reproduction and health should *not* be left to biological chance, as left alone, nature clearly makes many mistakes that produce great suffering. Rather, we should attempt to control health risks as much as possible. Although we cannot rid the world of disease and disability, if we can avoid heritable evils through medical technology, it may be our God-given responsibility and the beneficent thing to do. What, then, would a loving God expect of us in response to our new genetic capacities? What would God require as the most humane and beneficent use of them? This may be the question that clergy and counselors should pose to people of faith: Given the availability of genetic testing, what would a loving God require us to be and to do?

Clearly, Christian theology offers many avenues into thinking about genetic testing. The task for the pastoral counselor is to be conversant with as many of these alternatives as possible, open to exploring what seems to be the most meaningful and fulfilling approach for individuals confronting these issues. Perhaps the most important message to communicate is that we are all in this together, on a journey whose destination is unknown, and the best compass bearings we have reside in our commitments, our faith, and our personal ethics. These questions will have many answers, perhaps as many as there are individuals who ask them. The church should help us to explore them as honestly and openly as possible.

## NOTES

1. Genetic counselors generally prefer the term "client" rather than "patient" to reflect the profession's respect for the independence and autonomy of the person being served. For the purposes of consistency throughout this book, we will use the term "patient."

2. For more information on genetic counseling, see L. Andrews, J. Fullarton, N. Holtzman, and A. Motulsky, eds., *Assessing Genetic Risks: Implications for Health and Social Policy* (Washington, D.C.: National Academy Press, 1994), chapter 4.

3. For a more detailed discussion of pastoral concerns related to genetic testing and counseling, see Committee on Medical Ethics, Episcopal Diocese of Washington, D.C., *Wrestling with the Future: Our Genes and Our Choices* (Harrisburg, Pa.: Morehouse, 1998).

4. N. A. Holtzman and M. S. Watson, *Promoting Safe and Effective Genetic Testing in the United States* (Baltimore: Johns Hopkins University Press, 1998), xx.

5. M. S. Verp, A. T. Bombard, J. L. Simpson, and S. Elias, "Parental Decisions Following Prenatal Diagnosis of Fetal Chromosome Abnormality," *American Journal of American Genetics* 29 (1998): 613–622; A. Drugan, A. Greb, M. P. Johnson et al., "Determinants of Parental Decisions to Abort for Chromosome Abnormalities, *Prenatal Diagnosis* 10 (1990): 483–490.

6. Privacy about a pregnancy until testing is completed has been characterized as the "tentative pregnancy." See Barbara Katz Rothman, *The Tentative Pregnancy: Prenatal Diagnosis and the Future of Motherhood* (New York: Penguin, 1987).

7. A. B. Little, "There's Many a Slip 'twixt Implantation and the Crib," *New England Journal of Medicine* 319 (1988): 241–242.

8. For example, the Genetic Alliance, Inc., is an advocacy group that provides information and research on genetic disease, and professional and support group information (www.geneticalliance.org).

9. For a discussion of a number of contemporary Christian perspectives on abortion, see *Wrestling with the Future*, 88–91.

10. See Appendix 2, "Relevant Resolutions Adopted by the General Convention of the Episcopal Church," in *Wrestling with the Future*, 118–123.

11. In one study of genetic counselors, even counselors disagreed over the degree of severity of numerous diseases, including cystic fibrosis, Duchenne muscular dystrophy, alpha- and beta-thalassemia, and achondroplasia. For each disease, a number of counselors claimed it was lethal, others thought it was serious but not lethal, and still others thought it was not serious. Because each of these conditions has a wide range of expression, this variation may in part reflect each counselor's particular experience with the disorders in question. But if a group of similarly trained genetic counselors could not agree on the severity of suffering caused by relatively common genetic disorders, it is unlikely that these criteria will be an effective moral boundary for selective termination among the general public. See D. C. Wertz and B. M. Knoppers, "Serious Genetic Disorders: Can or Should they be Defined?" *American Journal of Medical Genetics* 108 (1) (2002): 29–35.

12. Americans with Disabilities Act (PL 101–336, 1990).

13. This question arose in two recent court cases: *Safer v. Estate of Pack* (291 N.J. Super. 619, 677 A.2d 1188 (App. Div.)) and *Pate v. Threlkel* (661 So. 2nd 278, (1995)).

14. Cynthia B. Cohen, "Wrestling with the Future: Should We Test Children for Adult-Onset Conditions?" *Kennedy Institute of Ethics Journal* 8, no. 2 (1998): 111–130.

15. For a thoughtful discussion of this distinction, see William Cronon, *Uncommon Ground: Rethinking the Human Place in Nature* (New York: W.W. Norton, 1995).

# 4

# Gene Transfer for Therapy or Enhancement

*Cynthia B. Cohen and LeRoy Walters*

Our growing ability to change and replace human genes promises to have a flesh and blood impact on our lives, our health, our hopes, and our descendants. It offers the possibility of preventing and treating serious diseases that have long plagued humankind. It also provides ways of enhancing and shaping human traits beyond the normal range of what we take to be required for good health. Indeed, as we increase our capacities to alter the human genome in more direct and specific ways than any we have previously imagined, some say, we are opening the door to alteration of the very meaning of what it is to be human. Even as we explore the scientific opportunities that our growing genetic powers set before us, we must also grapple with ethical, social, and theological questions that they raise as we envision using these powers to address human needs and aspirations.

If we were to hone genetic interventions to a point where they were safe and effective, would it be right to intervene into the genes of human beings? Is it consistent with God's purposes for us to modify our genes? If so, for what purposes? Should we limit our efforts to preventing and treating serious disease? Or should we also try to improve the characteristics of human beings so that they can function more effectively in an increasingly competitive world? Should social considerations be allowed to override the choices of individuals about the uses of gene transfer? In short, what ethical, social, and theological limits should there be to our efforts to treat and shape humankind?

In this chapter, we explore various responses to such questions given by Christian and secular thinkers. We do so in hopes of heightening our awareness of the range of reasons and beliefs on which those within our civic polity rely as we address ethical and social issues related to the new genetics. Religious and secular ethics share common ground and points of agreement that can provide a valuable and constructive resource for open public discussion. Moreover, the expression of religious understandings can enhance respect for individual freedom and reinforce those democratic practices that are at the foundation of our public life.[1]

We are persuaded that religious voices should be among those heard in public deliberations about the uses of our genetic capabilities in a democratic and pluralistic republic. However, we do not contend that they should provide the underlying justification for the conclusions written into public policy. Instead, they offer insights and arguments of importance to many in our civil society that may enable us to envision the significance of our genetic powers from a variety of perspectives and to develop an overlapping consensus in public policy. We proceed from these beliefs in this chapter, investigating the ethical, theological, and social import of genetic interventions in human beings to enlarge our understanding of how we ought to live.

## VIGNETTES OF POTENTIAL GENETIC INTERVENTIONS

What can we do with our growing genetic powers and how might we be able to use them in the future? How might they affect our lives and those of others in our society? The following vignettes provide some sense of what current genetic research might make possible. Only the situation characterized in the first vignette has been attempted in human beings as of this writing.

>    *Somatic cell intervention for therapy.* A couple requests that gene transfer be used for their son, who has severe combined immunodeficiency (SCID)—the disease that afflicted David, the boy in the bubble, in Houston, Texas, so that he can be free of this life-threatening condition.
>
>    *Germline intervention to prevent disease.* A husband and wife who both carry the gene for cystic fibrosis (CF), an ultimately fatal respiratory disease, ask scientists and researchers to modify embryos they have had produced through in vitro fertilization, so that their children and their children's descendants will not be at risk of having CF.
>
>    *Somatic cell intervention for enhancement.* Two short-statured parents ask their pediatrician to use gene transfer in their five-year-old son, who is also short, to increase his height to the normal range.
>
>    *Germline intervention for enhancement.* Scientists, with the informed consent of the biological parents, seek to modify embryos before they are implanted in the uterus to improve the long-term memory of children who might develop from these embryos.

*A borderline example that is between treatment and enhancement.* Scientists attempt to intervene genetically to prevent the aging of the human immune system, so that older people will be less susceptible to infectious diseases and cancers.

## DEVELOPING OUR CAPACITIES
## TO INTERVENE INTO OUR GENES

The story of how we came to embark on research that might ultimately give us the power to intervene into the human genome is relatively recent. It was in the middle of the twentieth century that scientists began to realize that genes—the name given to whatever it was that passed on inherited characteristics from one generation to the next—were made of deoxyribonucleic acid, better known as DNA. By the 1960s, they had discerned how the fundamental components of DNA molecules combine to form genes. They went on to crack the code by which DNA passes on the information that enables living beings to function. Since then, the technology of gene transfer, or of moving genes into cells to modify their activities and compensate for gene mutations, has been developing at an uneven pace.

Two revolutionary concepts are behind these efforts. One is that by gaining access to genes within human beings and correcting those that have gone awry, medical scientists can attack medical problems at their sources. Successful therapeutic gene transfer would represent an advance over the use of drugs or chemotherapy to treat disease. Another novel concept underlying these attempts is that by changing genes in ourselves and our children, we might alter and improve the human species. Indeed, some have suggested that our growing genetic capabilities could give us the power to remake humankind.[2]

Two ways of intervening into the genes of human beings could provide the means for realizing these goals: somatic cell and germline interventions.

### Somatic Cell Interventions

Somatic cell interventions would introduce genes into the somatic or nonreproductive cells found throughout the bodies of human beings. In the first vignette presented above, a somatic cell genetic intervention would be used to treat severe combined immunodeficiency, a rare and fatal condition, from which their son suffered. This somatic cell genetic intervention would affect only the genes of the individual into whom it is introduced. Such therapeutic somatic cell research has focused on treating conditions such as cystic fibrosis, hemophilia, AIDS, and cancer.

In the course of this research, scientists have attempted to use both viral and nonviral vectors, or ways of carrying inserting genes into somatic cells, hoping that some of this additional DNA would be "adopted" by cells and begin to function in them.[3] However, nonviral vectors, while likely to present fewer toxic and immunological problems than viral vectors, do not provide an efficient means for gene transfer. Moreover, they do not express the gene that has been inserted into them for an extended period of time. Therefore, researchers have turned to the use of viral vectors as the most efficient means of delivering genes to the cells of the human body.

Certain kinds of viruses infect us by inserting their genetic information into our cells, which then reproduce the invading virus. In some forms of gene transfer, scientists first attempt to disarm this sort of virus by removing from it the gene that causes infectious disease. Then the virus is sent into the person's somatic cells along with the replacement gene in hopes that it will do its therapeutic work. Hundreds of procedures that use such viral vectors are being tried out today in experimental gene transfer studies. So far, however, the research has produced few successes. A basic difficulty is that currently available vectors lack the capacity to take new DNA into the precise location where the mutated gene lies in order to counteract or replace it.[4] Further, the immune system sometimes reacts against the cells whose genes have been changed and diminishes them.

One therapeutic gene transfer experiment carried out in France involved treating ten children for a fatal form of SCID syndrome.[5] A viral vector was used to bring treated blood-producing stem cells into the bodies of these children, and they had seemed to do well. However, in the summer of 2002, one of them developed a leukemia-like syndrome that was treated with chemotherapy, and this trial was halted temporarily. Medical scientists think that this complication was caused by a viral vector that had entered the wrong region of a cell's genome and caused the cell to divide too rapidly.[6] The researchers contend that this molecular response was rare and unlikely to recur.

This unfortunate outcome raised further questions about the use of viral vectors in gene transfer attempts. Such attempts had already received a serious setback in 1999 when an eighteen-year-old man died while in gene transfer trials for ornithine transcarbamylase (OTC) deficiency, a liver disease. The death of Jesse Gelsinger, who had volunteered for a study that he hoped would help others who were more seriously ill, was directly attributed to the use of an adenoviral vector.[7] This tragedy made it evident that we need to anticipate and address more adequately the risks of delivering and integrating DNA into human somatic cells. It also made it clear that we need to develop better ways of informing human subjects about such risks.[8]

Scientists think that they will eventually overcome the problems that they have encountered in using viral vectors in attempts at gene transfer. Further, they hope that they will be able to develop methods of correcting or replacing mutated genes with genes that are well functioning, rather than having to resort to the current method of gene addition.

In our anticipation of the benefits that somatic cell genetic interventions might provide, we have developed the mistaken impression that therapeutic gene transfer is already successful. We have tended to overlook the reality that this research is highly exploratory and experimental. Although it is to be hoped that studies of recombinant DNA will lead to significant medical cures, we cannot currently provide definitive somatic cell therapies to those who are ill. Because such efforts are still on the drawing board, we think that it is more accurate to describe them as attempts at "gene transfer," rather than "gene therapy."

### Germline Interventions

In the second vignette set out above, parents consider using germline genetic interventions in embryos created with their gametes by means of in vitro fertilization. They seek to avoid having their children and their children's descendants afflicted with cystic fibrosis, a debilitating and ultimately fatal respiratory disease. The use of such a germline intervention would involve placing a specific, identifiable gene into an early embryo, thereby affecting all of its cells, including the reproductive cells that will develop during gestation and that, in turn, will become the egg or sperm cells of the resulting organism. These genetic changes would be manifest not only in the child, but also in his or her descendants.[9]

Germline interventions could, in theory, also be carried out directly in sperm and eggs, but efforts to introduce genetic changes into gametes in mice have had limited success. A third method of germline intervention would involve inserting an artificial chromosome into the early embryo that would add not just one gene to an embryo but hundreds, even thousands. This method, too, is currently impeded by serious technical problems.[10]

The use of therapeutic germline interventions would seem to offer a variety of benefits to human beings. Chief among these benefits is that they might treat or cure disease related to genes not only in the children who might be born after such interventions, but also in their descendants. It would seem easier and more efficient to use germline interventions to avoid the inheritance of gene-based diseases within a family than to use repeated somatic cell interventions into individuals in each generation of that family.

Germline interventions might offer certain additional benefits. They might provide the only way to prevent irreversible damage sometimes caused by mutated genes during fetal development. Such interventions also could, over a long period of time, lessen the frequency of certain inherited diseases in the human gene pool, since persons who were treated as carriers of deleterious gene mutations would not pass on these mutations to their children. Scientists who served on an American Association for the Advancement of Science (AAAS) working group on inherited genetic modifications, however, could find few circumstances in which germline interventions would provide the only available way to minimize genetic disease in future children.[11] They maintained that alternative measures that present fewer risks are available for use.

The use of germline interventions also carries certain disadvantages. Changes made in the genes of early embryos would be passed along to the descendants of the resulting children. This possibility raises distinctive issues of safety, for a gene that did not hit the right target could create a harmful mutation that would be transferred to later generations.[12] Since the long-term effects of these genetic manipulations on our descendants are largely unknown, there is no way, in principle, to learn what their impact might be on our children several years from now or on their descendants two hundred years from now. Consequently, some are reluctant to endorse germline interventions out of fear that they might have unpredictable and injurious effects on their recipients and their descendants.

In addition, critics have raised the issue of informed consent in connection with germline interventions. Some maintain that these interventions constitute a form of experimentation on future generations without their informed consent that is ethically unacceptable. To change the genes of those who come after us without their agreement, they argue, is prospectively to limit their control over their own bodies and to restrict the decisions that they can make about their own children. Proponents of germline interventions for therapeutic purposes respond that any reasonable future person would consent to germline interventions that counter serious disease that they would otherwise experience.[13] They add that we make many decisions that affect the genes of our descendants without their consent, as when we choose to marry a certain person or undergo radiation therapy that might cause genetic mutations in us. Proponents conclude that we should view ourselves as proxies for future generations, choosing on their behalf to bring them into the world free of serious disease.

Most mainstream scientists, ethicists, religious thinkers, and public policy makers hold that research into the use of germline interventions should not be attempted now. The AAAS working group mentioned above concluded that before germline interventions could proceed in human beings, standards should be developed for assessing the short-term risks of such interventions to tomorrow's children and the long-term risks to multiple future generations.[14] The working group also maintained that germline interventions raise ethical and social questions concerning justice, discrimination, governmental control, and the common good to which we should respond as a society before we consider using such interventions in human beings.

## ADDRESSING QUESTIONS RAISED BY INTERVENTIONS

### Enhancement

The same methods of genetic intervention that could be developed for therapeutic purposes, we are coming to realize, could also be used for enhancement. This possibility is illustrated in the third and fourth vignettes presented above, where interventions enhance living individuals or future children and their descendants. That is, certain genes are selected for transfer into human beings in order to improve normal human characteristics beyond what is necessary to sustain or restore good health.[15] Is it ethically acceptable to embellish certain traits in ourselves and our children by means of genetic measures—for example, intelligence, competitiveness, physical strength, altruism? Although such genetic interventions are, for the most part, fanciful, given our current knowledge, it is important to address them before they appear on the scene, so that we are prepared to respond to them.

Before we discuss the question of enhancement, though, we need to explore the question of how to distinguish between therapy and enhancement. A paradigm case of therapy would involve correcting or removing the gene associated with Huntington disease, a debilitating and eventually fatal neurological disease. A paradigm case of enhancement would involve inserting a gene associated with an eye color that is held in high regard within a culture to increase that child's attractiveness. The differences between treatment and enhancement, however, are not always obvious, as the fifth vignette displays. If we were to discover and modify genes associated with aging, enabling individuals to live a long life free from degenerative diseases, would that intervention be an example of therapy or of enhancement? An anti-aging procedure could be considered a form of treatment, for it would ameliorate a disabling human condition and would treat future disease in advance. Or it might seem a form of enhancement because it would improve normal human characteristics beyond what is typical for the human species. It is difficult to discern whether treatment or enhancement is involved in this borderline case. Examples that gnaw away at the distinction between therapy and enhancement will always be with us. These hard cases, however, do not destroy the usefulness of the distinction.[16] It provides a baseline for conducting a reasonable discussion of the ethics of genetic interventions and for assessing where we should draw lines around their uses.

The well-being of an individual with diabetes is compromised in a way that the well-being of an individual with average memory and health is not. The person with diabetes needs to be brought back to a level of normal functioning through available medical means, whereas it is difficult to argue that the person with average athletic ability needs to be brought to a higher level of athletic functioning by genetic means.

Some argue that, other things being equal, it is ethically justifiable to pursue such enhancements because it is preferable to live longer, in above-average health, and with more attractive personal characteristics and physical features. When the goal of enhancement is to improve the human condition, they maintain, there is nothing wrong with pursuing it. Further, they point out that we already engage in nongenetic enhancement in many ways in our ordinary lives and that this is not considered wrong. Thus, when we exercise our bodies to develop trim figures or employ orthodontics to straighten our teeth, we enhance ourselves. Indeed, parents are praised if they provide music lessons and special athletic coaching to assist their children to perform at a higher level. If we already enhance ourselves and our children in these ways without moral disapprobation, why should we not do so by genetic means as well?

There is an ethical difference between giving individuals greater opportunities to develop their skills and changing their genes in ways that make their own efforts, talents, and choices less relevant to their actions. What is new about such changes is not that they introduce enhancements into our lives, but the kind and extent of the enhancements that they make possible. When parents try to change their children by giving them music lessons or athletic coaching, for instance, they hope to improve certain abilities of their children. However, it is possible for their children to reject such changes. In contrast, when parents change their children by intervening in their genetic makeup, they introduce changes that it is more difficult for their children to undo. Their children's options are limited to a much greater extent when their genes have been changed.

Furthermore, it is arguable that such genetic changes could have a significant negative impact on those who undergo them and on the society in which they live. Suppose, for example, that gene transfer had advanced to a stage where we could significantly increase memory and ambition. To achieve high social status, individuals could use genetic interventions to create an above-average level of memory and ambition in themselves. If many people were to enhance themselves in this way, the average level of memory and ambition in the community would increase dramatically. Individuals might respond by using genetic means to produce an even greater increase in their own memory and ambition, thereby collectively creating an upward spiral of improvement seemingly without end. They could not withdraw from this spiral without condemning themselves to lesser social status.

The qualities that would give favored individuals a winning edge in such a society would not necessarily be those that are cherished within the Christian tradition or those that are beneficial to society as a whole. Having above-average memory and ambition might make a person more likely to succeed in meeting our society's cultural standards, but too much striving for individual success could foster self-centeredness and lack of concern for others. As Christians, we do not view ourselves as locked in a competitive battle that will result in the exclusion of many from the top tier of society. Instead, we are called by our faith to be members each of one another (Rom. 12:4–5), caring for one another and assisting those who are excluded from society. However, in a society where there is great pressure on individuals to compete for status and material rewards, civic-mindedness and solidarity could be so reduced as to endanger the very existence of that society as a communal enterprise.

This example suggests that as we move along the continuum from therapy to enhancement, it is wise to become more cautious. The question whether those without serious disease who undertake genetic enhancement would pose significant risks to society is sufficiently significant to merit much more public discussion than has been carried on to date.

### Eugenics

The history of the eugenics movement illustrates how efforts to enhance human capabilities by genetic interventions can go awry. The *Encyclopaedia Britannica* defines genetics as the study of human improvement by genetic means. The term was coined by Francis Galton in the late nineteenth century and derives from the Greek root meaning "good in birth." In the original version put forward by Galton, eugenics was intended to be a voluntary, socially encouraged program of upgrading the quality of the (British) population through the marriage and reproduction of the "fittest" group within society. However, in the twentieth century this kind of "positive" eugenics quickly gave way in several countries to attempts to prevent "unfit" persons from propagating their kind, that is, to "negative" eugenics. The initial method for preventing such propagation was the involuntary institutionalization and sexual segregation of those designated as unfit. However, the then-modern techniques of sexual sterilization—through vasectomy or the cutting of the fallopian tubes—quickly supplanted life-long institutionalization and were thought to be a more humane alternative to confinement.

To its shame, the United States was a pioneer in the passage of laws mandating sexual sterilization for the "unfit" and in the development of detailed lists of undesirable individuals and groups. More than thirty states passed mandatory sterilization statutes at one time or another, and in an infamous decision written by Justice Oliver Wendell Holmes in 1927 Virginia's mandatory sterilization law was found to be constitutional (*Buck v. Bell*, 274 U.S. 200 [1927]). The 1933 Nazi sterilization law was closely modeled on the writings of a U.S. eugenicist, Harry Laughlin, and the Japanese sterilization laws of 1940 and 1948 drew on both U.S. and German precedents. In the late twentieth century the Chinese Maternal and Child Health Act of 1994 reintroduced eugenic notions into public policy. (Under the terms of this law, couples are required to receive formal counseling before marrying and before conceiving children. Pregnant women must also be given medical advice. How strictly the Chinese law is enforced is a matter of some debate.) In fact, most industrialized nations, including Sweden, parts of Canada, and many Latin American countries, enacted mandatory sterilization laws at some point during the twentieth century. To its credit, the United Kingdom did not. Several Roman Catholic and Anglican thinkers in the United Kingdom were critical of the eugenics initiative.

Those designated as "unfit" usually fell into one of several categories. People termed "feeble-minded" were usually listed as among those to undergo sterilization in early sterilization statutes. Those afflicted with serious mental illnesses—especially schizophrenia or severe bipolar affective disorder—were also included, as were people with epilepsy and Huntington disease. In some cases people with physical disabilities like visual or hearing impairments were also singled out as candidates for sterilization. The "science" that underlay such efforts viewed these traits as unit characters—that is, unified and clear-cut traits—that were inexorably transmitted from one generation to the next.

In part because of the wild extremes to which Germany pushed its eugenics program in the late 1930s and early 1940s, mandatory sterilization programs are now in disrepute. In fact, China's current program has been roundly criticized by geneticists from many nations. Individuals and families are now the primary locus of decision making about reproductive matters, and federal rules and state statutes in the United States make it quite difficult to sterilize anyone—either a minor or an adult—without his or her explicit understanding of the procedure and informed consent.

In the latter part of the twentieth century and in the twenty-first century, questions analogous to those raised by state-mandated eugenics programs have been identified by several commentators. These questions focus on decisions by individuals and couples about whether to attempt a pregnancy, undergo preimplantation or prenatal diagnosis, or discard embryos or terminate pregnancies in cases where the embryo or fetus is likely to be afflicted with an identifiable condition—for example, cystic fibrosis or Down syndrome. One commentator, Troy Duster, has asked whether the decisions of individuals or couples enrolled in genetic screening and treatment programs might be leading us to a new kind of eugenics "through the backdoor," since these programs reflect a de facto policy of selecting among potential future persons on the basis of whether they are likely to be born with specific handicapping conditions.[17] Diane Paul and Philip Kitcher point out that "voluntary" is a slippery term and that strongly held social values can be partially coercive of individuals.[18]

There is probably little to be gained by lumping coercive state programs with patterns of free decision making by individuals and couples and then designating the latter as "eugenics." Individual choices are made with at least some degree of freedom. Further, insofar as social values affect who we are as individuals, a corrective to be taken when these values may be malign, in addition to making room for individual choice, is to encourage vigorous social debate about appropriate and just uses of various genetic interventions.

In the future, additional governments may follow China and at least encourage at-risk couples not to reproduce or else to undergo genetic testing or prenatal diagnosis in order to prevent the transmission of disease. Such programs could be based on reliable scientific information about the transmission of recessive or dominant disorders and could even be coupled with the offer of interventions to prevent the occurrence of those disorders. (The current offer of maternal serum alpha-fetoprotein testing to pregnant women could thus be a precursor of more ambitious future programs.) It is difficult to foresee all the conditions for which such programs might be proposed or all the directions in which they might go. In our view, it will be important for them to be voluntary rather than compulsory and for them to be coupled with efforts to help people with disabilities to achieve their full potential. Moreover, to prevent government from coercively imposing genetic interventions on its citizens, and to overcome social pressures that might lead to inequitable and unjust policies for their use, it will also be essential to use the avenues for public discussion and debate that are available in democratic societies.[19]

## INTERVENING INTO GOD'S CREATION

Some of the questions created by our growing genetic powers are the same as those raised by any novel techniques that heal or compensate for human diseases or disabilities. However, because some of these genetic powers involve directly altering bodily material for purposes never before entertained and in ways that might be transmitted to future generations, their possible use may raise unique ethical and theological questions. Thus, the gene transfer interventions discussed in this chapter raise in acute form some of the theological issues discussed earlier in chapter 2.

A theological question often voiced is whether the use of gene transfer and germline interventions would put us in danger of overstepping human limitations and defying God. Some have declared that to attempt to modify human genes is to invade territory forbidden to us by God.[20] Several religious and secular thinkers maintain that human genes should be regarded as untouchable as a matter of principle because genes are biologically essential to who we are as human beings. Indeed, they define who we are as human.

Some theologians who adopt this noninterventionist view call upon Scripture for additional support. The Bible, they indicate, teaches that to peer into "the book of life" (Exod. 32:32; Ps. 69:28; Rev. 20:12) and change what we find there amounts to presumptuous error akin to eating the forbidden fruit in the Garden of Eden. This view, however, would have us refrain from attempting to treat and prevent serious illness not only by genetic means but by any means. A refusal to intervene to overcome disease, we believe, contradicts our calling to heal the sick and to relieve their suffering. Moreover, the belief that "the book of life" referred to in Scripture is a document in which our entire lives are inscribed before we have lived them rests on a misreading of that text. "The book of life" was instead the record of the members of the community, a register of "everyone who has been recorded for life in Jerusalem" (Isa. 4:3), not a revelation of what the future holds.

Further, this approach misreads the role that our genes play in forming us. It assumes that genes determine human nature and that to change them would ipso facto be to change our very nature as human beings. Yet neither science nor the Christian tradition teaches us to regard ourselves as mere puppets who are predetermined by our genes to think and act in certain ways. When we attempt to modify genes in individuals that have mutated in harmful ways, we do not change the basic identity of those who bear such genes. For these and other reasons, few Anglican thinkers maintain that we ought to refrain from all genetic interventions.[21]

Some religious commentators from the opposite end of the spectrum have argued that it is wrong *not to* intervene into human genes to promote human well-being. The late Anglican Joseph Fletcher maintained that genetic manipulations undertaken to fix and control the human condition represent an ethical advance, rather than a regression. "Man is a maker and a selector and a designer, and the more rationally contrived and deliberate anything is, the more human it is," he declared.[22] He went on to state that "[t]o be civilized, is to be artificial."[23] In his view, human beings are called to use their technologies to shape the human genetic future and would be ethically remiss were they to refrain from remaking and improving humankind.

This prointervention approach accents the human capacity for free choice and places great faith in human ability to make wise decisions about the use of genetic interventions. It presumes that such interventions would give our children a sound physical and mental constitution,[24] but does not define just what it would mean to have such a constitution. It would set no limits to human interventions into our genes in spite of the possibly negative effects on individuals and society that have been postulated for some of these. The range and degree of acceptable interventions into human genes, on this approach, would be infinite. This lack of caution about the extent to which we should attempt to control human genes has struck many in the Christian tradition as a form of overreaching. To aim to remake humankind in our own image by means of genetic interventions, if not carried out in light of our understanding of our finite role in healing and nurturing others, could disregard God's sovereignty and wrongly interfere with creation.

The Anglican tradition would urge us to avoid attempting to aggrandize humankind by means of genetic interventions. Anglican thinkers, for the most part, join those who adopt a middle position between those who condemn all human genetic interventions and those who embrace them in their entirety. Commentators who fall into this mean between extremes can, in turn, be divided into two groups: The first emphasizes our role as stewards of what God has given to us in creation, while the second emphasizes our calling as ongoing cocreators with God in a dynamic and ever-changing world.

Those who focus on human stewardship of creation affirm that God has commissioned human beings to care for the natural order (Gen. 1 and 2). As we carry out this responsibility, we ought to recognize and honor the natural limits built into creation. On the stewardship approach, we should intervene into the human body only if it is clear that we are assisting natural processes to reach their intended ends. Anglican theologian Oliver O'Donovan, for instance, declares that we should not misuse our freedom in ways that would radically violate the natural order of creation.[25]

Those who adopt the stewardship approach generally accept the ethical legitimacy of using somatic cell genetic interventions for treatment and prevention of disease. Lutheran thinker Gilbert Meilaender, for instance, maintains that it is ethically permissible to proceed with somatic cell gene transfer for serious disease, since this might overcome disorders that hinder persons from carrying out biological functions necessary for personal or species survival.[26] When we attempt to modify our genes to rid ourselves and fellow creatures of illness and disability in this way, we cooperate with God in restoring human beings to their intended mode of functioning.

There is less agreement among those who adopt the stewardship view about whether to use germline genetic interventions in humans. Some stewardship proponents hold that we should not intervene into the human germline at all. Others, however, maintain that it would be ethically acceptable to use such interventions to treat serious disease if they were to prove more effective than somatic cell modifications for this purpose.

When the possibility of enhancing human beings enters the picture, however, those who adopt the stewardship view tend to draw back, maintaining that efforts to enhance human beings would push beyond the limits of the created order. To attempt to change our children and future generations in ways that exceed what is necessary to maintain good health and normal human functioning would open the door to making radical changes in humankind that would go well beyond God's intentions. Human pride and egoism will lead us to attempt to recreate the world in our own image, stewardship advocates maintain. In their view, human freedom is limited by the contours of our bodies and by our very finitude. This freedom is increased, not by expanding our power over creation, but by living well within the limits set by the God-given order of creation.

Cocreationists, who form the other group in the middle of the spectrum about the use of human genetic interventions, would intervene more extensively into nature and the human body. They see creation as an ongoing, dynamic process in which God is continuously active, influencing but not determining the direction in which creation moves.[27] At the heart of what it means for human beings to be created in God's image, these thinkers hold, is that we are to cooperate with God in the creative process. They maintain that the power to create is at the core of the dominion that God grants to human beings over creation in Genesis 1 and 2. By exercising our ability to shape and direct nature by means of genetic interventions, we cooperate in God's ongoing creative endeavors. Those who take this approach do not assert that we are equal to God, for, as "created cocreators," we are limited creatures who are affected by our environment, culture, and genes. Yet we possess the freedom to make ethically justifiable choices to intervene into nature.[28] Thus, Ted Peters observes: "Should we play God? No we should not play God in the promethean sense. But we should play human in the *imago dei* sense—that is, we should understand ourselves as created cocreators and express our scientific and technological creativity."[29]

Cocreationists agree with those who embrace the stewardship position in holding that it would be ethically acceptable to use somatic cell genetic interventions for therapeutic purposes, if this could be done safely and effectively. However, cocreationists go on to maintain that it would also be ethically appropriate to carry out germline interventions if they could be rendered safe and effective. Their primary support for this view is that we are expected, as God's companions in creating, to relieve human beings of the suffering caused by serious genetic disease as far into the future as we can. We ought to correct and restore genes that malfunction and seriously impair our health and that of our descendants as an essential aspect of our call to love our neighbor and seek the common good.

Thus, on both the stewardship and the cocreation views, it is morally acceptable, in principle, to modify somatic cell genes for therapeutic purposes. Further, when these views are combined, there is considerable support among them for the therapeutic use of germline interventions to overcome disease in multiple generations. When the question arises of whether we should attempt to enhance human beings through the use of either somatic cell or germline interventions, cocreationists tend to move forward toward that goal while stewardship advocates tend to draw back.

## REMAKING HUMANKIND

What is ultimately at issue for all of these thinkers is whether we should set out to remake human beings. Some who peer into the future fear that society or individuals acting under the pressure of socially defined norms will engineer human beings in ways that would radically change them to the point that they would no longer be human.[30] For instance, Leon Kass, the chair of the President's Council on Bioethics, has declared that:

> human nature itself lies on the operating table, ready for alteration, for eugenic and neuropsychic "enhancement," for wholesale design. In leading laboratories, academic and industrial, new creators are confidently amassing their powers, while on the street their evangelists are zealously prophesying a posthuman future.[31]

Genetic interventions, he contends, will necessarily modify the very essence or essential features of human beings. Yet these essential human features have inherent value, he maintains, and to change them by genetic or neuropsychiatric interventions would be to violate human dignity. Where would he have us draw an ethical line beyond which we should not go in using our genetic powers to change human beings? Kass, in a way akin to those who follow the stewardship approach, would have nature serve as an ethical guide to fixing such a line.

Other commentators, both secular and religious, would join with the co-creationists in maintaining that it is ethically appropriate to engage in genetic interventions that might reshape our notions of human nature. They believe that we are not lacking in analogies to guide our reflections about whether it would be right to alter humans in ways that would challenge our assumptions about what it means to be human. Past revolutions in technology and culture, such as the introduction of the wheel, the flowering of the Renaissance, the Industrial Revolution, the development of the theory of evolution, and the introduction of the germ theory of disease have done so in ways that we take to have been appropriate and beneficial. Further, in the view of those who adopt a dynamic view of human nature, we have an obligation to develop our inherited capacities, leaving behind "a fixed image of what was, is, and always ought to be." [32] Roman Catholic theologian Karl Rahner maintains that:

> This self-manipulation is not only carried out unconsciously, as was the case almost exclusively in the past, but deliberately planned, programmed and controlled. Man no longer makes himself merely with reference to eternity but with reference to history itself as such. . . . To a certain degree his ultimate essence has broken through to the outer regions of his existence. To a larger, more comprehensive, radical and tangible extent man has become what, according to the Christian understanding he is: the free being who has been handed over to himself.[33]

There are those who refuse to speculate about the possibility of changing and remaking humankind, or at least our understanding of what it is to be human, taking this as a form of science fiction. However, some of the genetic interventions posited by imaginative thinkers might in fact be implemented at some point in the future. If we were to decide against discussing whether we should genetically remake humankind today, we would risk failing to develop sound ethical guidance that we would need when faced with significant choices about the uses of genetic interventions tomorrow.[34]

At what point, if any, should we impose limits on the uses of such genetic interventions? A thoughtful Christian approach to this question takes into account not only the wishes and life plans of individuals, but also the values and goals of the wider community. It is true that Christians are individualists in that they value each person as a unique human being and child of God. Yet Christians are also communitarians in that they seek to create a cooperative society that considers the well-being and dignity of others and of the community as a whole. Thus, Christians are called to respect the genetic choices of individuals as far as possible, even as they recognize that, in some instances, individual choices about uses of our genetic powers should be limited because of their import for society. This viewpoint is not exclusively a Christian one. Notable secular thinkers who cherish individual freedom and seek the common good also recognize that at times "the interests of individuals sometimes yield to the good of all."[35]


## JUSTICE

Several commentators have raised important questions about whether the unfettered access of a relatively few individuals to genetic interventions for treatment and enhancement would create serious injustices within our society.[36] Some note that the prospect of financial reward, rather than considerations of justice, often drives decisions about which health care measures will be developed.[37] If genetic interventions were eventually to enter the marketplace, they would be expensive initially and would therefore only be within the reach of those with substantial financial resources. As these individuals purchased such interventions in increasing numbers, others who could not afford them would come to experience a greater proportion of disease and of socially disfavored traits than their well-to-do neighbors. Gradually, those who had not benefited from genetic interventions might come to be viewed as social pariahs, not only in the eyes of wealthier, healthier, and more beautiful members of society, but also, as they absorbed dominant cultural prejudices, in their own eyes. Thus, the introduction of expensive somatic cell and germline interventions for both therapy and enhancement eventually could lower the relative degree of well-being of those without access to them and harden social divisions that are already present in our stratified society. The well-off would prevail in terms of health and social position at the expense of those of more modest means. This outcome would fly in the face of the Christian and secular ethical traditions of egalitarian justice, which call for special attention to the needs of those who are less well-off and look askance at the perpetuation of social disparities that undermine the equal dignity of human beings.

Each of us bears a responsibility for the creation and preservation of a just society. In such a society, genetic research and its clinical applications would work to meet the needs not only of the wealthy, but also of its most vulnerable members, benefiting all members of society in an equitable manner. Jewish and Christian approaches to justice, as well as some contemporary secular views of justice, assign priority in access to care to the most needy. This theme recurs in Scripture, as seen in this passage: "Since there will never cease to be some need on the earth, I therefore command you, 'Open your hand to the poor and needy neighbor in your land'" (Deut. 15:11). Among the early Christians, "there was not a needy person," for those who lacked the basics were attended to by their neighbors (Acts 4:34). A linchpin of John Rawls's influential theory of justice holds that the needs of the least well-off members of society represent a primary consideration in an adequate theory of justice.[38]

On this view of justice, it would be unfair to promote the genetic health and well-being of those who are well-off without concern for the effects on marginalized individuals and communities. Society and its members thus have a responsibility to assist the vulnerable, poor, or disabled to meet their significant needs—even if that means that others might not obtain all they might desire in the way of genetic treatments and enhancements. To elevate individual autonomy to the exclusion of all other values would be to ignore some of the basic requirements of justice.[39] We should attempt to ensure that our health care resources are distributed fairly and justly, recognizing that those who can pay for access to medically and ethically sound genetic treatments have a responsibility to contribute to the care of those who cannot. Fair distribution of basic health care resources is essential to a just human community in which the well-being of each individual is a high priority.

According to many Christian and secular ethicists we also have a responsibility to challenge the use of genetic interventions that could deepen social or economic stratification and diminish diversity within the community. Individual choices to use our growing genetic powers, taken collectively, could exacerbate social inequalities and economic divisions and deepen existing forms of social discrimination.[40] The use of genetic enhancements, in particular, could worsen prejudices that lead to the inequitable treatment of persons on the basis of race, gender, or age.

Human diversity—sexual, racial, ethnic, and cultural—is a valued aspect of the human condition within the Christian and the secular traditions. Genetic diversity has enabled human beings to survive, evolve, and adapt to new situations and helped us to appreciate the richness and variety of creation. If genetic interventions were eventually to become more affordable and more common, however, their use could lead to a gradual reduction of diversity within society as socially disfavored differences were eradicated.

Members of the disability rights community have been especially concerned that the use of genetic interventions to prevent disabilities might create an environment more hostile to them. As research on genetic interventions advances in a culture that emphasizes competition and youth, marketing and other resources will inevitably be pumped into genetic enhancement in particular.[41] The contemporary social movement to address the needs of those with disabilities more adequately, which was slow to develop, could diminish in force if genetic measures to prevent disabilities were employed with increasing frequency. Thus, some within the disabled community believe that our new genetic powers could threaten to marginalize those with disabilities.

We should resist genetic interventions that would reduce or downplay the range of diversity that pervades and enriches society.[42] This stance does not commit us to aiming for unlimited diversity. It would be wrong to perpetuate diseases such as cystic fibrosis, Alzheimer's disease, and Huntington disease in order to preserve human diversity. However, it is important to discern when genetic interventions would, as a whole, encourage the development of arbitrary standards of proper human functioning and of beauty that would lead to discrimination against those who did not adhere to them.

## CONCLUSION

The Anglican tradition has always evinced great respect for scientific and medical discoveries, particularly those directed toward the amelioration of disease. In keeping with that tradition, we believe that we are called to use God's gifts of medicine and science to respond to the needs of those who face illness and disability due to genetic malfunction. This affirmation is the principal basis for our assertion *that it is ethically warranted to proceed with research into somatic cell genetic interventions that are directed toward therapy,* provided that precautions are taken to protect the safety of the individuals involved and ensure their voluntary consent.

In utilizing an ethically sound experimental model for cutting edge research into somatic cells, investigators should provide the individuals involved with the complex information about the risks and benefits of a trial in language that is conceptually clear and understandable to nonscientists. Moreover, participants in gene transfer experiments should be told that, as yet, very few such experiments have demonstrated benefit to their subjects. They should not be given misleading promises of therapeutic results that would compromise the consent process and prey on those with mistaken and unrealistic hopes.

We believe that research into *germline genetic interventions for the prevention of disease,* while ethically acceptable in principle, should not be undertaken in human beings until at least three conditions related to safety have been met and significant ethical and social questions have been addressed. First, germline interventions should have reached the stage where they replace deleterious genes, rather than simply add genes. Second, we should have developed a method for evaluating the risks and the benefits of germline interventions over several generations of human beings, insofar as they can be known, and of comparing them with the risks and benefits associated with currently available interventions for the same diseases. The underlying principle behind this standard is that the risks and benefits of germline interventions for future persons, insofar as they can be known, should be no greater than the risks and benefits of being born with the genetic condition at issue. Third, we should have ascertained that germline techniques have been tested thoroughly on laboratory animals—preferably including nonhuman primates—and have been demonstrated to be safe, reliable, and reproducible. Finally, before germline interventions directed toward the prevention of disease are introduced into clinical practice, the social and moral implications of doing so should have been publicly discussed. Such discussion would give special attention to basic questions of what we mean by individual well-being and what is required to use them justly.

We are more cautious about the use of both somatic cell and germline interventions to *enhance* human beings. Mindful of our past misuses of God's gifts, we are concerned that the quest to improve human capabilities could easily go too far and too fast. However, we recognize that enhancement may be justifiable in some situations, especially for the alleviation of human suffering.

In our judgment, uses of genetic interventions for enhancement should not be publicly funded at present. Further, any attempts to perform genetic enhancement, even if financed by private funds, should be subjected to a prior public review process, in which their safety and social impact are carefully assessed, before they proceed.

We believe that our society should promote public discussion and education about the scientific, social, and ethical implications of the use of somatic cell and germline interventions. To do so would be to facilitate communication and understanding between scientists/researchers and the public and would lay the foundation for justified public trust in the effort to develop genetic interventions in human beings. It would also support and strengthen our democratic institutions and increase the likelihood that all centrally located decisions about the development of genetic interventions would be transparent to public view and subject to public assessment. In our view, decisions about the use of genetic interventions in human beings should be made in light of our religious and secular vocation to treat one another as immeasurably valuable and our calling to serve the common good and foster justice within the human community.

## NOTES

1. James F. Childress, "Religion, Morality, and Public Policy: The Controversy about Human Cloning," in Dena S. Davis and Laurie Zoloth, *Notes from a Narrow Ridge: Religion and Bioethics* (Hagerstown, Md.: University Publishing, 1999), 65–86; Courtney S. Campbell, "In Whose Image? Religion and the Controversy of Human Cloning," *Second Opinion* no. 1 (September 1999): 24–43; Cynthia B. Cohen, "Religious Belief, Politics, and Public Bioethics: A Challenge to Political Liberalism," *Second Opinion* no. 6 (May 2001): 37–52.

2. Paul Ramsey, *Fabricated Man: The Ethics of Genetic Control* (New Haven: Yale University Press, 1970); Joseph Fletcher, *The Ethics of Genetic Control: Ending Reproductive Roulette* (Garden City, N.Y.: Anchor Press/Doubleday, 1974); Lee M. Silver, *Remaking Eden: How Genetic Engineering and Cloning Will Transform the American Family* (New York: Avon Books, 1997); George Annas, "The Man on the Moon, Immortality, and Other Millennial Myths: The Prospects and Perils of Human Genetic Engineering," *Emory Law Journal* 49 (2000): 754–782; Francis Fukuyama, *Our Posthuman Future: Consequences of the Biotechnology Revolution* (New York: Farrar, Straus and Giroux, 2002); Leon Kass, *Life, Liberty, and the Defense of Dignity: The Challenge for Bioethics* (San Francisco: Encounter Books, 2002).

3. Nikunj Somia and Inder M. Verma, "Gene Therapy: Trials and Tribulations," *Nature Reviews: Genetics* 1 (November 2000): 91–98, reprinted in Tom Beauchamp and LeRoy Walters, *Contemporary Issues in Bioethics*, 6th edition (Belmont, Calif.: Wadsworth, 2003), 526–530.

4. Ibid.

5. M. Cavazzana-Calvo et al., "Gene Therapy of Human Severe Combined Immunodeficiency (SCID)-X1 Disease" *Science* 288 (2000): 669–672; S. Hacein-Bey-Abina et al., "Sustained Correction of X-Linked Severe Combined Immunodeficiency by *ex vivo* Gene Therapy," *New England Journal of Medicine* 346 (2002): 1185–1193.

6. Eliot Marshall, "Gene Therapy A Suspect in Leukemia-like Disease," *Science* 298 (2002): 34–35.

7. Somia and Verma, "Gene Therapy," 528.

8. Theodore Friedmann, "Principles for Human Gene Therapy Studies," *Science* 287 (March 24, 2000): 2163–2165, reprinted in Beauchamp and Walters, *Contemporary Issues*, 522–525.

9. LeRoy Walters and Julie Gage Palmer, *The Ethics of Human Gene Therapy* (New York: Oxford, 1997), 63–67; Mark S. Frankel and Audrey R. Chapman, *Human Inheritable Genetic Modifications: Assessing Scientific, Ethical, Religious, and Policy Issues* (Washington, D.C.: American Association for the Advancement of Science, 2000), 2.

10. Frankel and Chapman, *Human Inheritable Genetic Modifications*, 16.

11. Ibid., 7, 13–14.

12. Walters and Palmer, *Ethics of Human Gene Therapy*, 72–74, 80.

13. Ibid., 86.

14. Frankel and Chapman, *Human Inheritable Genetic Modifications*, 3.

15. Eric Juengst, "What Does Enhancement Mean?" in Erik Parens, ed., *Enhancing Human Traits: Ethical and Social Implications* (Washington, D.C.: Georgetown University Press, 1998), 29–47.

16. Juengst, "What Does Enhancement Mean?" 34.

17. Troy Duster, *Backdoor to Eugenics* (New York: Routledge, 1990).

18. Diane Paul, "Is Genetics Disguised Eugenics?" in Robert F. Weir, Susan C. Lawrence, and Evan Fales, eds., *Genes and Human Self-Knowledge: Historical and Philosophical Reflections on Modern Genetics* (Iowa City: University of Iowa Press, 1994); Philip Kitcher, *The Lives to Come* (New York: Simon and Schuster, 1996).

19. Cynthia B. Cohen, "Creating Tomorrow's Children: The Right to Reproduce and Germline Interventions," in Audrey R. Chapman and Mark S. Frankel, eds., American Association for the Advancement of Science, *Designing Our Descendants: The Promise and Perils of Genetic Modifications* (Baltimore: Johns Hopkins University Press, 2002).

20. Ramsey, *Fabricated Man*, 151.

21. Committee on Medical Ethics, Episcopal Diocese of Washington, D.C., *Wrestling with the Future: Our Genes and Our Choices* (Harrisburg, Pa.: Morehouse, 1998), 15–18.

22. Joseph Fletcher, "Ethical Aspects of Genetic Controls," *New England Journal of Medicine* 285, no. 14 (1971): 776–783.

23. Joseph Fletcher, *The Ethics of Genetic Control*, 15.

24. Fletcher, "Ethical Aspects of Genetic Controls," 776.

25. Oliver O'Donovan, *Begotten or Made?* (New York: Oxford University Press, 1984), 29.

26. Gilbert Meilaender, "Mastering our Gen(i)es: When Do We Say No?" *The Christian Century* (October 3, 1990): 872–875.

27. Ronald Cole-Turner, *The New Genesis: Theology and the Genetic Revolution* (Louisville, Ky.: Westminster John Knox Press, 1997), 99.

28. Philip Hefner, *The Human Factor* (Minneapolis: Fortress Press, 1993), 35–42.

29. Ted Peters, *Playing God? Genetic Determinism and Human Freedom* (New York: Routledge, 1997), 161.

30. Ramsey, *Fabricated Man*; Annas, "The Man on the Moon"; Fukuyama, *Our Posthuman Future*; Kass, *Life, Liberty, and the Defense of Dignity*.

31. Kass, *Life, Liberty, and the Defense of Dignity*, 23.

32. James F. Gustafson, "Genetic Engineering and the Normative View of the Human" in Preston N. Williams, ed., *Ethical Issues in Biology and Medicine* (Cambridge, Mass.: Schenkman, 1973), 46–58.

33. Karl Rahner, *Theological Investigations*, trans. Graham Harrison (New York: Herder & Herder, 1972) 9: 205–224. Cited in LeRoy Walters, "Human Genetic Intervention and the Theologians: Cosmic Theology and Casuisitic Analysis," in Lisa Sowle Cahill and James F. Childress, eds., *Christian Ethics: Problems and Prospects* (Cleveland: Pilgrim Press, 1996), 235–249.

34. Allen Buchanan, Dan W. Brock, Norman Daniels, and Daniel Wikler, *From Chance to Choice: Genetics and Justice* (New York: Cambridge University Press, 2000), 23.

35. Ibid., 11–12.

36. W. French Anderson, "Human Gene Therapy," *Science* 256, no. 5058 (1992): 808–813; Allen Verhey, " 'Playing God' and Invoking a Perspective," *Journal of Medicine and Philosophy* 20 (1995): 347–364; Walters and Palmer, *Ethics of Human Gene Therapy*, 83, 129, 132; Lisa Sowle Cahill, "Genetics, Ethics and Social Policy," in Maureen Junker-Kenny and Lisa Sowle Cahill, eds., *The Ethics of Genetic Engineering* (London: SCM Press, 1998), vii-xiii; Buchanan, Brock, Daniels, and Wikler, *From Chance to Choice*, 309–314.

37. Cahill, "Genetics, Ethics and Social Policy," xi.

38. John Rawls, *A Theory of Justice* (Cambridge: Harvard University Press, 1971).

39. Buchanan, Brock, Daniels, and Wikler, *From Chance to Choice*, 13.

40. Frankel and Chapman, *Human Inheritable Genetic Modifications*, 9–10.

41. Mark S. Frankel and Michele Garfinkel, "To Market, To Market: The Effects of Commerce on Germ Line Intervention" in Chapman and Frankel, *Designing Our Descendants* (Baltimore: Johns Hopkins University Press, 2002).

42. Richard A. McCormick, "Genetic Technology and Our Common Future," in Richard A. McCormick, *The Critical Calling: Reflections on Moral Dilemmas* (Washington, D.C.: Georgetown University Press, 1989), 261–272.

# 5

# Creating and Shaping Future Children

*Cynthia B. Cohen and Mary R. Anderlik*

We are on the verge of extending our powers to modify and select human genes beyond those found in adults and children to those we detect in early embryos. Currently, couples can create embryos in a laboratory dish and then select those that are free of genes associated with disease to transfer to a woman's uterus. This practice, known as preimplantation genetic diagnosis (PGD), avoids creating children who have genes associated with certain diseases. In the future, couples will be able to alter or replace such genes in early embryos, in effect treating genetic disease before these embryos are transferred to women's bodies. Such germline interventions will also allow couples to alter and enhance the features of future children by modifying their genes at the early embryonic stage.

This stunning repertoire of genetic technologies must be used in combination with in vitro fertilization or a novel technology hovering over the contemporary scene, reproductive cloning. The power that these merged technologies would give individuals and society over the creation of children raises fundamental questions about the limits of human finitude and about our understanding of procreation and parenthood.

If we were to create disease-free children via the petri dish and DNA chip, would that constitute a form of procreation? If we were to employ these techniques to treat and enhance future children, would we come to view them as products of our own making, rather than as gifts and creatures made in the image of God? Would the very availability of these novel technologies inevitably attract us to design the "perfect" child or to create a mini-Me? Could it become an obligation of parenthood to shape and mold future children in socially prescribed ways? In short, what it would mean to procreate children and to serve as their parents in a future in which we could produce and design children at will?

Rather than offer "a view from nowhere" in response to such questions, this chapter draws especially on the resources of the Anglican or Episcopal theological and moral tradition regarding procreation and parenthood, even as it attends to the broad Christian tradition and mainstream secular thought. Delving into a religious tradition such as Anglicanism, which honors its roots in Scripture and tradition, emphasizes the use of reason and the relevance of secular thought, and consciously seeks a "middle way" between extremes, can enrich theological and secular ethical analysis in at least two ways. First, it can offer a framework for analysis that is thicker and deeper than that suggested by invocations of choice or utility. Further, by attending to a lively discussion over time among thinkers at once rooted in a tradition and engaged in their societies, it can contribute to the development of a fuller and more meaningful understanding of procreation and parenthood.

## OUR NEW GENETIC POWERS

How we have gotten to this point? What has led us to develop the power to create children and to affect their health and features in significant ways? But first, just what do our novel genetic and reproductive powers enable us to do with early embryos?

Attempts to select and alter the genes of early embryos have followed fast on the heels of the new reproductive technologies. Interest in these novel ways of bringing babies into the world skyrocketed at the end of the last century as couples sought technological assistance to overcome infertility. Some used in vitro fertilization (IVF), in which sperm and egg are merged in a laboratory dish and, if they are fortunate, a fertilized egg results that is transferred to the uterus of a woman. This technique results in a successful pregnancy in about a quarter of such transfers on the average. IVF has enabled some couples to get around daunting physiological barriers that had blocked their earlier efforts to have children through coitus.

Some who were not infertile but who were at risk of transmitting inherited disease to their children soon turned to IVF. Since one or both of them carried a gene related to a serious disease, they initially sought to use a gamete from a donor who did not bear this gene, along with a gamete from the unaffected spouse. Some couples, however, felt that this approach left too much to chance, for they had no guarantee that the donated gametes did not bring with them some other medical risks. Moreover, some were morally and psychologically uncomfortable about inviting third parties to become progenitors of their children.

Meanwhile, medical scientists had gained direct access to the early embryo through IVF, which gave them the power to engage in hands-on embryonic manipulation. As a result, some couples in recent years have sought to avoid passing deleterious genes to their children by evaluating and selecting embryos outside the uterus, using certain reproductive and genetic measures, and then transferring the chosen embryos to the woman's body. Medical specialists anticipate the advent of still other technologies that might enable couples to create children who are free of inherited disease, including reproductive cloning. The following vignettes give an inkling of the current and future possibilities that these various technologies offer.

> *Using donated eggs to avoid genetic disease.* A couple eager to have a child is concerned about proceeding because the wife has a gene mutation that leads to Huntington disease, a fatal neurological condition that affects persons in mid-life. To avoid passing this gene to their child, they select an egg "donor" from among those listed in the catalog of an egg broker and agree to pay the broker $5,000 in exchange for her eggs, provided that she is tested and found to be free of the Huntington gene. When tests reveal that the donor does not have the gene, they accept her eggs, which are then surgically extracted from the donor and merged with the husband's sperm in a lab dish by means of IVF. Several embryos result, and four are transferred to the wife's uterus. Ultimately she gives birth to a healthy baby girl who is free of the gene associated with Huntington disease.
>
> *Creating multiple embryos to screen for genetic disease.* A couple with twins who have cystic fibrosis, a condition that creates severe respiratory disease and is ultimately fatal, learn that the twins were affected because both parents carry a genetic mutation linked to cystic fibrosis. For their next pregnancy, they decide to use preimplantation genetic diagnosis (PGD) to avoid having other children who will suffer from this condition. PGD allows them to learn whether any the embryos they have had created by means of IVF is free of the gene associated with cystic fibrosis. If so, they will have that embryo transferred to the woman's uterus with the hope that it will implant and develop into a child who will not have cystic fibrosis. They have chosen to use PGD because it does not involve abortion, a procedure that is of moral concern to them.
>
> *Providing treatment for genetic disease to a child not yet born.* In the future, couples may be able to use germline interventions, which involve repairing or replacing genes in embryos, to avert serious disease in their children. This technology, for instance, could help a couple avoid passing a gene associated with early onset Alzheimer's disease, which the husband bears, to their children. Embryos would be created by means

of IVF, and the gene at issue would be changed or removed before one or more embryos were transferred to the uterus. Such germline interventions would render their children and their children's children free of this version of Alzheimer's disease.

*Treating a future child for genetic disease and enhancing him as well.* In another futuristic scenario, a woman gives birth to a boy who is not at risk of inheriting adolescent-onset colon cancer and has red hair, blue eyes, a good memory, and great athletic abilities. His mother had initially decided to use a germline intervention to ensure that her child would not inherit familial colon cancer. While she was at it, she also decided to create a boy with physical and mental characteristics that she considered desirable.

*Reproductive cloning to avoid genetic disease.* In a final vignette that is set in the future, picture a husband and wife who want to have a biologically related child but are concerned about proceeding by means of coital reproduction because the wife carries the gene associated with muscular dystrophy. To avoid passing this gene to their child, they elect to have the husband cloned. The nucleus of a cell from his body is fused with his wife's egg, from which the nucleus has been removed. This egg is stimulated to develop into an embryo, which is then implanted in the woman's uterus. They feel assured of having a boy who will resemble his father in almost all ways and who will not fall prey to muscular dystrophy.

To discern whether it would be ethically acceptable to exercise the unprecedented sort of control over future children illustrated by these stories, we begin this chapter with an exploration of Christian understandings of the meaning of procreation and parenthood. We then draw out the implications of these understandings for individuals, families, churches, and society as they grapple with moral questions about appropriate uses of our growing genetic and reproductive powers to create children.

## THE SIGNIFICANCE OF PROCREATION

Many in our society initially embraced in vitro fertilization, which is currently used for carrying out genetic interventions in early embryos, because it promised to help couples overcome infertility. Yet some among us are becoming concerned that the increasing use of this and other novel means of creating children will lead us inadvertently to convert procreation into a barren process of the manufacture of children. How can we retain an understanding of procreation as a loving act of bringing children into the world when a by-product of embracing these technologies may be that we come to view procreation as the mechanical production of offspring? To delve into this issue, we first consider scriptural and traditional Christian resources that address the significance of procreation

## Procreation in Scripture and the Christian Tradition

The first command of God found in Scripture concerns procreation. In the Priestly account of Creation (Gen. 1:1–2:4a), God tells Adam and Eve to "be fruitful and multiply." The Jewish tradition has taken this passage to mean that procreation is a leading purpose of sexuality within marriage.[1] Having children and raising them to carry on the traditions of the community is a vital religious duty in Judaism because it promotes social identity and ensures the survival of Israel as a people. That is why, when a man and a woman are married in a Jewish ceremony, they sign a contract in which they agree to perform their respective parts so that they will bring children into the world to bear the identity of their parents and their people into the future.[2]

Christian understandings of procreation were strongly influenced not only by the Priestly account of Creation in Genesis so important to Judaism, but also by the Jahwist account (Gen. 2:4b–3:24).[3] In it, God forms Adam from the dust of the ground and then declares, "It is not good that Adam should be alone" (Gen. 2:18). Thereupon, God creates woman from Adam's rib as he sleeps. Man and woman are made for one another; emerging from one flesh, they are called once again to unity. This account of Creation suggests that companionship is a leading purpose of sexuality within marriage.[4]

A companionate view of marriage is consistent with several Gospel passages that portray the observations of Jesus. In Mark, for example, Jesus responds to a question about whether it is lawful for a man to divorce his wife (which was allowed within Judaism if she were barren, among other reasons) by saying:

> From the beginning of creation, "God made them male and female." "For this reason a man shall leave his father and mother and be joined to his wife, and the two shall become one flesh." So they are no longer two, but one flesh. Therefore what God has joined together, let no one separate. (Mark 10:6–8)

Here and in other passages (Matt. 19:3–6; 1 Cor. 7:10–11), Jesus suggests that marriage is centered on a commitment of husband and wife to one another. The commandment that appears in Genesis, "Increase and multiply," is not repeated in the Gospels when Genesis is cited in Mark 10 and Matthew 19.

Elaine Pagels observes that:

> By subordinating the obligation to procreate, rejecting divorce, and implicitly sanctioning monogamous relationships, Jesus reverses traditional priorities declaring, in effect, that other obligations, including marital ones, are now more important than procreation.[5]

The companionate view of marriage that underlies these Gospel passages does not understand marriage as a contractual agreement in which the relationship between husband and wife is established in order to bring about something else.[6] It takes the relationship between husband and wife as one of mutual love, regardless of the consequences. This is not to deny that procreation is viewed in a positive light in the Gospels, as when a mother feels "joy that a man is born into the world" (John 16:21). It is to point out that its value is not emphasized.[7]

Yet during the centuries after the New Testament was written, a procreative ethic developed within the Christian tradition that culminated in the thought of the fourth-century theologian Augustine. He integrated the various strands of asceticism about sex of his time, which were largely Stoic in origin, to take the position that sexual intercourse is morally acceptable only for the purpose of procreation. Sexual desire, Augustine maintained, is God's crowning punishment for Adam and Eve's disobedience, and sexual union solely to fulfill that desire is wrong.[8] Only the intention of having children can justify engaging in sexual intercourse, he held. Augustine commended marriage in view of three goods toward which he maintained it was directed. These are, in descending order of priority, procreation, faithfulness of partners, and sacrament or an indissoluble union.[9] He recognized, in the second good, that companionship is also an element in the marriage bond, but maintained, along with the Stoics, that a man ought to love his wife with judgment, not affection. Procreation remained the primary end of marital intercourse in his view.

Critics debate whether Augustine's ethical analysis of human sexuality is consistent with the Gospels and other strands of the Christian tradition that frame sex within a generous love.[10] Even so, they recognize that Augustine's theology had a powerful influence on subsequent Christian thought.[11]

The view that companionship is a primary end of marriage was not lost during the reign of this procreative ethic. In the fourth century, John Chrysostom, for instance, dwelt eloquently on the injunction to spouses in Ephesians 5 to love one another. He declared that "The love of husband and wife is the force that welds society together" and that "Marriage is not a business venture, but a fellowship for life."[12] The love between man and wife is embodied in procreation, Chrysostom taught, for when a child is born to a couple, the three become one flesh.

Among those influenced by Augustine's procreative ethic was the thirteenth-century theologian Thomas Aquinas. He maintained that all sexual acts that are not initiated with procreative intent deviate from natural law and are therefore wrong.[13] Aquinas's view of sexual desire was more accepting than that of Augustine, for he construed sexual pleasure as a form of sin that is allowable in order to bring children into the world.[14] However, if the unitive (companionate) end expressed in the sexual relation between husband and wife were not focused on procreation, that unitive end could not be fully realized. Thus, the Gospel view of procreation as the joyful outcome of a loving companionate marriage, but not its be-all and end-all, was transformed within the Christian tradition into the primary end of marriage.

During the Reformation, the companionate view of marriage reappeared and gained ground, nurtured within a budding social model of marriage. According to Luther, marriage is at the very foundation of society and its institutions; it is an indispensable agent of social order and communal cohesion. That is why God commanded all persons to marry, he declared, and why few are exempt from this ordinance.[15] Luther went on to adopt a more companionate view of marriage than that held earlier within the Christian tradition. Not only procreation, but also companionship is part of the natural institution of marriage,[16] he declared; neither takes precedence over the other. "There is no sweeter union," he wrote, "than that in a good marriage."[17] In short, having children, for Luther, was the outcome of a loving relationship between husband and wife and was looked upon with favor and joy by God and the community. However, it was not the overriding purpose of marriage.

Calvin, who was influenced by Luther, developed a more explicit covenantal model of marriage, which, in turn, affected his view of the place of procreation and companionship in marriage. Just as God enters into a covenant with the elect believer, he held, so God draws husband and wife into a covenant relationship with one another.[18] The society that is forged between them as a result has three major purposes: their mutual love and support, the procreation and nurture of children, and their mutual protection from sexual sin.[19] Husband and wife are called to complete the life and love of one another.[20] Marriage also forges a society between the couple and the community, as exhibited in the requirement that parents, peers, ministers, and magistrates participate in the formation of the covenant of marriage. To omit any of them was, in effect, to omit God.[21] Thus, Calvin, too, developed a more explicitly companionate and covenantal view of marriage, enveloping it within the social context.

These approaches to marriage, companionship, and procreation taken by Luther and Calvin strongly influenced developing Anglican thought in the sixteenth century. Anglican views of the ends of marriage came to the fore in a cyclical pattern, often circling back to encompass positions that had seemed wholly displaced earlier. For instance, *The King's Book* of 1543 named "mutual aid and comfort" as the chief purpose of marriage, followed by procreation and deterrence from sin.[22] However, the 1549 version of the *Book of Common Prayer* took procreation as the primary end of marriage.[23] Bucer reverted to the earlier approach in 1551, maintaining, on the basis of Genesis 2:18, that mutual society, help, and comfort were the main ends of marriage.[24] Becon also asserted during this period that marriage was a covenant between a man and a woman directed toward three ends: love, procreation, and deterrence from sin, in that order of priority.[25] Eventually, the companionate view of marriage emerged as primary from out of these cycles of Anglican thought.

In the seventeenth century, a commonwealth model of marriage developed within Anglican thought that embraced and went beyond earlier sacramental, social, and covenantal models.[26] Although this model was not universally accepted among Anglicans, it was adopted by a broad range of English theologians. Marriage, on this model, was instituted to serve the commonwealth, or the common good, of the couple, children, the church, and the state. The companionate emphasis on marital love went hand-in-glove with this model of marriage, for at its core was a mutual covenant between a man and a woman who cherished one another. Yet the importance of procreation was not overlooked, for marriage required the desire to have children who would become the future generations of the commonwealth. This commonwealth model of marriage was not held steadily within Anglican thought, but rose and fell as political leaders with varying theological views gained and lost power. As it gradually came into ascendancy, however, it reinforced the companionate view of marriage without losing sight of its procreative end.

This companionate view of marriage was beautifully expressed in the seventeenth century by Anglican divine Jeremy Taylor. He observed that marriage is:

> the proper scene of piety and patience, of the duty of parents and the charity of relatives; here kindness is spread abroad, and love is united and made firm as a centre; marriage is the nursery of heaven . . . marriage fills up the numbers of the elect, and hath in it the labour of love, and the delicacies of friendship, the blessing of society, and the union of hands and hearts.[27]

The covenantal love and fidelity of spouses, affirmed before and upheld by the community, now became the fixed center of Anglican thought about marriage.

This Anglican understanding had a strong impact on later English religious and secular thinkers. Eighteenth-century theologian and philosopher John Locke called upon the Anglican covenantal and companionate understanding of marriage in his view of it as a loving relationship into which man and woman enter as equals in the state of nature.[28] They set the terms of their marital relationship in a contract that he considered superior to all other governing norms that might be set by the state. Locke's followers, however, dropped the covenantal aspect of marriage insofar as it involved a promise made by the couple before God and moved exclusively to a contractual model.[29] John Stuart Mill moved even further toward a private contract model in making fulfillment of the mutual preferences of husband and wife the primary end of marriage.[30] Thus, the understanding of marriage developed among Anglican theologians reappeared as Western philosophical and political thought about the ends and form of marriage took shape. However, it was gradually transformed into a narrower, contractual view in which, we shall argue, neither procreation nor companionship played a necessary role.

## Contemporary Approaches to Procreation

Today, the Anglican tradition within the United States retains the view that marriage is primarily companionate and covenantal. It is a union entered into before God by a man and a woman for the sake of mutual love and support, procreation, and protection.[31] We find this understanding expressed in the *Book of Common Prayer* of the Episcopal Church. There the priority of love and companionship is reflected in the marriage vows, in which man and woman take each other "for better for worse, for richer for poorer, in sickness and in health, to love and to cherish, until we are parted by death."[32] In that same service, the couple is reminded that "[t]he union of husband and wife in heart, body, and mind is intended by God for their mutual joy; for the help and comfort given one another in prosperity and adversity; and, when it is God's will, for the procreation of children and their nurture in the knowledge and love of the Lord." Thus, husband and wife gain identity and fulfillment in their love for one another. That love turns outward to welcome and embrace children, should they be blessed with them. Having children is a valued outcome of human sexuality and marriage, and yet not everyone is called to be a parent.

The contemporary Anglican tradition also encompasses those who take procreation as the primary end of marriage and sexual union.[33] These thinkers hold, as did Aquinas, that the unitive and the procreative aspects of sexual intercourse in marriage are inseparably connected. Such differences have led to an ongoing Anglican dialogue in which a nuanced "middle way" between the companionate and procreative ends of marriage has developed.

By the twentieth century, secular Western society had widely adopted the view that the primary purpose of marriage is to enhance mutual love and comfort. Love, commitment, and friendship between husband and wife were no longer seen as ancillary goods but as basic ends of marriage. Moreover, marriage and its associated goods, including procreation, were seen as embedded within a social context. This view, however, is being challenged today. We are gradually moving toward an understanding of marriage as grounded in a contract created by the wills of the parties, governed by their desires, and aimed at their individual fulfillment. In effect, this view, which developed from one strand of the thought of Locke, among other sources, is becoming the rule. Couples can choose to make primary whatever ends they take to be desirable.

This understanding has been expressed in the legal sphere with regard to the generation of children under the rubric of "procreative liberty." The central tenet of this contemporary view of procreation is that individuals have a constitutional right not only to produce children coitally, but also to use reproductive technologies to implement their procreative preferences.[34] Indeed, some legal scholars maintain that implementing the desires of individuals and couples to control children's features by manipulating their genes is also a matter of fundamental right.[35] In their view, the new reproductive and genetic technologies simply enlarge the realm for the exercise of individual reproductive freedom of choice. They argue against interfering with this choice absent a demonstration of direct harm to others. Talk of the primary ends of marriage and of the relative importance of a companionate versus a procreative ethic has no place in this stripped down, individualistic approach. Social meanings and "symbolic" ethical considerations have little, if any, weight.

There are good reasons to make individual freedom of choice the ethical bedrock for decisions about procreation in particular. As observed in the previous chapter, history reveals many instances of the abuse of state and professional power in relation to reproduction and sterilization. Hence there is much to be said for a society in which individuals have rights and considerable freedom of thought, expression, decision, and action, rather than one in which such freedom is suppressed. However, it is questionable whether the expansion of individual choice with regard to technological means of creating children always enhances individual freedom. The appearance that those who have a wider range of options have greater freedom of choice can be illusory. The multiplication of reproductive choices may lead to the loss of the very structures and limits that give such choice meaning. Moreover, where power is concentrated in the hands of those who provide the technology, individual freedom of choice can be attenuated and even lost.

A basic concern raised by the procreative liberty approach is that procreation is coming to mean the technological union of body products—sperm, eggs, and cells—by any means necessary to produce a baby. Reproduction is carried out with minimal regard for the welfare of the women involved, the good of the resulting children, or the integrity of significant familial and social roles. The larger network of biological and social relationships that has long framed individual orderings of procreation is set aside by the procreative liberty approach, leaving nothing in its place except the desires of would-be parents. This loss of the understanding of procreation that has long undergirded both religious and secular thought about what it means to become and be a parent should not be passively accepted as a necessary aspect of social evolution in the face of the introduction of new genetic and reproductive technologies. While we need not return to a procreative ethic that would compel reproduction in the name of natural law, we also need not succumb to the unrestrained manufacture of children in the name of procreative liberty.

## ON BECOMING AND BEING PARENTS

In considering whether it is right to employ the new reproductive and genetic technologies to bring children into the world, questions inevitably come to the fore about the values and virtues at the core of the parent–child relationship. What are parents permitted or required to do to further the welfare of a future child? Should they use available technology to avoid bringing into the world children who would bear the genes for serious disease? Should would-be parents design children in specific ways to fulfill their own desires? To make their children better prepared to deal with a competitive world? To assist us to address such questions, we explore understandings of the meaning of parenthood and its obligations found in Scripture and the Christian tradition, with emphasis once again on Anglican thought. We then turn to contemporary views of parenthood to assess where we stand today and where we ought to stand.

### Parent and Child in Scripture and the Christian Tradition

The child in both Scripture and Christian tradition is generally considered a gift from God. We see this understanding repeated over and over again in such biblical stories as that of Abraham and Sarah (Gen. 17:15–19; 21: 1–3), Hannah (1 Sam. 1:1–2:21), Elizabeth (Luke 1:11–24), and Mary (Matt. 1: 18–25; Luke 1: 26–38). Perhaps no biblical story exhibits it more starkly than that of Abraham and Isaac (Gen. 22), in which God tests Abraham by commanding him to give up the gift of his son. The story implies that children are our trusts, rather than our possessions, and that they ultimately belong to God. It also honors the significance and depth of the relationship between parent and child, for when Abraham is about to dispatch Isaac, God's angel pulls him back, returning Isaac to Abraham's care.

The Bible, to be sure, also presents us with stories of parental partiality among children, misuse of offspring, and downright wickedness toward heirs. Parental love in Scripture can be grudging, meager, or arbitrary. Children, at times, are viewed as capricious and ignorant creatures in need of strict discipline (2 Kings 2:23–24; Isa. 3:4; Wis. 12:24–25; 15:14; Prov. 22:15; Sir. 30:1–13). Such scriptural stories do not present us with models or norms of good parental behavior but rather represent to us the ways in which parenthood can be cruelly and wrongfully played out.

The New Testament includes few references to children, yet it is clear that Jesus was known for his concern for children. Although children occupied a low estate in the culture of his time, he taught that they are owed special love and protection; he is often pictured as blessing and healing them (Mark 10:13–16; Matt. 19:13–15; Luke 18:15–17). "Take care that you do not despise one of these little ones; for, I tell you, in heaven their angels continually see the face of my Father" (Matt. 18:10–11). Jesus equates welcoming a little child in his name to welcoming himself and God (Mark 9:33–37; Matt. 18:1–2; Luke 9:46–48). The relationship of parent to child is significant for Jesus. In several texts, most prominently the story of the Prodigal Son, he draws an analogy between this relationship and that of God to humans (Matt. 18:2–5 and 19:13–15; Mark 9:36–37 and 10:13–16; and Luke 9:47–48 and 18:15–17). Neither of these relationships is contractual nor instrumental; both are grounded in love. Further, parents, in Jesus' stories, are naturally concerned about their children, not for any advantage that these offspring might offer them, but for the sake of the children themselves (Matt. 15:21–28; Mark 7:24–30; John 4:46–53).

The view of the early church that sexual relations could be justified only when open to procreation was not inevitably accompanied by an affirmation of the importance of rearing the resulting children. Even so, it is clear that the well-being of children was of great concern to early Christians. They are said to have appealed to loving parenthood more often than any other religious group of their time.[36] Yet as Christianity grew, many Christian thinkers came to accept without severe moral condemnation parents' abandonment or sale of children, whether carried out because of poverty or self-interest.[37] John Boswell maintains that:

> By insisting that sexuality be directed always and only to the procreation of children, and by prohibiting every means of contraception or terminating pregnancy, the prevailing moral and legal systems of Catholic Europe all but forced Christian parents into coping with an abundance of offspring, and many responded to this by abandoning some of them.[38]

As Christianity grew and held sway over Europe, the obligation to rear the children who were the fruit of uncontrolled procreation was put at peril to a surprising degree, given Christian teachings.

During the Reformation an explicit focus on the good not only of having, but also of rearing children appeared in Protestant writing. Luther, for instance, considered parenthood a holy calling and wrote of the wonders of pregnancy, childbirth, and child rearing. He urged parents to engage in the mundane tasks of child care in a spirit of joy and trust.[39] Children should be brought into the world for their own sake, he held, rather than to satisfy their parents' desires. Indeed, Luther berated the royal families of his day for trying to engineer the birth of children in order to cement political alliances.

Calvin, too, held that parents should care for and educate their children, not because that would fulfill their own personal ambitions, but because children are to be nurtured as a "mirror of God's grace," a sign that God cares for the family.[40] He urged parents to view themselves as models for their children and make conscious efforts to be worthy of their imitation. Thus, the Protestant Reformers explicitly focused attention on children's welfare. Nurturing and rearing children in love came to be seen as an important obligation in Protestant teachings.

The Anglican approach to parenthood was considerably influenced by the Protestant Reformers. Anglican thinkers held that the love between husband and wife at the core of covenantal marriage overflows to embrace children who are born into the family. Children were seen as innocent, uncultivated creatures whose capacities for reason and virtue needed to be developed, rather than as selfish masses of desires in need of instruction in virtue and piety. A "poisonous pedagogy"[41] that depicted them as depraved and stubbornly willful did not find a home within Anglican thought. Indeed, the call to parents to love and nurture children is so strong within this tradition that Anglican F. D. Maurice in the nineteenth century could declare that the parent–child relationship is the foundation for an ethic of universal brotherhood.[42]

The liturgy of the Episcopal Church reflects this view. A prayer in the marriage rite in the *Book of Common Prayer* calls on parents to nurture and rear their children on behalf of God. The service of "Thanksgiving for the Birth or Adoption of a Child" includes a prayer that God will "give them strength and patient wisdom as they seek to bring this child to love all that is true and noble, just and pure, lovable and gracious, excellent and admirable. . . ."[43]

Contemporary Anglicans still see children as gifts from God, rather than products, projects, or possessions of their parents. The primary task for parents is to nurture in their children a loving and upright character. Parents are not enjoined to confer traits on their children that will maximize the children's health or bring them social advantages, nor are they invited to manipulate their children according to their own particular preferences. This does not mean that it is considered wrong for parents to desire a healthy child or to take steps to improve a child's well-being. To the contrary, parents have a responsibility to attend to their children's physical and mental good. The error would lie in sacrificing the unconditional and loving acceptance that should define the parent–child relationship in order to achieve a lesser good such as social success.

In keeping with this approach, Anglican Oliver O'Donovan takes it as a misunderstanding of parenthood to view children as projects of parental will and design. To adopt such a view is to imply a radical inequality between children and parents, for it is difficult to consider as equal that which we make.[44] Instead, O'Donovan maintains, children are to be seen as begotten, not made, as possibilities and ends in themselves. Parents are to raise them in ways that equip them for independent life as adults, rather than to attempt to control their nature and development from their earliest moments. O'Donovan and several other contemporary Anglicans maintain that we are to rear children within a basic framework that accepts and cares for them lovingly with all their perceived frailties and imperfections—much as we hope they will later accept and care for us.

## Contemporary Approaches to Parenthood

We live in a curious social and cultural context in which we juggle two different versions of how parents should view children. Some speak of children as the "products" of conception and "a special kind of 'property.'"[45] On the version of the parent–child relationship that they presume, children are beings whom parents obtain in order to serve their own interests and desires. Advocates of this view argue that those who would be parents should be free to acquire whatever kind of child they desire by whatever reproductive and genetic means they can afford as long as they do no material harm to others. To obtain the results they desire, parents may need to exercise "quality control" over the production of their children; it is ethically acceptable to select early embryos or to change their genes in order to achieve this end. The needs of the children themselves do not figure significantly in this view of parenthood. Instead, children are primarily seen as a means to achieving parental satisfaction.

In the future, this approach to parenthood may make it easy for parents to slip unreflectively from the assertion of control in order to benefit the child to the simple assertion of control in order to benefit the parent. In one of the vignettes that opened this chapter, an opportunity to select against a genetic mutation associated with an above-average risk of colon cancer readily becomes an opportunity to select for traits that match the preferences of the would-be parent. Although this scenario is speculative, if there are no moral constraints on parental decision making other than direct harm to the resulting child, it is likely that future prospective parents will be presented with a menu of genetic interventions from which they may choose without regard to such important concerns as the good of the future child.

Others recognize a different version of the parent–child relationship, one that is indebted to the Christian view of parenthood without necessarily adopting specific Christian beliefs. On this version, children are not to be acquired on grounds that they meet parental specifications and desires but are to be welcomed as persons in their own right, regardless of their traits.[46] In law, this view appears in the guise of the "best interests of the child" standard for decision making in cases involving children. It is also reflected in the work of secular bioethicists such as Thomas Murray, who puts the relationship between parent and child at the center, thus stressing the benefits to adults as well as children when adults learn to focus on beings and relations beyond themselves.[47] This second version of the parent–child relationship counsels against attempts by parents to seek control over every aspect of the being of their children. Clearly, in its emphasis on the good of children rather than the self-interest of parents, it places sharper limits on parental choice than does the first view.

Thus, we live with a tension between accepting children as they come to us and seeking to control and alter them. The social meaning of parenthood and the weight that we give to children's welfare are at stake as we mediate between these two views. So, too, is the meaning of procreation, for we risk losing something important about procreation when we try to control its every aspect. As Gilbert Meilaender, a Lutheran thinker, expresses it, "Within this life we can exercise a modest degree of control, but if we seek to do more than that we have fundamentally altered the nature of what we are doing and of the beings to whom we give rise."[48]

## ETHICAL ISSUES RAISED BY THE MERGER OF NEW GENETIC AND REPRODUCTIVE TECHNOLOGIES

The understandings of procreation and parenthood that run through Christian thought, we have suggested, have influenced not only the views of contemporary religious thinkers, but also those of a more secular bent. Many contemporary secular commentators also assert that procreation is not merely the manipulation of human biological materials in order to produce children and that it is more than a private matter between husband and wife, although it surely is at least that. Having children is a familial and social activity, an enterprise in which individuals should cooperate, not only out of love for one other, but also out of love for their children and out of concern for certain significant social goods. Many secular writers also maintain that children are not to be categorized as parental products, projects, or possessions but as human beings of value in themselves.

Thus, a variety of Christian and secular thinkers have enunciated broader understandings of procreation and parenting. We now bring these understandings to bear on questions about whether certain new genetic and reproductive technologies should be used to create and shape future children and, if so, where to draw ethical lines around the uses of these technologies. To reach supportable conclusions, we explore ethical issues related to the use of in vitro fertilization (IVF), third-party gamete donation, preimplantation genetic diagnosis (PGD), germline interventions, and reproductive cloning—when these techniques are specifically used to avoid genetic disease in children.

## The Use of IVF to Avoid Genetic Disease in Future Children

In vitro fertilization (IVF) is a reproductive technology on which almost all of these novel genetic interventions depend. Therefore, we first consider whether its use is, in itself, morally acceptable and then evaluate whether it is morally sound to merge it with certain genetic technologies to ensure that future children will be free of inherited genetic diseases.

One criticism of the use of IVF is that it diminishes the importance of the body in bringing forth children. Conceiving children in a laboratory dish seems a far cry from the understanding of procreation that we explored earlier as the fruit of an intimate loving relationship between husband and wife. Although the use of reproductive technology undoubtedly diminishes the significance of the physical relationship between spouses, that alone does not require that we reject IVF. We should not overemphasize the physical dimension of the marital relationship by making it an absolute requirement for every act of procreation. The loving conjugal bond between infertile couples can be as strong and real when they cooperate in using IVF to bypass physical obstacles to having children as it would be were they able to have children coitally.[49] To insist that procreation must always be accompanied by sexual intercourse is, as Lisa Sowle Cahill, a Roman Catholic thinker, observes, to derive "moral norms too simply from the observable or physical structure of human reproduction without sufficient regard for its affective, cognitive, and volitional character."[50]

A related concern expressed by some Christian and secular thinkers is that the use of reproductive technologies such as IVF, by separating the unitive and procreative aspects of sexual intercourse, violates natural law and runs the risk of instrumentalizing the process of procreation. The production orientation inherent in a technology such as IVF could overwhelm the receptive orientation that is part of a richer understanding of procreation explored above, reducing it to the manipulation of raw bodily materials in order to produce a child. It could also distort the ways in which we approach our children, leading us to view them as artifacts whom we produce at will and by design.

Some concerned commentators maintain that these dangers are so serious and likely to be realized that we should abjure the use of technological reproduction altogether. Oliver O'Donovan, for instance, argues that:

> What we "make," then, is alien from our humanity. In that it has a human maker, it has come to existence as a human project, its being at the disposal of mankind. It is not fit to take its place alongside mankind in fellowship, for it has no place beside him on which to stand: man's will is the law of its being. That which we beget can be, and should be, our companion; but the product of our art—whatever immeasurable satisfaction and enjoyment there may be both in making it and in cherishing it—can never have the independence to be that

"other I," equal to us and differentiated from us, which we acknowledge in those who are begotten of human seed.[51]

This view, although not in the ascendance today in the United States, has tempered the influence of those within Anglicanism who would embrace all new reproductive and genetic technologies as morally sound just because they are distinctively human endeavors. These technology enthusiasts include Joseph Fletcher, who made the claim that:

> Laboratory reproduction is radically human compared to conception by ordinary heterosexual intercourse. It is willed, chosen, purposed and controlled, and surely these are the traits that distinguish *Homo sapiens*. . . . Coital reproduction is, therefore, less human than laboratory reproduction. [52]

Yet this view has not overcome a cautious but generally accepting position toward the application of IVF taken by Episcopalians. Couples who encounter physical barriers to procreation would dearly love to have children in a way that does not involve the use of technological means. Yet they cannot. Adoption can be a significant way for them to experience parenthood, but it requires a renunciation of some of the goods of procreation, such as the physical intimacy of pregnancy and the genetic connection between parents and children. Much as it is morally acceptable for those with physiological problems that diminish normal physical functioning to go through onerous medical procedures to overcome them, so it is morally acceptable for those who face physical barriers to procreation to go though the demanding procedures associated with IVF in order to be able to function reproductively.

It is not that a couple's desire to overcome infertility trumps all other considerations, but that a couple's decision to use IVF to bypass physical obstacles to procreation can be a responsible and loving choice. This conclusion has been accepted by the General Convention of the Episcopal Church, which has adopted several resolutions supporting the use of IVF by those who are infertile.[53] However, that the use of IVF by couples can be morally acceptable does not mean that couples and individuals have ethical license to use this technology in any and all ways possible. It is important that couples are not pressured into proceeding with increasingly burdensome interventions in the cause of having a biologically related child. We do not condone the continuing dissemination of reproductive technologies without foresight or oversight or the remarkable lack of systematically collected data about their outcomes for the resulting children. Much more needs to be done to protect the men, women, and children involved in the use of IVF from the physical, psychological, and social risks that it may entail. It is important that couples are not pressured into proceeding with increasingly burdensome interventions in the cause of having a biologically related child. Moreover, greater effort needs to be extended to develop appropriate ethical and social limitations to the uses of this technology.

## The Use of Gamete Donation to Avoid Serious Genetic Disease in Children

The morality of using donated sperm or eggs, along with IVF, to avoid passing disease-related genes from parents to children, as in the Huntington disease example presented above, has been the subject of considerable debate among both Christian and secular thinkers. Some have questioned whether it is ever morally acceptable to set aside one of the major features of procreation—that it is exclusive—as occurs in gamete donation. Some commentators question whether averting serious disease in future children justifies the use of reproductive materials provided by third parties.[54] In their view, gamete donation nullifies the exclusive nature of the relationship between husband and wife. Paul Ramsey hints that it resembles adultery.[55]

Yet gamete donation, unlike adultery, does not violate the covenant of mutual fidelity into which married couples enter. Some members of a working party of the Church of England have expressed this argument as follows: "[T]here is no offence against the married partner, there is no breaking of the relationship of physical fidelity and there is no relationship with a person outside of marriage."[56] Couples who turn to gamete donation see it as the only way in which they can have a healthy child who is as close to them biologically as it is safe to be.

Critics maintain further that the use of third-party gametes will unjustifiably diminish the importance of the biological relationship between parents and children. Gilbert Meilaender, for instance, points out that our lines of kinship and descent situate us within particular relationships and communities and argues that this reality imposes limits on individual freedom of reproductive choice.[57] Gamete donation vitiates these familial lines and, if increasingly used, may eventually lead to the reconceptualization of the family.

Surely the biological bond between parents and children is a significant element in a normative understanding of parenthood. Yet in the circumstances that we are addressing, the child would bear genes from only one parent *solely because* that is necessary to ensure that he or she will not inherit a deleterious gene from the other parent. These parents are not pursuing gamete donation in order to play out what Brent Waters terms "an ideological account of freedom as autonomy in which the family is a contractual arrangement enabling personal fulfillment. . . ."[58] Instead, they are using it in an attempt to ensure the health of the child. Moreover, it is unlikely that gamete donation would be carried out in such large numbers as to make a discernible difference in the structure of the family as we know it.

Further, in adoption, the biological and social relationship between parents and children is sundered, and the obligations of the biological parents are alienated. Yet we accept adoption as morally sound because it is carried out for the sake of the children and because it is compatible with a view that love is expansive. That suggests that it is also acceptable to allow such separation in the context of gamete donation when it is initiated to avoid genetic disease in children.

Critics of gamete donation respond that what we value about adoption is that children who already exist and who cannot be raised by their biological parents are therefore given over for nurture to adoptive parents. In the case of gamete donation, in contrast, a child is deliberately created by means of IVF in order to be given to at least one nonbiological parent for rearing. That amounts to deliberate preconception abandonment by the gamete donor, these critics maintain. The practices of gamete donation and adoptions, they conclude, are therefore radically different in moral terms.[59]

We disagree. Those who put a child up for adoption have good reason to suppose that this child will be reared with love and care by a stable family. If gamete donors have the same assurance, it is difficult to judge third-party donation wrong. As Anthony Dyson has observed, the principal question is whether the rearing parents will provide a stable environment in which the welfare of the child is a central focus of concern.[60]

Concern about the welfare of the child is at the core of a related objection to third-party gamete donation: this practice might have a detrimental psychological and social impact on the resulting children. David H. Smith, for instance, observes that our genetic and social origins are an integral part of the story of who we are. He writes of children who do not know of their genetic origins:

> The child growing up in such a situation perceives a gap between the roots of self and the roots of body; the child's world is fractured in some ways that others' worlds are not . . . it is a problem, that a child conceived with donor gametes asks "Who am I?" in ways that other persons do not.[61]

This observation raises a significant ethical issue that is the subject of exploration and debate among psychologists. As yet, we do not have sufficient information about the impact of gamete donation on children to ban it as seriously detrimental to them. However, we do have some insights drawn from adoption about the negative effects of secrecy about their origins on adopted children.[62] It is reasonable to suspect that the secrecy about their origins would have the same impact on children born of gamete donation. It would be wise, therefore, to carry out gamete donation with greater openness, taking account of the age, maturity, and psychological and social context of the specific child.[63]

A final issue raised by critics of gamete donation is that it is leading to the commercialization of procreation. Our current practice of paying significant sums to some egg donors comes uncomfortably close to baby buying and flies in the face of our view of children as creatures endowed with dignity and value. To respond to this genuine concern and avoid the commercial overtones of the current practice of gamete donation, we need to develop ways of thanking those who donate gametes in ways that do not rely on exorbitant financial inducements.[64]

Those who are concerned about passing genes associated with serious disease to their children use gamete donation to have healthy children whom they can raise within a nurturing family. This core reason for the practice provides presumptive grounds to allow its use when that is the only way available to couples to enter into responsible procreation. Adoption is a viable ethical option that couples in this predicament should seriously consider, although it, too, can be onerous, expensive, and ethically complex.

### The Use of Preimplantation Genetic Diagnosis (PGD) to Avoid Serious Genetic Disease in Children

Another recent technological advance that allows would-be parents to avoid bringing children into the world who suffer from serious genetic disease is preimplantation genetic diagnosis (PGD). This technique was described in chapter 1 and in our cystic fibrosis vignette above. In PGD, embryos created by means of IVF are tested to determine whether they have a gene associated with a serious genetic disease. Embryos that do not have the gene of concern are transferred to the woman's uterus, and those that do have the suspect gene are discarded.

A major question about the use of PGD concerns the moral status of the early embryo. We address this vexed question in chapter 6, where we conclude that early human embryos are not individual human beings but that they are potential human beings who are owed a degree of moral consideration. However, their moral status is distinctively different from that of fetuses and born human beings, and what is owed to them morally, therefore, is somewhat different. This discussion leads to the question whether it is morally permissible to discard early embryos that bear genes associated with serious disorders, as occurs in PGD.

The early embryos examined by means of PGD have been created in the hope that some will not have genes associated with serious disease and can be brought to birth. They are the same in this respect as embryos that are created by means of in vitro fertilization (IVF) to overcome infertility. Not all of the embryos created in IVF can be used in one attempt, and the remaining ones are stored for future use. Some of these stored embryos, however, may ultimately not be needed by those who had them created if they are fortunate enough to succeed in their first attempts to have a child. Thus, both embryos that remain when IVF has been completed and early embryos revealed by PGD to bear genes associated with disease are alike, in that they were created for a procreative purpose but cannot be used for that purpose. It is not wrong to create embryos for infertile couples and to discard them when it is realized that they are no longer needed. Similarly, it is not wrong to create embryos for couples who bear genes associated with a genetic disease and to discard those that reveal such genes. Indeed, to do the latter is to mirror what often happens in nature. Scientific evidence indicates that early embryos with genetic anomalies that are created by means of sexual intercourse are often miscarried.[65] To discard early embryos created in vitro that exhibit genetic anomalies, therefore, is to do the same. While it is regrettable to lose these early embryos, it is not a violation of the degree of care that we owe them to discard them to avoid genetic disease in future children.

Some have expressed concern that the use of PGD may create a social climate that is biased against already living children who have serious genetic disease. The fear is that others may treat them as lesser persons whose lives are not worth living, implicitly conveying to them that they should never have been born. Some of those who are living with such gene-associated conditions as hemophilia and cystic fibrosis feel demeaned by efforts to avoid bringing children with these conditions into the world. Moreover, parents of such children may come to be viewed as pariahs who acted wrongly by allowing the children to be born.

This difficult matter is addressed more fully elsewhere. Here we stress that much more needs to be done to provide such individuals and their families with appropriate medical treatment and social support. We owe to those with serious genetic disease access to health care and to opportunities for a full life. We also observe that those who decide against having children with serious genetic disease are not usually motivated by the belief that such children are somehow inferior or to be despised. Many have an affected child whom they cherish. They are often hopeful that their future children will be spared the suffering that they have seen their living children undergo.

That is why many find it morally perplexing for some families deliberately to select early embryos with a gene associated with a disease or disability to bring into the world. Some within the deaf community, for instance, favor using PGD to select early embryos with genes associated with deafness to transfer so that they might have a child who will be deaf. They prefer having a child who will fit into the deaf environment to a hearing child. This preference strikes many who are not deaf as wrong, for they believe that we ought to seek the welfare of our children. Being deaf, in their view, does not promote a child's welfare. They consider it better to be able to hear. Indeed, parents who gave birth to a hearing child and then deliberately caused him or her to become deaf would be condemned morally and legally for child abuse. It also seems wrong to these critics to use PGD intentionally to bring a deaf child into the world. In this case, as in our vignette above in which children's specific traits are enhanced, the point of the intervention is to shape these children for a particular destiny, to control their future in ways that cannot be reversed. Persons seeking such interventions should ask themselves whether it is truly the welfare of the child that is being served or the welfare and convenience of the parents.

We conclude that preimplantation genetic diagnosis can provide an ethically acceptable way of screening early embryos to learn whether they bear genes associated with serious genetic disease. It is morally appropriate to carry out such testing in order to ensure that children who are born to parents who themselves bear genes associated with serious disease will not be stricken with such disease.

## Use of Germline Interventions to Avoid Serious Genetic Disease in Children

If in the future it were to become safe to use germline interventions in early embryos to overcome serious genetic disease in future children, doing so would be consonant with our Christian call to heal and restore those who would be stricken by disease. It would be right to attempt to overcome disease in already living children by modifying their genes if we could do so safely, as observed in the previous chapter. Similarly, it would be right to attempt to overcome disease in future children by modifying their genes at the embryonic stage if we could do so safely. However, since we cannot carry out such germline interventions without incurring extremely serious risks for future children, it is not morally acceptable to employ them currently. So while it is ethically acceptable in principle to carry out germline interventions, it is not acceptable to do so in practice today.

Moreover, when we contemplate using germline interventions for purposes of enhancement—an even more futuristic possibility at this time—serious moral questions surface. A major issue about which several Christian thinkers have expressed concern is that if we were to embark upon a program to improve future children genetically, it could become more difficult to love these children for themselves.[66] The role of parents, these thinkers argue, as we have above, is not to control the quality of their children but to accept and cherish them for who they are.

Moreover, the quest for a perfect child could create a social environment that is hostile to children who do not live up to certain standards of perfection.[67] Indeed, society might elect to limit support for children born with genetic disease if their parents could have avoided their birth in the first place. For such reasons, Christian and other thinkers have tended to maintain that it is wrong to use genetic technologies, including germline interventions, to produce enhanced children shaped to meet parental standards of perfection.

These concerns are well placed. However, not all germline interventions directed toward enhancement need be the product of overbearing parents bent on controlling the genetic makeup of their future children. In some instances, these interventions might be motivated by the hope of enriching the lives of these children, much as parents do when they send their children to school or provide them with art and music lessons. A middle way must be found between arrogant parental control over the genetic makeup of future children and the abdication of parental responsibility to foster the good of their children.

As a society, we have not even attempted to discuss and discern where to draw the lines around appropriate uses of the new reproductive and genetic technologies. The tension between accepting children for themselves and responsibly seeking to alter their circumstances must be addressed openly within our society before the possibility of using germline interventions for enhancement purposes becomes a reality. The shadow of the eugenics movement hovers over such well-meaning but socially dangerous reproductive choices and once again raises the question of what sort of society we would and should become.

### Use of Reproductive Cloning to Avoid Serious Genetic Disease in Children

The possibility that we might have the power to use cloning to bring children into the world is unsettling and morally abhorrent to many Christian and secular thinkers. They view human beings as unique and precious creatures who ought not be reproduced by a process that they believe stands procreation on its head. Others, however, would welcome human cloning because it would offers a variety of benefits, particularly that it might allow parents to have children free of inherited disease.

There is little question that the use of reproductive cloning to avoid having children with genetic disease would radically change our understanding of what it means to have children. Procreation, as we know it, unites the gametes of a man and a woman. Cloning, in contrast, uses the gamete of only one person, the female egg. In this respect it differs from the creation of identical twins or triplets, for each of these children is the issue of the union of gametes from two different persons. Is it wrong to create a human being from a single cell taken from the body of one individual? Critics of reproductive cloning are concerned that its use could destroy the long-standing core view of human procreation as a biological and relational partnership between two people who are in a loving, committed union.

Moreover, critics of reproductive cloning believe that it would introduce confusion into our understandings of parenthood. Who would be the parent(s) of the cloned child? The donor of the cell that is inserted into the enucleated egg? The donor of the egg? The cloned child's grandparents? The lines between father and son, mother and daughter would be blurred by reproductive cloning in a way that they are not by coital procreation or IVF. Cloning would bypass connections within families and among generations—parents, sisters, brothers, grandparents, and ancestors—that seem integral to human identity and well-being.

Should reproductive cloning be used to avoid serious disease in a future child? Surely God rejoices when those who would be parents attempt to avert genetic disorders in children. Yet critics of human cloning see it as more than just another reproductive technology that might enable a child to be born healthy. Instead, they take it as a tool that would put complete control over the genes of another into the hands of one person. Donald Bruce, a representative of the Church of Scotland, argues that we ought not deliberately predetermine the entire genetic composition of a new individual.[68] Our genetic constitution, he points out, is not an add-on that we can throw off in the way that we can renounce our upbringing or our social institutions. It is, in a sense, part of who we are. Although to control the genes of another is not to control that individual's very being, it is to have a significant influence over who that person is and who he or she will become.

Although the call to procreative liberty resonates in our individualistic culture, our uses of procreative freedom have ethical limits. These limits emerge fully at the point where human reproductive cloning enters. Sufficient questions have been raised about the risks of reproductive cloning, not only in terms of its safety for the resulting children, but also in terms of our understanding of procreation as emerging from a loving relationship between two people, our call to nurture our children to become persons in their own right, and our view of family members as standing in predictable relationships to one another, that uses of this technology should be questioned and challenged. In light of the physical, personal, moral, and social risks posed by reproductive cloning, it is grossly irresponsible for would-be cloners to play upon the emotions of those who are desperate to have healthy children for the purpose of gaining grist for their terrible but remunerative experiments.

Those who would look to reproductive cloning as a way to avert serious genetic disease in their children should not to be turned away lightly from this technology. Nevertheless, we are in danger of serious distortions of our life together if we forge ahead with the use of this procedure without much more forethought and open debate. Reproductive cloning does not offer the only available or most reliable way for couples to overcome serious disorders in their children. Given its personal, ethical, and social drawbacks, those who hope to avoid having children who are free of genetic disease would be better served by using means other than reproductive cloning to reach that goal.

## CONCLUSION

Respect for individual freedom is an important value within the Christian tradition, particularly the Anglican tradition. Yet this tradition also maintains that the way in which children are brought into the world is of great social and religious concern. For many Anglican thinkers, the potential of the new reproductive and genetic technologies to alter our understandings of procreation, parenthood, and the family weighs against treating the uses of these technologies solely as a private matter. If we are to develop fundamentally new understandings of such basic social goods, we should do so reflectively as a community, rather than as isolated individuals. While we should limit the use of reproductive and genetic interventions on grounds of harm to others, we should also consider whether to limit their use in certain respects on grounds of a shared sense of what is required to sustain a society that seeks the common good.

We can use our new genetic and reproductive powers responsibly to bring children who are free from terrible diseases into the world. Yet we can also use them in ways that would seriously distort how we live our lives together. There are undoubtedly some circumstances in which couples would face great tragedy if they did not have access to in vitro fertilization and gamete donation or preimplantation genetic diagnosis. In other circumstances the lives of couples would be diminished if they were denied access to such interventions as germline modifications or reproductive cloning. Yet if we hope to sustain understandings of procreation and parenthood that anchor our lives and our social institutions, we cannot simply embrace them all without forethought. Sadly, it will not always be possible to resolve such tragic human realities as disease and disability through the use of our genetic and reproductive powers. Upon reflection, we have found the personal, social, and ethical risks of using these technologies worth bearing in some circumstances. Nevertheless, we have found in other cases that we have questioned whether we should go forward with the use of some of these technologies. Our ultimate touchstone should be that we offer to tomorrow's children and the families in which they will live a framework of meaning and values that grounds and makes sense of the interventions used to bring children into being and to shape who they may become.

## NOTES

_We are indebted to Professor Timothy F. Sedgwick of Virginia Theological Seminary for several helpful conversations about the development of Anglican thought regarding procreation and marriage, although he is not responsible for the approach to these matters taken here._

1. David M. Feldman, _Health and Medicine in the Jewish Tradition_ (New York: Crossroad, 1986), 56–58; Eliot N. Dorff and Arthur Rosett, _A Living Tree: The Roots and Growth of Jewish Law_ (Albany: State University of New York Press, 1988), 485–486; Peter Brown, _The Body and Society: Men, Women, and Sexual Renunciation in Early Christianity_ (New York: Columbia University Press, 1988), 61–65.

2. Dorff and Rosett, _A Living Tree_, 451–454.

3. Although the Jahwist writing comes later in sequence in scripture than the Priestly writing, it was given its edited form some 300 years earlier, which suggests that originally it came first. Cf. Lisa Cahill, _Between the Sexes: Foundation for a Christian Ethics of Sexuality_ (Philadelphia: Fortress Press, 1985), 53–56.

4. Timothy F. Sedgwick, "The Transformation of Sexuality and the Challenge of Conscience" in Charles Hefling, ed., _Our Selves, Our Souls and Bodies: Sexuality and the Household of God_ (Cambridge, Mass.: Cowley Publications, 1996), 30–32.

5. Elaine Pagels, _Adam, Eve and the Serpent_ (New York: Random House, 1988), 13.

6. Sedgwick, "Transformation of Sexuality," 33.

7. John T. Noonan Jr., _Contraception: A History of Its Treatment by the Catholic Theologians and Canonists_ (Cambridge, Mass.: Harvard University Press, 1965), 41.

8. Augustine, _City of God_, trans. Henry Bettenson, ed. David Knowles (New York: Penguin Books, 1972), XIV.16–23; Augustine, _Marriage and Virginity: The Excellence of Marriage, Holy Virginity, The Excellence of Widowhood, Adulterous Marriages, Continence_, trans. Ray Kearney, ed. David G. Hunter (Hyde Park, N.Y.: New City Press, 1999), 33–61; Peter Brown, _Augustine of Hippo_ (Berkeley and Los Angeles: University of California Press, 1967).

9. Augustine, "On the Goods of Marriage," in David G. Hunter, ed., _Marriage in the Early Church_ (Minneapolis: Fortress Press, 1992), 102ff.

10. Thomas E. Breidenthal, _Christian Households: The Sanctification of Nearness_ (Cambridge, Mass.: Cowley Publications, 1997), 124–128; Ted Peters, _For the Love of Children: Genetic Technology and the Future of the Family_ (Louisville, Ky.: Westminster John Knox Press, 1996), 121–126.

11. Margaret A. Farley, "Sexual Ethics" in _Encyclopedia of Bioethics_, 2nd ed. (New York: Macmillan, 1995), vol. 5, 2363, 2367.

12. John Chrysostom, "How to Choose a Wife," in _St. John Chrysostom on Marriage and Family Life_ (Crestwood, N.J.: St. Vladimir's Press, 1986), 89–114, cited in John Witte Jr., _From Sacrament to Contract: Marriage, Religion, and Law in the Western Tradition_ (Louisville, Ky.: Westminster John Knox Press, 1997), 21.

13. Thomas Aquinas, _St. Thomas Aquinas: Summa Theologica_, translated by the Fathers of the English Dominican Fathers (Allen, Tex.: Thomas More Publishing, 1981), II-II.154.5, 64.5 ad 3.

14. Thomas Aquinas, _Summa Contra Gentiles_, trans. Anton C. Pegis (Notre Dame, Ind.: University of Notre Dame Press, 1997), III-II.122–9.

15. Martin Luther, "The Estate of Marriage," *Luther's Works,* ed. Helmut T. Lehmann (Philadelphia: Fortress Press, 1966), vol. 45, 17–21.

16. Martin Luther, "Table Talk," *Luther's Works,* vol. 54, 324.

17. Ibid.

18. Jean Calvin, *Institutes of the Christian Religion,* ed. John T. McNeill, trans. Ford Lewis Battles (Philadelphia: Westminster Press, 1960), Book 2, chaps. 10–11.

19. Jean Calvin, *Commentary on Genesis, Calvin's Commentaries* (Grand Rapids, Mich.: Associated Publishers and Authors, 1971), 1:27, 1:28, 2:18, 2:21, 2:22.

20. Ibid., 1:27.

21. Witte, *From Sacrament to Contract,* 94–96.

22. *The King's Book,* 57, cited in Witte, *From Sacrament to Contract,* 173.

23. Marion J. Hatchett, *Commentary on the American Prayer Book* (San Francisco: HarperCollins, 1995), 429, 432.

24. Ibid., 433.

25. Thomas Becon, *Booke of Matrimonie,* folio DCxvi, 1560, cited in Witte, *From Sacrament to Contract,* 144.

26. Witte, *From Sacrament to Contract,* 131–133.

27. Jeremy Taylor, "The Marriage Ring" in *Jeremy Taylor: Selected Works,* ed. Thomas K. Carroll (Mahwah, N.J.: Paulist Press, 1990), 261–267.

28. John Locke, *Two Treatises of Government,* ed. Peter Laslett (Cambridge: Cambridge University Press, 1960), vol. II, 57–63.

29. Witte, *From Sacrament to Contract,* 196–198.

30. John Stuart Mill, *On Liberty and Other Essays,* ed. John Gray (Oxford and New York: Oxford University Press, 1991).

31. A Canon of the Episcopal Church (Title I, Canon 17, Section 3) adopted in 1949 lists mutual fellowship, encouragement, and understanding as the primary cause of marriage, then "procreation (if it may be) of children," and finally the safeguarding and benefit of society. Cf. Hatchett, *Commentary* , 432–433.

32. "The Celebration and Blessing of a Marriage," *The Book of Common Prayer According to the Use of the Episcopal Church* (1979), 427.

33. Oliver O'Donovan, *Begotten or Made?* (New York: Oxford University Press, 1984), 32, 40; Harmon L. Smith, "Decorum as Doctrine: Teachings on Human Sexuality" in Timothy Sedgwick and Philip Turner, eds., *The Crisis in Moral Teaching in the Episcopal Church* (Harrisburg, Pa.: Morehouse, 1992), 15–40.

34. Lori B. Andrews, "Cloning Human Beings: The Current and Future Legal Status of Cloning" in National Bioethics Advisory Commission, *Cloning Human Beings,* Vol. II. *Report and Recommendations of the National Bioethics Advisory Commission. Commissioned Papers* (Rockville, Md.: National Bioethics Advisory Commission, 1997), F3–F58 at F-6, F 37–39; John A. Robertson, *Children of Choice: Freedom and the New Reproductive Technologies.* (Princeton: Princeton University Press, 1994); Lawrence Wu, "Family Planning through Human Cloning: Is there a Fundamental Right?" *Columbia Law Review* 68 (1998): 1461–1515.

35. John A. Robertson, "Genetic Selection of Offspring Characteristics," *Boston University Law Review* (1996): 76, 421–481.

36. John Boswell, *The Kindness of Strangers: The Abandonment of Children in Western Europe from Late Antiquity to the Renaissance* (Chicago: University of Chicago Press, 1988), 177.

37. Ibid., 264.

38. Ibid., 168–169.

39. Martin Luther, "Sermon on the Estate of Marriage," *Luther's Works*, vol. 44, 12–13.

40. Barbara Pitkin, "The Heritage of the Lord: Children in the Theology of John Calvin" in Marcia J. Bunge, ed., *The Child in Christian Thought* (Grand Rapids, Mich.: Eerdmans, 2001), 160–193, 173.

41. Marcia Bunge, "Introduction," *The Child in Christian Thought*, 5.

42. F. D. Maurice, *Social Morality: Twenty-One Lectures Delivered in the University of Cambridge* (London and Cambridge: Macmillan, 1869).

43. *Book of Common Prayer*, 443.

44. O'Donovan, *Begotten or Made?* 2, 17, 86.

45. Robertson, "Genetic Selection of Offspring Characteristics," 481.

46. Thomas H. Murray, *The Worth of a Child* (Berkeley: University of California Press, 1996).

47. Peters, *For the Love of Children*, 133.

48. Gilbert Meilaender, *Body, Soul, and Bioethics* (Notre Dame, Ind.: University of Notre Dame Press, 1995), 84–85.

49. Paul Lauritzen, *Pursuing Parenthood: Ethical Issues in Assisted Reproduction* (Bloomington and Indianapolis: Indiana University Press, 1993), 10–12.

50. Lisa Sowle Cahill, "What is the 'Nature' of the Unity of Sex, Love, and Procreation?" in Edmund D. Pellegrino, John Collins Harvey, and John Langan, eds., *Gift of Life: Catholic Scholars Respond to the Vatican Instruction* (Washington, D.C.: Georgetown University Press, 1990), 137–148.

51. O'Donovan, *Begotten or Made?* 1.

52. Joseph Fletcher, "Ethical Aspects of Genetic Controls: Designed Genetic Changes in Man," *New England Journal of Medicine* 285, no. 14 (1971): 776–783.

53. Resolution A067, "Approve the Use of 'In Vitro' Fertilization," *Journal of the General Convention*, 1982; Resolution A101, "Reaffirm the Recommendation Considering External Fertilization," *Journal of the General Convention*, 1991.

54. Paul Ramsey, *Fabricated Man: The Ethics of Genetic Control* (New Haven: Yale University Press, 1970), 107–111, 128–129, 133, 136; David H. Smith, *Health and Medicine in the Anglican Tradition* (New York: Crossroad, 1986), 82–84; Hessel Bouma III, Douglas Diekema, Edward Langerak, Theodore Rottman, and Allen Verhey, *Christian Faith, Health, and Medical Practice* (Grand Rapids, Mich.: Eerdmans, 1989), 195–202; Brent Waters, *Reproductive Technology: Towards a Theology of Procreative Stewardship* (Cleveland: Pilgrim Press, 2001), 53–55.

55. Ramsey, *Fabricated Man*, 133, 136.

56. Church of England, Board of Social Responsibility, *Personal Origins* (2nd rev. ed. 1996).

57. Meilaender, *Body, Soul and Bioethics*, 61–88.

58. Waters, *Reproductive Technology*, 78.

59. O'Donovan, *Begotten or Made?* 36–37; Lisa Sowle Cahill, "Moral Concerns about Institutionalized Gamete Donation" in Cynthia B. Cohen, ed., *New Ways of Making Babies: The Case of Egg Donation* (Bloomington: Indiana University Press, 1996), 70–88.

60. Anthony Dyson, *The Ethics of IVF* (London and New York: Mowbray, 1995), 108–120.

61. Smith, *Health and Medicine in the Anglican Tradition*, 83.

62. Annette Baran and Reuben Pannor, *Lethal Secrets: The Shocking Consequences and Unsolved Problems of Artificial Insemination* (New York: Warner, 1989).

63. Cynthia B. Cohen, "Parents Anonymous" in *New Ways of Making Babies*, 88–105.

64. Cynthia B. Cohen, "Selling Bits and Pieces of Humans to Make Babies," *Journal of Medicine and Philosophy* 24, no. 3 (1999): 288–306.

65. Errol R. Norwitz, Danny J. Shust, and Susan J. Fisher, "Implantation and the Survival of Early Pregnancy," *New England Journal of Medicine* 345, no. 19 (2001): 1400–1408; K. Hardy et al., "From Cell Death to Embryo Arrest: Mathematical Models of Human Preimplantation Embryo Development," *Proceedings of the National Academy of Sciences* 98, no. 4 (2001): 1655–1660; A. J. Wilcox, C. R. Weinberg, J. F. O'Connor et al., "Incidence of Early Loss of Pregnancy," *New England Journal of Medicine* 319, no. 4 (1988): 189–194.

66. Allen Verhey, " 'Playing God' and Invoking a Perspective," *Journal of Medicine and Philosophy* 20 (1995): 347–364.

67. Murray, *Worth of a Child*, 12, 27, 32.

68. Donald Bruce, "Ethics Keeping Pace with Technology in Ronald Cole-Turner, ed., *Beyond Cloning: Religion and the Remaking of Humanity* (Harrisburg, Pa.: Trinity Press International, 2001), 39–40.

# 6

## The Moral Status of Early Embryos and New Genetic Interventions

*Cynthia B. Cohen*

The moral status of early human life has been the focus of sharp debate recently and it is not surprising that this issue has appeared at several points in this book. However, the contexts in which it arises here—that of whether to use preimplantation genetic diagnosis and, more hypothetically, germline modifications in early embryos—differ in significant respects from the main context in which it has come to the fore elsewhere—whether to engage in abortion.

The primary ethical question at stake when abortion is considered is how to balance the life, health, and well-being of a pregnant woman against that of a fetus that is inadvertently putting these in jeopardy. However, that question is irrelevant when contemplating preimplantation genetic diagnosis or germline interventions, for early embryos, rather than fetuses, are under discussion and those embryos place no woman's life, health, and well-being at risk. Instead, the central question is whether it would be wrong either to discard embryos at five or six days after fertilization (upon receiving a negative report from preimplantation genetic diagnosis of early embryos) or possibly to put them at risk (by attempting germline interventions to modify genes associated with serious disease found in early embryos). Thus, responses to the question whether it would be right to engage in abortion will not necessarily apply to the question whether it would be right to use preimplantation genetic diagnosis or germline interventions in early embryos. As Lutheran thinker Gilbert Meilaender points out, "No doubt it is, in our society, impossible to contemplate this question [of the moral status of early embryos] without feeling sucked back into the abortion debate," but it "is a separate question."[1]

Therefore, in this chapter we do not address the question of the morality of abortion of fetuses.[2] Instead, we ask whether early embryos at approximately five days after fertilization have the moral status of actual human beings, potential human beings, some other moral status, or no moral status at all. By moral status, we mean to have moral importance in one's own right, to be owed moral consideration by others, to have one's needs and well-being given weight by them.[3] To reach a conclusion about this, we call upon the rich resources of Scripture, the writings of Church Fathers, other facets of the Christian tradition, the science of embryology, contemporary Christian thinking, and the work of authors of other religious traditions and of those who stand outside any religious tradition. We then consider the implications of our conclusions about the moral status of early embryos for the question whether it is right to use preimplantation genetic diagnosis or germline interventions in which early embryos might be discarded or put at risk.

We do not claim to provide the final word about the moral status of early embryos and how that should figure in efforts to carry out novel genetic and reproductive interventions. We claim only to provide documented and reasoned grounds for our conclusions from a Christian understanding. We do so in hopes that this exploration will encourage further discussion of these significant and morally difficult matters within our pluralistic secular society. It is important to grasp the nuances of Christian views of the moral status of early embryos not only because these are of interest in themselves and are of special interest to Christians, but also because Christian thought, both conservative and liberal, has had a major, pointed impact on public discussion of this question in the United States and abroad.

## SCRIPTURE AND THE MORAL STATUS OF EARLY EMBRYOS

We begin with an exploration of scriptural texts that might help us to reach an understanding of a Christian approach to the moral status of the embryo. Although these texts provide no explicit, systematic discussion of this question, some seem to bear directly and immediately on this question, while others do so indirectly. We also highlight certain themes that appear and reappear throughout the Bible that seem relevant to this investigation.

Genesis has been a rich source of insights into the meaning and development of human life. Some Christians read the creation story in Genesis 1:26, which states that human beings are created in "the image of God," to indicate that early human embryos necessarily bear "the image of God." They maintain that because of their divine imprint, these embryos should be treated as human beings from the time of conception.

A major difficulty with this view is that it assumes its conclusion. That is, it simply asserts that early embryos bear "the image of God" without further explanation and then declares that they are therefore human beings from the instant of conception. This begs the question. What it means to bear "the image of God" and whether the fertilized egg does so are matters at issue; our conclusions about them cannot be assumed at the start. Further, early embryos do not figure in this Creation story. Adam and Eve are newly created adults; they have not gone through prenatal life and birth. Therefore, we cannot read from the value that God accords to them the moral value that early embryos might have. Genesis 1:26, consequently, provides no clear basis for the claim that early embryos constitute human beings and have the moral status of such beings.

Some take Jeremiah 1:5 to indicate that we should consider early human embryos as morally equivalent to human beings. In this passage, God speaks to Jeremiah, saying: "Before you were in the womb I knew you, before you were born I set you apart; I appointed you as prophet to the nations." This suggests to some scholars that since God knew Jeremiah as an individual human being even before he was in the womb, God must surely have known him as an individual human being once he entered the womb. They reason that the same must hold for all other human beings. From this they extrapolate that all embryos are individual human beings from the instant that they are conceived and that early embryos have the same moral status as human beings.

Others, however, maintain that if the text in Jeremiah were taken as a description of when the prophet first became an individual human being, it would indicate that he lived in some other world where God knew him before he entered the womb. The Christian tradition, however, rejects the belief that individual human beings dwell in some preexisting realm before they enter this one. It seems a misreading to take this passage as declaring just when individual human beings come into existence. This text is a poetical and metaphorical passage that tells of God's love and care for Jeremiah and for us. This and similar texts, such as Isaiah 49:1, Galatians 1:15, and Ephesians 1:3–4, express wonder about God's knowledge and plans, even as they celebrate God's call to us throughout all time. They do not indicate whether the early embryo is to be considered an individual human being from the instant of conception.

Some commentators find that Psalm 139:13–16 declares that an individual human being is present at the moment of conception. That text reads:

> For it was you who formed my inward parts;
> you knit me together in my mother's womb . . .
> my frame was not hidden from you,
> when I was being made in secret,
> intricately woven in the depths of the earth.
> Your eyes beheld my unformed substance.
> In your book were written all the days that were formed for me,
> when none of them as yet existed.

They take this passage to convey that since God knit David together in the womb, he must have been an individual human being from the moment of conception.[4] They generalize from this to conclude that all other early embryos are also individual human beings and have the moral status of such beings from the moment of conception.[5]

This passage, however, seems to convey something different about how human beings come into existence. It surely indicates that God was intimately involved in David's coming into being. However, it does not state that he was an individual human being from the moment of conception or that all embryos are individual human beings at that moment.[6] Instead, it indicates that making each human being is a process in which God engages but does not state when that process begins or ends. Moreover, like the text from Jeremiah, this passage does not speak in factual language but in poetic, religious language. It and similar texts, such as Job 31:15, tell of God's presence, reliability, and providential care of us, but they do not specify when human life begins.[7]

The Jewish tradition provided guidance to early Christians about the interpretation of passages in the Old Testament even as it does today. The text cited most often by Jewish scholars to explain their view of the moral status of nascent human life is Exodus 21:22–25,[8] which reads:

> If two men fight, and wound a woman who is pregnant (and is standing nearby) so that her fruit be expelled, but no harm shall befall (her) then he shall be fined as her husband assess, and the matter placed before the judges. But if harm befall her, then shalt give life for life.

This passage, which is in the Septuagint translation, requires a monetary penalty for ending fetal life but the death penalty for ending the life of a living human being. Thus, it presupposes that neither the fetus nor, by implication, the embryo that precedes it has the moral status of an individual human being. Yet the fetus has some value as a form of property, according to this passage, and its loss therefore requires compensation. Here the Jewish tradition deals with the destruction of a fetus according to property law, rather than according to the law of murder. This text prescribes the penalty of "life for life" if the embryo is "formed." This passage was given great weight within the later Christian tradition, which, as we shall see, related the penalty imposed on one who brings about the loss of early human life to its gestational age.[9]

Jewish scholars have generally held that until the fortieth day after conception embryos are, as stated in the Babylonian Talmud, "as if they were simply water."[10] They have taken Genesis 2:7, in which God breathes life into Adam, to signify that an individual human life begins with *ruach*, the Hebrew term for breath. This leads them to conclude that an individual human being is not present until the head or the greater part of the breech is delivered from the birth canal and the infant has taken a breath.[11] Thus, within the Jewish tradition, the early embryo is viewed as owed special consideration but is not treated as an individual human being.[12]

Such varying interpretations of scriptural passages about nascent human life have led some within the Christian tradition to conclude that specific biblical texts cannot resolve the question of the moral status of early embryos. They believe that this conclusion is confirmed by Ecclesiastes 11:5, which reads, "As you do not know how the breath comes to the bones in the woman's womb, so you do not know the work of God, who makes everything," for it suggests that the question of what sort of moral status to ascribe to nascent human life is unanswerable by humans. Those who take this view remain agnostic about the moral status of both early embryos and fetuses based on what they can find in Scripture.

If we turn to biblical themes, rather than to specific passages, the constantly recurring theme of divine creation implies the need for respect and concern for all human and other life. Scripture calls us to serve and support the vulnerable throughout creation and to love our neighbor. These themes suggest that we are to care for nature and the wide range of forms of life found within it. Yet these broad themes do not provide specific conclusions about whether early human embryos constitute individual human beings. As a group of Anglican, Roman Catholic, Orthodox, and Reformed Christian theologians has observed, scriptural passages do not establish when an individual human life begins.[13] This view is also expressed by Meilaender, who states, "We cannot, I think, claim that the Bible itself establishes the point at which an individual life begins, although it surely directs our attention to the value of fetal life."[14]

## THE CHRISTIAN TRADITION AND EARLY EMBRYOS

Christian theologians have debated the question of when an individual human being comes into existence for centuries.[15] No one answer to this question has been universally accepted. However, the predominant view has been that there is an ontological and moral distinction between early and later fetuses and that the destruction of the latter, but not the former, is akin to homicide.

Theologians disagreed during the first millennium about whether the soul preexisted the body, as Plato had held; was transmitted by the parents; or was infused by God into the body at a certain time.[16] Gradually many, although not all, drew a distinction between "unformed" and "formed" nascent human life. This distinction was based on whether or not such life could be recognized as having a human soul that formed and animated it. The soul was thought of as the "form" of the body, as contrasted with the "unformed" matter of the body; the soul gave the body its particular contours and unique characteristics. It "formed" the body at a certain point in its development and at that point, a human being came into existence. This distinction between "unformed" and "formed" life was derived from Aristotle, who held that the fetus undergoes "progressive ensoulment" from a vegetable soul via an animal soul to a human soul.[17]

Many early Church Fathers embraced this distinction between "unformed" and "formed" life, including Lactantius (240–ca. 320), Gregory of Nyssa (330–395), Jerome (347–419), Augustine (354–430), Cyril of Alexandria (ca. 375–444), Ambrose (ca.340–397), and Theodoret (393–457).[18] It carried the implication that "unformed" life does not have the same moral status as "formed" life because it is not a living human being. Thus, Gregory of Nyssa maintained that:

> . . . it would not be possible to style the unformed embryo a human being, but only a potential one—assuming that it is completed so as to come forth to human birth, while so long as it is in this unformed state it is something other than a human. . . .[19]

Other Church Fathers, however, including Clement of Alexandria (?–215), Tertullian (160–240), and Basil (330–379), questioned the distinction between "formed" and "unformed" life and considered it seriously wrong to end nascent human life at any stage. Tertullian argued that the embryo has a soul after conception and that it is man when it attains its final form.[20]

John Noonan states that the dominant view among Christian theologians was that the embryo becomes a man only when "formed."[21] Estimates of when "unformed" nascent human life became "formed" and "animated" and therefore physically developed enough to receive a human or spiritual soul varied, but centered on about two months after conception. This point was derived from Aristotle's view that in the male such life becomes "formed" at forty days and in the female at eighty days.[22] The female takes longer to receive a soul because she results from the corruption of the male seed, Aristotle maintained. Texts from several Church Fathers also reach the conclusion that an embryo is not ensouled and constituted as an individual entity until, at the earliest, forty days after fertilization.[23] This view was affirmed in the thirteenth century by Thomas Aquinas.[24] It appeared and reappeared in canonical penances and in canon law.

The destruction of "formed" but not "unformed" life was regarded as homicide or the killing of a human being.[25] Jerome took this position when he said of ending "unformed" and "formed" life that ". . . seeds are gradually formed in the uterus, and it is not reputed homicide until the scattered elements receive their appearance and members."[26] Augustine, too, expressed this view, writing that:

If the embryo is still unformed, but yet in some way ensouled while unformed . . . the law does not provide that the act [ending its life] pertains to homicide, because still there cannot be said to be a live soul in a body that lacks sensation, if it is in flesh, not yet formed and thus not yet endowed with senses.[27]

The destruction of "unformed" life was a lesser sin. This was because such an act was viewed as akin to contraception, rather than to the killing of a human being. As observed in chapter 5, a procreative ethic that held that sexual intercourse was morally justified only if its goal was to procreate was solidified within the Christian tradition by Augustine. He rejected the use of contraceptives, which he termed "the poisons of sterility," because they frustrated the procreative purpose of coitus.[28] Augustine considered the destruction of an "unformed" embryo to be wrong on the same grounds.[29] Thus, Augustine did not maintain that destroying an "unformed" embryo was wrong because it involved killing a "live soul," or human being, but because it frustrated the primary purpose of marital intercourse, procreation.

By the late Middle Ages, most Western Christian theologians had come to hold this view, maintaining that the early embryo was not an individual human being and that abortion of "unformed" life was a different and lesser sin than abortion of "formed" life. The latter ". . . was looked upon as anticipated homicide, or interpretive homicide, or homicide in intent, because it involved the destruction of a future man. It was always closely related to homicide."[30] Abortion of "unformed" life, in contrast, did not involve ending the life of a "future man."

These conclusions were influenced by the biology with which these thinkers were familiar. They were aware of three different theories of procreation.[31] The first, derived from Aristotle, was that "the seed of the man" was the active principle of human generation and that the female menses provided the passive matter on which it worked. Among the theologians who adopted this view were Lactantius, Clement of Alexandria, Jerome, and Augustine. Most of these thinkers were led by this Aristotelian biological theory also to accept the Aristotelian distinction between "unformed" and "formed" life, for the matter being worked upon had to be animated and ensouled at a certain point in its development. A second theory was that the male sperm contains both moisture and "pneuma," the spiritual element, whereas the female contains only "pneuma." The male and female "pneuma" combine in the uterus, so that the soul of the embryo springs from both parents but the body springs only from the father's seed. This view, which was primarily held by Stoics but also by some Christians, also distinguished between soul and body but did not set a point at which the former infused the latter. The third theory did not credit the woman with any substantive contribution to the creation of the embryo, as did the other two, but viewed her as merely a depository for the male seed. This theory was adopted by Tertullian, who maintained that there is no difference in the moral status of the "unformed" and the "formed" embryo, since once it was conceived, no female contribution could make a difference to its progression; its essence was fixed by the male seed at conception. Thus, the understanding of the biology of procreation that individual Christian thinkers adopted had a significant impact on their views of the moral status of the early embryo.[32] If the theory adopted by a thinker turned out to be only partially correct, this would pose a serious challenge to his view of the morality of ending early embryonic life.

The science of the development of nascent human life was not well understood among ancient and medieval Christian scholars. They knew nothing about the female oocyte and, therefore, little about fertilization. They had had no access to techniques of embryo research and no reason to imagine the development of the microscope. Thus, their views about the morality of destroying "unformed" and "formed" embryos rested on limited and precarious scientific grounds. In the seventeenth century, an "embryological revolution" began that led to the progressive abandonment of Aristotelian concepts of biology[33] and with them the distinction between "unformed" and "formed" embryos.

In 1678, Anton van Leeuwenhoek directly viewed sperm, using his newly invented microscope. He claimed to see a *homunculus*, or miniature human being, through it, thereby supporting what has come to be known as the "preformation" theory. According to this theory, which is related to the third biological theory of procreation above, the male sperm contains the preformed human being, while the female remains a passive receptacle for fertilization. The material provided by the woman, it was believed, merely sparked off the growth of the *homunculus* within the sperm and provided the necessary food for its nourishment. Over the following century and a half, however, scientists began to dispute this view.

In 1827, Karl Ernst von Baer discovered the human oocyte and scientists began to attribute a more prominent role to the female element in the process of fertilization. This made it more difficult to hold either the Aristotelian theory of a series of animating life principles or souls or the preformation theory of the existence of a *homunculus*. Christian theologians abandoned these theories[34] and instead adopted the notion of immediate rational human ensoulment at conception. Acceptance of this view was among the factors that led Pope Pius IX to strike the distinction between "unformed" and "formed" life from the canon law of the Roman Catholic Church in 1869. That law had previously imposed excommunication only for the abortion of a "formed" fetus but now imposed excommunication on those who had an abortion at any stage of the development of nascent human life.

These changes in Christian thought and the eventual Christian rejection of classical and medieval biology indicate that scientific discoveries about the growth and development of the embryo are of importance to the development of Christian teachings regarding the moral status of the embryo. Although science alone cannot resolve the question when an individual entity with the moral status of a human being begins to exist, insights and information from embryology are necessary to reach a reasonable and supportable conclusion about this. We therefore turn to explore what is known today by scientists about the development of the human embryo.

## THE BIOLOGICAL DEVELOPMENT OF EARLY EMBRYOS

Each one of us is here today as a result of the merger of an egg of a woman and a sperm of a man. From our current perspective as living human beings, this merger is extremely significant, for if that egg and that sperm had not joined, we would not be here. Some conclude that since everyone who is alive began as a merger of a sperm and an egg, all fertilized eggs must constitute individual living human beings and have the moral status of such beings.

However, when we look forward from the point at which sperm and egg merge, rather than back in retrospect after a fertilized egg has developed into an individual human being, it seems less obvious that all fertilized eggs must be individual human beings. We know that sometimes more than one sperm penetrates an egg, creating a fertilized egg that will never develop further[35] and that some fertilized eggs become tumors or hydatidiform moles. Such fertilized eggs are not individual human beings. We also know that some fertilized eggs split into several embryos that are multiples, ranging from twins to octuplets.[36] These cannot be individual human beings at the point of fertilization, for they do not become individuated until later in the process of development. We know as well that if a cell is removed from an early stage embryo and put into a hospitable environment, that cell can be grown into a separate embryo distinct from the original. This, too, puts into question whether the fertilized egg can be considered an individual entity. We also know that between 75 and 80 percent of fertilized eggs fail to implant but instead die.[37] It is difficult to accept that God calls individual human beings into existence at conception and then allows over three-quarters of them to die.[38]

All of this suggests that if we look forward from the time of conception, rather than back from our current state as living human beings, it is not clear that fertilized eggs constitute individual human beings. However, recent research, as we shall see, suggests that there may be a significant relationship between the fertilized egg and the later embryo.[39] It becomes evident from such research in embryology that we need to examine available scientific information if we are to understand the moral status of early embryos.

When the cell membranes of the sperm and egg fuse, the sperm, with its haploid complement of twenty-three chromosomes, enters the cytoplasm of the egg. Within the next eighteen to twenty-six hours, the second polar body with its surplus chromosomes is ejected from the egg, leaving it with twenty-three chromosomes. The chromosomes of egg and sperm now merge within the nucleus of the resulting cell, creating a genetically unique fertilized egg with forty-six chromosomes. This cell, which is now termed a zygote, undergoes a series of divisions into smaller cells called blastomeres. The genes in these blastomeres are identical to those in the initial cell.[40] By three days, the zygote consists of six to twelve cells and by four days, it consists of sixteen to thirty-two cells.

Up to the eight-cell stage, each of these genetically identical cells or blastomeres is totipotential—that is, each cell is able to develop into a complete individual embryo distinct from the others. If a cell is separated skillfully from the rest of the cells of the zygote at this stage, it will grow into a new individual embryo and the remaining cells of the zygote will not be damaged. This separation occurs in nature when identical (monozygotic) twins, triplets, and higher multiples form. The reverse can also take place, in that separate and distinct zygotes can fuse to form one single cell, creating what are called chimeras. A leading embryology text concludes from this that during the first fourteen days "[a] genetically unique but non-individuated embryo has yet to acquire determinate individuality, a stable human identity."[41]

Scientists have maintained that the fertilized egg and the cells that develop from it during these early stages are undifferentiated, meaning that they have no distinguishing characteristics. There is no way to identify which cells in the zygote will subsequently form the membranes and placenta and which will form the primitive streak. However, some researchers have found that newly fertilized eggs of mice, and therefore by implication of humans, have a defined top-bottom axis that is transmitted to the cells into which they split. They have also proposed that the cell created at fertilization contributes preferentially to the inner cell mass from which the fetus arises.[42] This suggests to some that fertilized eggs and the blastomeres that develop from them are not wholly undifferentiated and that the zygote plays some role in the development of the later embryo from the very start.

Beginning at the eight-cell stage, "the originally round and loosely adherent blastomeres" begin to flatten and to differentiate and "cell-to-cell contact among the blastomeres at the center of the mass" now develops.[43] Cells multiply further and a hollow ball termed a blastocyst begins to appear. The cells on the inside and outside of this ball now begin to behave differently from each other. Those on the inside form a cluster of some forty cells. These cells are pluripotent, meaning that they can differentiate and branch out into all the specialized cells that constitute the tissues and organs of the human body. It is this inner cell mass that grows into the fetus. The outer ring of cells, known as the trophoblast, develops into the placenta and other extra-fetal tissues that are cast off if the early embryo proceeds to develop.[44]

The early embryo travels along the oviduct and between the third and fourth day after fertilization enters the uterus. By the fifth day, the blastocyst is "now naked of all of its original investments and can interact directly with the endometrium."[45] It is still not possible to know at the blastocyst stage whether fertilization has produced an entity that will develop beyond a cluster of cells. Indeed, an early embryo at this stage is highly likely to die.[46] It is believed that chromosomal anomalies are responsible for 40–50 percent of these spontaneous abortions.[47]

During the second week, the early embryo splits into two layers, one of which will become "the embryo proper"[48] and the other, the placenta and related peripheral structures. As implantation takes place and the blastocyst gradually moves into the uterine wall, new tissue, such as chorionic villi, and the amniotic and chorionic cavities develop. On the thirteenth day, the definitive yolk sac appears and the primary yolk sac dissolves. The embryo proper is attached to the wall of the chorionic cavity by a connecting stalk and implantation is completed on the fourteenth day.

The first major event of the third week, gastrulation, commences with the appearance of the primitive streak at or around the fourteenth or fifteenth day. This is at first a faint groove along the midline of the germ disc that by day sixteen becomes part of a structure termed the craniocaudal body axis that establishes bilateral symmetry in the body. Gastrulation also "brings subpopulations of cells into proximity so that they can interact to produce the tissue precursors . . . that give rise to the organ system of the body."[49] In other words, cells begin to differentiate, the primitive streak that forms the axis of the body appears, and the precursors of the central nervous system and bodily organs arise.[50] At this point, it is irrevocably settled whether there are one, two, or more individuals.

From the fourth to the eighth week, formation of the major organ systems is completed and the neural tube appears. Electrical activity in the brain commences at the eighth week. A neurological pathway develops which accounts for reflexive responses to stimuli. At this time, limbs of the embryo extend into legs and arms. The embryonic period, which extends from the third through the eighth weeks,[51] now ends and transition to the fetus begins.

Why is this scientific information about the development of embryos morally important? It is significant because it can indicate, as we shall discuss in some detail, whether embryos at five or six days after fertilization have developed the biological substratum necessary to constitute an individual human being.

## CONTEMPORARY CHRISTIAN AND SECULAR THOUGHT ABOUT THE MORAL STATUS OF EARLY EMBRYOS

Recent religious and secular thinkers have given four main answers to the question whether early embryos have the moral status of individual human beings. These are the "fixed point in development" view, the developmental view, the "personhood" view, and the agnostic view. Different commentators give various shadings to these four answers. We present the core of their positions here.

### The "Fixed Point in Development" View

The first answer, which we have dubbed the "fixed point in development" view, is that an individual human entity is present at a certain critical biological point in the development of embryos and fetuses. When the embryo or fetus reaches this threshold, those who take this approach say that it has the moral status of either an actual or a potential human being. (By a potential human being, they mean an entity that, in the normal course of its development, will become an actual human being unless some agent or force unexpectedly intervenes.) They differ about which point in the biological development of nascent human life marks the beginning of an actual or potential human being.

Some among them hold that an actual human being exists at conception, when egg and sperm merge and the unique genotype of the individual human being is established. Thus, Noonan declares:

> at conception the new being receives the genetic code. It is this information which determines his characteristics, which is the biological carrier of the possibility of human wisdom, which makes him a self-evolving being. A being with a human genetic code is a man.[52]

Those who take this stand rest their belief on the genetic completeness of the conceptus. They hold that the rest of its growth involves working out and developing what has been established genetically at conception. Recent research, they believe, supports the view that the fertilized egg directs the subsequent development of the cells that spring from it.[53] Studies in animals show that axes form in the initial fertilized cell before cleavage and that this cell preferentially contributes to the inner cell mass from which the fetus later arises.[54] This research leads these commentators to maintain that the genome of the zygote directs its cleavage into several cells and the differentiation of its tissues that begins at the fourteen-day stage. Therefore, they hold, the zygote must be an individual human being and must be owed the same respect as children or adults.

Others maintain that it is a mistake to take the formation of a genotype as the point at which an individual human being comes into being. They accept that the early embryo is human, in the sense that it possesses a human genotype, and it is living, in that it exhibits all the biological signs of being a living cell. However, they say, it is not an individual human being. Donald Evans argues that "[a]n individual mass of cells alone does not constitute an individual life, even though those cells may be human and alive. (Consider, for example, a blood sample.)"[55] A report of the Board of Social Responsibility of the Church of England states that:

> [I]t is not true that every human being has a unique genetic code (as the phenomena of twinning and embryo fusion make clear), nor that every human entity which has a unique genetic code is a human being, for all the following are genetically unique: every sperm and ovum, many tumours and hydatidiform moles which are products of conception formed when two sperm fuse with an egg cytoplasm, having placental but never embryonic development.[56]

Thus, that an individual, undifferentiated cell has a certain genotype, responding commentators argue, is not a sufficient distinguishing mark of a human individual. More than a human cell containing a genotype is needed to claim that an individual human being is present at conception.

These critics argue further that if the fertilized egg is organized as a single entity, it should exhibit signs of containing specific instructions for the development of differentiated tissues, organs, or limbs. Yet they maintain that it does not. Instead, the activation of the genes in each cell into which the zygote divides is influenced by such factors as the location of each cell, its previous history, cell-to-cell contacts, and cytoplasmic, electric, and biochemical signals.[57] The way in which the fertilized egg develops is due to a cascade of effects within and between cells, rather than to a blueprint found in the zygote.

These critics place strong emphasis on evidence that each cell that separates from the initial cell up to the eight-cell stage is capable of becoming a distinct and separate individual embryo. If, as recent research could be taken to suggest, the fertilized egg is an individual entity that directs its own development, the emergence of several individuals from it must be explained. If an individual ensouled human being is present in the original fertilized egg and it then divides into twins and triplets, what happens to the original individual? Is that individual with his or her soul sacrificed to these subsequent individuals with their souls? Or does the original individual contain several different souls? If all these individuals are present in the original fertilized egg and they merely separate from one another, as some commentators have reasoned, it is difficult to understand how this occurs "unless we revert to a dualistic approach where, upon division, the soul(s) is added in."[58]

These early cells, or blastomeres, are distinct cells, according to these commentators, but they are not organized bodies. Ford points to an experiment in sheep to support the contention that an ontologically single individual has not yet developed at the four-cell stage. He explains:

> When single cells from four-cell white, black, and brown sheep embryos are aggregated in an empty zona pellucida and placed in a recipient ewe, a white, black, and brown chimeric sheep can be formed. Such a sheep does not begin at fertilization. If the cells of *genetically dissimilar* embryos can be aggregated to form a chimeric sheep, this suggests *that genetically similar* embryonic human cells could *normally* do the same.[59]

The apparently undetermined nature of these blastomeres and the fact that none is essential to the early embryo, in that they can be lost or removed without detriment to the rest of the cells, has persuaded many prominent Christian thinkers that an individual human being does not exist at the time of conception.[60] They maintain that a certain biological stability is required in an organism before it can be claimed that the substratum necessary for the development of an individual human being is present. Since there appears to be no such stability in the early embryo during the first fourteen days, these commentators conclude, it cannot be considered an individual human being before that time.

They find that it is when the primitive streak appears at around day fourteen that the early embryo becomes an organized entity and the physical basis for individuality is established. In short, they claim that the embryo at fourteen days after conception is developmentally single and either it is, or might become, an individual human being. "Then, and only then, is it clear that another individual cannot come from the cells of this embryo," Shannon and Wolter maintain.[61]

Others identify a later point at which they say that an individual human being or an individual entity that might develop into a human being is present. Some locate this point at eight weeks after conception when electrical activity is discernible in the fetal brain, providing the initial basis for self-awareness.[62] Others maintain that it is when the connection between the brain stem and the neocortex is made between the twenty-first and twenty-fourth weeks, for this provides the biological rudiments of thinking and sensing.[63] Still others hold that an individual human being is not present until birth.[64] And some say that it is when the entity has self-consciousness and a concept of a self that it is human and owed moral protection.[65] Arguments have been given for and against each of these views and still other points have been suggested at which an individual human being is present.[66] It is notoriously difficult to pin down one of these views as correct, for they vary depending on the criteria that are taken to be essential for ascertaining when an individual human being is present and the degree to which these criteria are met.[67]

## The Developmental View

The second answer, the developmental view, does not maintain that nascent human life attains human moral status at a particular point along the spectrum of development. Those who adopt this approach can find no obvious threshold point on the basis of which to draw the traditional distinction between an "unformed" and "formed" embryo.[68] Therefore, they maintain that slowly and gradually in a continuous process nascent human life grows into a discrete individual human being and that as a human organism develops various biological, psychological, and social traits, it gains increased moral status.[69]

Bouma and colleagues, from within the Reformed tradition present a version of this view. They state that "human zygotes are not beings that already have human capacities (waiting to be actualized) but they are the kind of beings that will acquire these capacities in the normal course of their development."[70] They go on to argue against fixing on a particular stage in human development at which the life of an individual human being decisively begins. Instead, they adopt a potentiality position, stating:

> We believe that attending to the implications of a developing human being's potential is a less problematic way of accounting for its moral and theological status than is the effort to find some point before birth (or even after birth) when it becomes a person. We accept the following potentiality principle: if, in the normal course of its development, a being *will become* an imager of God, then by virtue of this potential it already deserves some of the reverence due imagers of God.[71]

As the potential of nascent human life to become an actual individual human being increases, in their view, its moral status also increases. Most who take this approach maintain that the early embryo is owed respect because in the normal course of its development, it will become an actual human being. However, it has a lesser moral status than the fetus.

There is no one point at which all of those who adopt a developmental view agree that a human being is finally present and owed protection against destruction. They concur that as nascent human life develops and attains increasing moral standing, stronger moral justification is needed to discard or destroy it. Most do not accord the early embryo sufficient moral status to warrant preventing its death.

## The "Personhood" View

Some secular and religious thinkers have proposed that it is not when one becomes a human being that one is owed protection from destruction, but when one becomes a person. By "a person" some refer to an individual who has a certain set of capacities that entitle him or her to be treated as a moral agent.[72] The bearer of these capacities need not be human; certain animals with these capacities are to be considered persons. These commentators often enumerate such attributes as consciousness and self-awareness, sentience and ability to feel pain, and some minimal capacity to relate to others.

Clearly early embryos do not have such capacities, these thinkers observe, because their nervous systems are not sufficiently developed. Thus, in their view, embryos are not persons. They argue that while the precise onset of the ability to have even rudimentary experiences, such as the perception of pain, is controversial, the physiology of pain perception makes it unlikely that fetuses have experiences of any kind before the end of the second trimester.

Conscious awareness is important to the moral status of an entity, these commentators say, because only conscious, sentient beings have "interests." Steinbock declares that "a being can have interests only if it can matter to the being what is being done to it . . . if nothing at all can possibly matter to a being, then that being has no interests."[73] That is, an entity has moral status only if it can perceive and understand its "interests." The early embryo, however, cannot know or care about what happens to itself and, therefore, has no moral status, on this view. Consequently, its interests need not be taken into account when making a decision about its fate. Whether early embryos are preserved or destroyed may be very important to others, but this is of no interest or concern to them.

A major difficulty with this view is that it would rule out some whom we take indubitably to be owed protection from destruction—those who are comatose, elderly people with dementia, those who are seriously disabled developmentally, and even newborn infants on some versions of the personhood view. Yet individuals who have lost or not yet developed certain human capacities for perceiving and experiencing are not nonpersons. They are considered persons in both common and legal parlance. This odd result arises because this version of the personhood view confuses two different senses of the term "interest." One can "have an interest in" something, in the sense that one can focus special concern on it, and one can "have an interest" in the sense that something can be for one's good, can help promote one's well-being. Those who have lost or not yet developed certain human capacities still have "interests" in that certain decisions and actions can work toward their good, even though they cannot be aware of or take an "interest in" that good. They are persons, but persons who are among the weakest and most disadvantaged members of the human community. They are not to be dismissed as nonpersons without moral status who can be destroyed as it is convenient.

## The Agnostic View

The fourth answer to the question of the moral status of the early embryo is that we do not know the answer. According to this view, we have not been able to ascertain when an individual entity with the moral status of a human being is present as nascent human life develops. Our lack of certain knowledge about this has ethical consequences.

One version of the agnostic position was enunciated in a declaration of the Roman Catholic Church in 1974, which stated, "This Declaration deliberately leaves aside at what moment in time the spiritual soul is infused. On this matter tradition is not unanimous and writers differ."[74] It went on to state that "From a moral point of view this is certain: even if a doubt existed concerning whether the fruit of conception is already a human person, it is objectively a grave sin to dare to risk murder." That is, Roman Catholic thinker Germaine Grisez explains, if one does not know with certainty whether an entity is not a human being and one is willing to destroy an early embryo, this is precisely the same as being willing to destroy a human being.[75] Any reasonable doubt about the moral status of the zygote or early embryo must count in favor of that zygote or early embryo. Since there is reasonable doubt about whether the early embryo is a human being, we should treat it as a human being.

This view, which is known as tutiorism, maintains that if the life of an entity that might be a human being is at issue, one should not resolve doubts about this on the basis of the degree of probability of being right. If there is any probability that it is a human being, no matter how small, it would be gravely wrong to end its life. Thus, tutiorism maintains that it would be wrong to proceed with an action that might involve the destruction of an early embryo since absolute certainty about whether it is human has not been attained.

However, we rarely have absolute certainty when we make moral choices and we need not achieve such certainty before we can act morally. A person is judged morally for his or her actions on the basis of what it is reasonable to believe is the case. That is why Anglican thinkers for the past three hundred or more years have rejected tutiorism. The best summary of the rationale for this rejection remains the work of Anglican theologian Kenneth Kirk.[76] He maintained that tutiorism reflects an excessive focus on one's own moral purity, it suggests that moral knowledge can aspire to a greater degree of certainty than is possible, and it removes from individuals and communities the responsibility for serious moral reasoning about difficult matters. Kirk maintained that there can be more than one morally reasonable course open in contested cases and that even if one of those courses seems less probable than another, as long as it reasonable, one may take it. Jeremy Taylor, a prominent seventeenth-century Anglican theologian, in contrast with Kirk, favored choosing the more reasonable course rather than any reasonable one.[77]

On this alternative to tutiorism, even though it cannot be proven conclusively whether early embryos are individual human beings, those who argue that they are not such beings present a *reasonable* argument. It is morally sound for them to judge that it is not wrong to discard early embryos *if there are good reasons to do so*. However, it does not follow morally from this that when such reasons exist, early embryos can be destroyed at whim. What follows is that it is not always wrong to discard them.

## THE MORAL STATUS OF EARLY EMBRYOS

Several contemporary Anglican thinkers have taken the development of the primitive streak at approximately fourteen days after conception as the time after which early embryos are owed moral consideration.[78] They have accepted this approximate point on the basis of the predominant teaching of the Church Fathers, the Christian tradition, and what is known scientifically about the development of human embryos.

Scientists have found that at about day 14 a significant change occurs in early embryos. The primitive streak, a thickening plate of cells among the loosely assembled cluster of cells, now appears and develops rapidly into the nervous system. The cells in the cluster of cells known as the zygote begin to differentiate into their future organic and neural functions, and the cells that form the embryo proper become distinguished from those that form the placenta. Further, this is the last time when identical twins can form. It is difficult to regard the early embryo during the fourteen-day period as a single entity and one that is identifiable with a single later human being.

Some Anglican theologians disagree with this conclusion and side with the teachings of some Church Fathers that it is prohibited to destroy nascent human life from the point of conception onward. Those Anglicans who were signatories to "A Theologians' Brief," including Rowan Williams, the Archbishop of Canterbury, maintain that the Church Fathers held that it was seriously wrong to destroy any early embryo, whether this occurred before or after forty days had elapsed.[79]

We have concluded, however, that the predominant view of the Church Fathers, which is also the view written into the canon law and penitential literature of the church, was that the intentional destruction of early embryos before forty days was not a mortal sin. These Church Fathers did not take early embryos to have the same moral status as fetuses. In their view, it was wrong to end the life of early embryos, not because they were human beings, but because this frustrated the primary end of coitus, which they took to be procreation. However, as observed in chapter 5, several Christian denominations, including the Anglican, have moved away from this Augustinian view and back to the concept of the Gospels and the early church that the primary end of coitus is companionship and love. This means that it is no longer considered wrong to engage in marital sexual intercourse only for the sake of love and companionship rather than to procreate and that the objection of these Church Fathers to ending the lives of early embryos therefore no longer holds.

We join those Anglican theologians who conclude that early embryos before approximately fourteen days are not individual human beings. Should we consider them potential human beings? There are some problems with this view. A potential entity will, in the normal course of its development, go on to become an actual entity of its kind unless unexpected events, forces, or agents intervene to prevent this, as Bouma and colleagues state.[80] Yet in the normal course of its development, the early embryo does not have the capabilities, powers, and inner directedness to become an actual human being. We have learned that nearly 80 percent of such embryos do not survive a host of hazards to reach day 14, often because they lack the capacity to develop the structure and organization of a human being. This makes it difficult to claim that early embryos are potential human beings since, in the normal course of their development, most will not become actual human beings. While it is possible that a specific early embryo will implant in the uterus and go on to become an actual human being, it cannot be said that early embryos *in general* are potential human beings, since that will not occur in the normal course of their development.

Yet early embryos are more than possible human beings. Possible entities, according to Bouma and colleagues, could, under certain causally possible conditions, become actual ones. A sperm, for example, is a possible human being, for it could, if merged with an egg and implanted in the uterus of a woman and brought to birth, become an actual human being. However, this will not occur in the normal course of its development, for millions of sperm die and do not fertilize eggs that implant and develop into human beings. Therefore a sperm is a possible, rather than a potential human being. An early embryo, however, is further along the path to becoming an actual human being than is a sperm. It has forty-six chromosomes, rather than twenty-three, and has begun to divide into several cells that will, in a minority of cases, go on to develop the structure of a single entity, implant, and eventually be born as an actual human being. The early embryo therefore seems closer to a potential than a possible human being.

Because of this, we maintain that it is morally sound to treat the early embryo as having the moral status of a potential human being. Since we cannot find a clear cutoff point at which a possible human being becomes a potential human being, we are led to accept the developmental view of the moral status of human life. That is, we maintain that as nascent human life develops, it increases in moral status, or in the moral consideration that it is owed by others. On this developmental approach, early embryos do not have the same moral status as born human beings or of, say, four-month fetuses, for these embryos are at a much earlier stage of the development. Yet early embryos do have some moral status and are to be treated with some degree of care and respect because some of them will enter the spectrum of human development.

G. R. Dunstan also concludes that the early embryo is not an individual human being, stating that:

> The principle embodied in the [Christian] historical tradition was that the protection due to the embryo or foetus advanced step by step with its own growth toward maturity. The critical period now, however, is not forty days but fourteen.[81]

He goes on to consider the significance of this conclusion for the moral status of the early embryo and argues that it is morally acceptable to discard early embryos before day 14 but that after this, nascent human life is owed greater moral consideration.

Is this consistent with the care and respect that we should accord to early embryos? Embryonic human life is not the same as the life of an individual human organism, yet it is, in the minority of cases, life that might still go on to develop into an individual human being. What does it mean for such early embryos to have some degree of moral status?

It means, to begin with, that they should not be treated arbitrarily. They should not be treated as mere clusters of cells that can be discarded at whim. They are owed greater protection than sperm or than animal embryos. We should have very serious reasons morally for knowingly damaging or discarding them. However, they are not owed all of the protections that we are obliged to provide to human beings. The kind and degree of loss that the early embryo would undergo if discarded or put at risk of death must be weighed against the moral seriousness of the reasons for doing so.

It can be morally justifiable to discard or end the life of early embryos in some limited circumstances. It would be morally acceptable to do so to avoid possibly bringing into the world a human individual who is afflicted with a serious inherited disease. That an early embryo would, if it navigated the treacherous passage to birth, suffer from a devastating disease, is a morally serious reason that justifies the discard of a five-day embryo. It would also be morally acceptable to end the life of early embryos that remain after in vitro fertilization procedures have been completed in order to aid research aimed at preventing serious illness in already living human beings. The goal of preventing illness and even death in living human beings is a morally weighty one that justifies the use of early embryos that would otherwise be discarded. However, we do not believe that it is morally sound to discard or otherwise end the lives of early embryos for reasons that are less serious morally, such as to avoid having a child with the "wrong" color hair or the "wrong" gender.

In reaching these conclusions, we have attempted to engage in a process of discernment that remains faithful to basic Christian convictions and teachings while taking into account contemporary embryological findings. We have sought to provide reasons for our conclusions whose intelligibility is open to scrutiny by others. We acknowledge that faithful, reasonable people can disagree about these conclusions. Therefore, we invite all to ponder them and to provide alternative conclusions that they take to be more justifiable morally should they find our conclusions wanting.

## THE EARLY EMBRYO AND
## PREIMPLANTATION GENETIC DIAGNOSIS

Preimplantation genetic diagnosis (PGD) involves testing early embryos for genes associated with serious genetic disease or conditions and implanting those that are free of such genes. Those early embryos that, upon evaluation, are found to have such genes are discarded. This allows parents to bring children into the world who will not bear the burdens of serious, and perhaps lethal, disease.

Is it wrong to create early embryos knowing that some may be discarded to avoid bringing the children into whom they might develop into the world with serious diseases? It is important to point out that we already accept the discard of some early embryos. That is, the usual protocol for carrying out IVF involves inspecting those early embryos that have been created in vitro to discern whether they appear normal. Those embryos that seem impaired in some way are neither implanted nor frozen but are discarded. This is done to avoid bringing children into the world who will be seriously ill or have serious disabling conditions. PGD is carried out using a similar procedure. In PGD, however, early embryos are not just visually inspected but are directly and specifically tested to learn whether they have genes that might lead to serious disease in a later child if they were implanted. Thus, PGD and visual inspection of the early embryo created through IVF are both carried out for the same reason.

If it is morally acceptable to examine early embryos and to discard some that appear abnormal in shape and configuration, as is sometimes the case when IVF is used, it is also morally acceptable to test early embryos even more closely and to discard those with genes clearly connected with serious illness, as is sometimes the case in PGD. Since we accept the discard of early embryos in IVF as necessary to ensure that we do not bring into the world children who will be terribly ill, it seems morally acceptable to do the same when we use PGD.

For instance, should PGD indicate that a future child who might eventually develop from an early embryo would be affected by a severe gene-based disease, such as Lesch-Nyhan disease or Tay-Sachs disease, it would be morally acceptable to discard that early embryo to avoid the possibility of bringing a seriously ill child into the world. Since that child would suffer from illness, disability, and ultimately, death, it would be a morally sound choice to decide against transferring the early embryo of concern to a woman's uterus for implantation. Here the negative import of the suffering of the future child over a life of limited span morally outweighs the care that is owed to the early embryo.

However, it is more difficult to justify discarding early embryos when PGD indicates that the later child would have only moderate disease or late-onset disease that might not affect it until adulthood. Because of this difficulty, a decision about whether it would be right to implant such embryos and possibly bring the resulting children into the world, we believe, is appropriately made by the parents who are most likely to have the good of the particular child at heart. However, many on our task force believe that it is not morally sound to discard an early embryo because it bears genes for traits unrelated to health, such as those associated with short height or a hair color that its creators do not want their future child to have. As we have observed at several points in earlier chapters, it is morally questionable to reject possible later children because of qualities they would bear that are not to parental taste.

## THE EARLY EMBRYO AND GERMLINE INTERVENTIONS

Germline interventions for therapeutic purposes require the creation of early embryos in vitro. However, they do not call for the discard of such embryos. Instead they involve altering or replacing genes in those embryos that have gone awry and that would lead to serious illness or disability in the future child.

As we have discussed at several points in previous chapters, genes in themselves are not sacrosanct. There is nothing inherently wrong in altering or repairing them when this is done to avoid serious genetic disease in the later child and its descendants—if this can be done safely. The difficulty is that we have not yet developed methods for carrying out germline interventions in ways that will not damage the early embryo. Much more research needs to be done in this area before such interventions could be employed in human early embryos with an assurance of safety. If this were eventually accomplished—and there is serious question about whether the safety not only of the embryos who receive such germline interventions, but also the safety of their descendants, could be adequately assured—it would exhibit appropriate care for early embryos to use such interventions in them. Thus, it is morally acceptable, in principle, to engage in germline interventions into early embryos for therapeutic purposes.

## NOTES

1. Gilbert Meilaender, "Some Protestant Reflections," in *The Human Embryonic Stem Cell Debate*, ed. Suzanne Holland, Karen Lebacqz, and Laurie Zoloth (Cambridge: MIT Press, 2001) 141–147.

2. The General Convention of the Episcopal Church has maintained that abortion is morally acceptable in cases where "the physical or mental health of the mother is threatened seriously, or where there is substantial reason to believe that the child would be born badly deformed in mind or body, or where the pregnancy has resulted from rape or incest." (Sixty-Seventh General Convention of 1982 (B-9S), reaffirming a resolution passed in 1967.) In a later resolution, the General Convention stated that "[w]e emphatically oppose abortion as a means of birth control, family planning, sex selection, or any reason of mere convenience." (Seventy-First General Convention of 1994 (A-054s), reaffirming and expanding a resolution passed in 1988.)

3. Mary Anne Warren, *Moral Status: Obligations to Persons and Other Living Things* (Oxford: Oxford University Press, 1997) 3.

4. Oliver O'Donovan, *The Christian and the Unborn Child* (Bramcote, England: Grove Books, 1986) 15.

5. David Atkinson, "Some Theological Perspectives on the Human Embryo (Part 2)," *Ethics and Medicine: A Christian Perspective* 2, no. 23 (1986): 23ff, 32.

6. James C. Peterson, *Genetic Turning Points: The Ethics of Human Genetic Intervention* (Grand Rapids, Mich.: Eerdmans, 2001), 114–115.

7. Anthony Dyson, "At Heaven's Command?: The Churches, Theology, and Experiments on Embryos," in *Experiments on Embryos*, ed. A. Dyson and J. Harris (London: Routledge, 1992), 82–104.

8. Laurie Zoloth, "The Ethics of the Eighth Day: Jewish Bioethics and Research on Human Embryonic Stem Cells," in *The Human Embryonic Stem Cell Debate*, ed. Suzanne Holland, Karen Lebacqz, and Laurie Zoloth (Cambridge: MIT Press, 2001), 95–112.

9. G. R. Dunstan, "The Moral Status of the Human Embryo: A Tradition Recalled," *Journal of Medical Ethics* 1 (1984): 38–44.

10. Immanuel Jakobovitz, *Jewish Medical Ethics* (New York: Bloch, 1975), 275.

11. Zoloth, 100.

12. David Feldman, *Marital Relations, Birth Control, and Jewish Law* (New York: New York University Press, 1995), 257–266.

13. "A Theologians' Brief," *Ethics & Medicine: An International Journal of Bioethics*, 17, no. 3 (Fall 2001): 22.

14. Gilbert Meilaender, *Bioethics: A Primer for Christians* (Grand Rapids, Mich.: Eerdmans, 1996), 29.

15. John T. Noonan Jr. "An Almost Absolute Value in History," in *The Morality of Abortion—Legal, and Historical Perspectives*, ed. John T. Noonan Jr. (Cambridge: Harvard University Press, 1972), 1–59.

16. Carol A. Tauer, "The Tradition of Probabilism and the Moral Status of the Early Embryo," *Theological Studies* 45 (1984): 3–33.

17. Aristotle, *History of Animals*, 7.3, and *De Anima* 402a.6ff.; see Dunstan, "The Moral Status of the Human Embryo," 39 and G. R. Dunstan, "The Embryo, from Aristotle to Alton," *Cross Currents* 38, no. 47 (April 1998): 6–8.

18. John Connery, *Abortion: The Development of the Roman Catholic Perspective* (Chicago: Loyola University Press, 1977) 40, 50–52, 56.

19. Gregory of Nyssa, *Adversus Macedonianos*, cited by G. R. Dunstan, "The Moral Status of the Embryo," 40.

20. Tertullian, *The Soul* 25.2, 37a, cited in John T. Noonan Jr., *Contraception: A History of Its Treatment by the Catholic Theologians and Canonists* (Cambridge: Harvard University Press, 1965) 90.

21. Noonan, *Contraception,* 89.

22. Ibid., 89–90.

23. "A Theologians' Brief," 4.

24. Thomas Aquinas, *Summa Contra Gentiles* IV.5; *Commentary on Book III of the Sentences* 3.5.2.

25. Church of England, Board of Social Responsibility, *Personal Origins* (2nd rev. ed., 1996), 34.

26. Jerome, *Epistles* 121.4, cited in Noonan, *Contraception*, 90.

27. Augustine, *On Exodus* 21.80, cited in Noonan, *Contraception*, 90.

28. Augustine, *Marriage and Concupiscence* 1.15.17.

29. Ibid.

30. Connery, 306.

31. Noonan, *Contraception*, 89–90.

32. *Personal Origins,* 35.

33. Ibid.

34. Noonan, "An Almost Absolute Value in History," 38.

35. Keith L. Moore and T.V.N. Persaud, *The Developing Human: Clinically Oriented Embryology*, 6th ed. (Philadelphia: Saunders, 1998) 37; see also T. W. Sadler, *Langman's Medical Embryology* 6th ed. (Baltimore: William and Wilkins, 1990), 27, and C. R. Austin, *Human Embryos: The Debate on Assisted Reproduction* (Oxford: Oxford University Press, 1989) 9.

36. M. G. Bulmer, *The Biology of Twinning in Man* (Oxford: Clarendon Press, 1970).

37. Errol R. Norwitz, Danny J. Shust, and Susan J. Fisher, "Implantation and the Survival of Early Pregnancy," *New England Journal of Medicine* 345, no. 19 (2001): 1400–1408; K. Hardy et al., "From Cell Death to Embryo Arrest: Mathematical Models of Human Preimplantation Embryo Development*,*" *Proceedings of the National Academy of Sciences* 98, no. 4 (2001): 1655–1660; A. J. Wilcox, C. R. Weinberg, J. F. O'Connor et al., "Incidence of Early Loss of Pregnancy," *New England Journal of Medicine* 319, no. 4 (1988): 189–194; Clifford Grobstein, "External Human Fertilization," *Scientific American* 240, no. 6 (1979): 57–67.

38. Meilaender, *Bioethics*, 30; Karl Rahner, *Theological Investigations*, trans. Graham Harrison, vol. 9, chap. 14, 236.

39. K. Piotrowska et al., "Blastomeres Arising from the First Cleavage Division Have Distinguishable Fates in Normal Mouse Development," *Development* 128 (2001): 3739–3748; R. L. Gardner, "Specification of Embryonic Axes Begins before Cleavage in Normal Mouse Development," *Development* 128 (2001): 839–847; R. L. Gardner, "The Early Blastocyst is Bilaterally Symmetrical and its Axis of Symmetry is Aligned with the Animal-Vegetal Axis of the Zygote in the Mouse," *Development* 124 (1997): 289–301.

40. Robert G. Lee and Derek Morgan, *Human Fertilisation and Embryology: Regulating the Reproductive Revolution* (London: Blackstone Press, 2001), 62; William J.

Larsen, *Human Embryology,* 2nd ed. (New York: Churchill Livingstone, 1997) 17–51; Ronan O'Rahilly and Fabiola Müller, *Human Embryology and Teratology* (New York: Wiley-Liss, 1992), 20; Sadler, 29.

41. O'Rahilly and Müller, 6.

42. Gardner, "Specification of Embronic Axes;" Gardner, "The Early Blastocyst is Bilaterally Symmetrical."

43. Larsen, 19.

44. Norwitz et al., 1402

45. Larsen, 19–20.

46. Norwitz et al.; Hardy et al.; Wilcox et al.; Grobstein.

47. Larsen, 22; O'Rahilly and Müller, 56.

48. Larsen, 19, 33, 35.

49. Larsen, 49.

50. Larsen, 51.

51. Larsen, 47.

52. Noonan, "An Almost Absolute Value in History," 57.

53. Helen Pearson, "Your Destiny from Day One," *Nature* 414 (2002): 14–15; Richard M. Doerflinger, "The Ethics of Funding Embryonic Stem Cell Research: A Catholic Viewpoint," *Kennedy Institute of Ethics Journal* 9 no. 2 (1999): 137–150.

54. Piotrowska, "Blastomeres Arising from the First Cleavage Division;" Gardner, "Specification of Embryonic Axes;" Gardner, "The Early Blastocyst is Bilaterally Symmetrical."

55. Donald Evans, "Pro-Attitudes toward pre-Embryos," in D. Evans, ed., *Conceiving the Embryo: Ethics, Law and Practice in Human Embryology* (The Hague: Kluwer, 1996), 27–46, 34.

56. *Personal Origins,* 41.

57. Norman M. Ford, *The Prenatal Person: Ethics from Conception to Birth* (Oxford: Blackwell Publishers, 2002), 67–68; Lewis Wolpert, *The Triumph of the Embryo* (Oxford: University Press, 1991), 31–32, 37–40, 84, 199–202.

58. Stephen Beasley, "Contraception and the Moral Status of the Early Human Embryo," in D. Evans, ed., *Conceiving the Embryo* (The Hague: Kluwer, 1996), 89–118, 96.

59. Ford, *The Prenatal Person,* 66.

60. Norman Ford, *When Did I Begin?* (Cambridge: Cambridge University Press, 1988), 102–121; Richard A. McCormick, "Who or What Is the Pre-Embryo?" *Kennedy Institute of Ethics Journal* 1 (1991): 1–15; T. Shannon and A. Wolter "Reflections on the Moral Status of the Pre-Embryo," *Theological Studies* 51 (1990): 603–626; James Diamond, "Abortion, Animation, and Biological Humanization," *Theological Studies* 36 (1975): 305–324; Andre Hellegers, "Fetal Development," *Theological Studies* 31 (1970): 3–9.

61. Shannon and Wolter, 614.

62. Michael Lockwood, "When Does a Life Begin?" in Michael Lockwood, ed., *Moral Dilemmas in Modern Medicine* (London: Oxford University Press, 1985), 9–31; Baruch Brody, *Abortion and the Sanctity of Human Life* (Cambridge: Cambridge University Press, 1975); Robert M. Veatch, *The Basics of Bioethics* (Upper Saddle River, N.J.: Prentice Hall, 1999).

63. Helga Kuhse and Peter Singer, "Individuals, Humans and Personhood: The Issue of Moral Status," in Peter Singer et al., eds., *Embryo Experimentation: Ethical, Legal and Social Issues* (Cambridge: Cambridge University Press, 1990), 65–75.

64. Tom Regan, "Introduction," *Matters of Life and Death*, ed. T. Regan (New York: Random House, 1980), 3–27.

65. Michael Tooley, "Abortion and Infanticide," *Philosophy and Public Affairs* 2, no. 1 (Fall 1972): 37–65.

66. See Committee on Medical Ethics, Episcopal Diocese of Washington, D.C., *Wrestling with the Future: Our Genes and Our Choices* (Harrisburg, Pa: Morehouse, 1998) 90.

67. Richard M. Doerflinger, "The Ethics of Funding Embryonic Stem Cell Research: A Catholic Viewpoint," *Kennedy Institute of Ethics Journal* 9, no. 2 (1999): 137–150; Ronald M. Green, *The Human Embryo Research Debates: Bioethics in the Vortex of Controversy* (Oxford: Oxford University Press, 2001), 43–52.

68. *Personal Origins*, 2.

69. M. Forrester, *Persons, Animals, and Fetuses* (Dordrecht: Reidel, 1996).

70. Hessel Bouma III, Douglas Diekema, Edward Langerak, Theodore Rottman, and Allen Verhey, *Christian Faith, Health, and Medical Practice* (Grand Rapids, Mich.: Eerdmans, 1989), 27–49, 39.

71. Ibid., 45.

72. Warren, *Moral Status*, 148–177.

73. Bonnie Steinbock, *Life Before Birth: The Moral and Legal Status of Embryos and Fetuses* (New York: Oxford University Press, 1992), 10.

74. Sacred Congregation for the Doctrine of the Faith, *Declaration on Abortion* (Washington, D.C.: U.S. Catholic Conference, 1975); See also Sacred Congregation for the Doctrine of the Faith, *Donum vitae (Instruction on Respect for Human Life in Its Origin and on the Dignity of Procreation) Origins* 16 (1987): 697–711.

75. Germaine Grisez, *Abortion: The Myths, the Realities and the Arguments* (New York: Corpus Books, 1990), 306, 344.

76. Kenneth E. Kirk, *Conscience and Its Problems: An Introduction to Casuistry*, introduction by David H. Smith (1927; reprint, Louisville, Ky.: Westminster John Knox Press, 1999), 207–209.

77. Albert R. Jonsen and Stephen Toulmin, *The Abuse of Casuistry: A History of Moral Reasoning* (Berkeley: University of California Press, 1988), 161–162; see also Tauer, "The Tradition of Probabilism and the Moral Status of the Early Embryo."

78. Gordon Dunstan, "The Moral Status of the Human Embryo," in *Philosophical Ethics in Reproductive Medicine*, ed. David R. Bronham, Maureen E. Dalton, and Jennifer C. Jackson (Manchester: Manchester University Press, 1988), 2–14; Richard Harries, "Report of House of Lords Select Committee on Stem Cell Research," *Hansard* 62, 1, no. 16, col. 35.37; John Habgood, in *Report of the Committee of Inquiry into Human Fertilisation and Embryology. The Warnock Committee* (London: Her Majesty's Stationery Office, 1984), 60.

79. "A Theologians' Brief."

80. Bouma et al., *Christian Faith*, 39; Philip E. Devine, *The Ethics of Homicide* (Ithaca: Cornell University Press, 1978), 94. There is a vast literature on the disputed concept of "potentiality." See, for example, Jim Stone, "Why Potentiality Matters," *Canadian Journal of Philosophy* 17, no. 4 (1987): 815–830; John Andrew Fisher, "Why Potentiality Does Not Matter: A Reply to Stone," *Canadian Journal of Philosophy* 24, no. 2 (1994): 261–280; Jim Stone, "Why Potentiality Still Matters," *Canadian Journal of Philosophy* 24, no. 2 (1994): 281–294.

81. Dunstan, "The Moral Status of the Early Embryo," 8.

# 7

# Genetics and Genetic Technology in Social Context

*Bruce Jennings and Elizabeth Heitman*

No science or technology, least of all genetics, exists in a social, cultural, or historical vacuum. Like most human activities, science is a social practice, and the application of genetic knowledge is influenced by historical experience and social values.[1] The relationship between science and society is not simple, but it is clear that the influences run both ways. Social forces shape science and technology, even as new scientific knowledge and new technological powers shape society and culture. Science affects us individually and shapes us collectively and institutionally. Science has personal and even moral and spiritual effects. New genetic knowledge leads individuals to view their bodies and their health differently. Moreover, this knowledge may inspire different views of nature and the rights and freedoms of others. No less important, some individuals may find themselves affected spiritually; confronted by new scientific findings, they may develop a new perspective on their religious faith. Families, governments, corporations, and churches also react to genetics and genetic technology—increasingly, it seems, these institutions are allowing genetics to set their agendas and to define many of their deepest concerns.

With scientific and clinical advances in genetics come tremendous opportunities for alleviating suffering and restoring health. But genetic science and technology also carry considerable ideological, social, and ethical dangers. One significant danger is that through careless or ill-informed use of scientific concepts as metaphors, we will come to think of ourselves and others in ways that hinder our ability to relate to God. And, what comes perhaps to the same thing, we risk thinking about genetics in ways that hinder the establishment of "right relationships" among persons; that is to say, relationships including love, caring, service, mutual respect, dignity, protecting and promoting the rights of others, and fulfilling duties of justice.

The social and cultural reception of genetics—and not the intellectually appropriate understanding of genetics per se—is the subject matter of this chapter. Here we address a number of questions: Will genetics give us a new understanding of disease and disability, and how should society respond to such redefinition? Are genetic knowledge and genetic technology morally neutral? In the end, these questions lead to two other, larger ones: Can humankind be trusted to use genetic knowledge and technology properly and wisely? Given the human propensity for sin, blindness, and evil, what safeguards and regulations should govern our use of genetics?

## THE CURRENT CLIMATE

Chapter 4 provides an overview of the terrible history of American, English, and Nazi German social policy intended to "improve" the human race through eugenics. Talk of improving the genetic health of the human population still raises the specter of state-mandated testing and forced eugenic intervention for society's alleged benefit, but in current practice, voluntary, individualistic, and clinical uses of genetics are the norm, and the concept of population-based activities is rarely raised even in theory. Mandatory sterilization programs are now viewed as a serious violation of human rights. Reproductive rights advocates, theologians, and geneticists from many nations have roundly criticized China's current program of limiting families to one child and promoting, if not requiring, abortion and sterilization. In the United States, individuals and families are now the primary locus of decision making about reproductive matters, and federal rules and state statutes make it quite difficult to sterilize anyone without his or her explicit understanding and informed consent. After a long hiatus, the field of public health is once again working in what is now known as "public health genetics," but in that area experts are particularly careful to support only programs, such as newborn screening, designed to lead to better medical care and enhanced access to health services rather than to any kind of stigmatization or discrimination.[2]

Nonetheless, it is not hard for critics to see potentially eugenic purposes behind some contemporary uses of genetics. Individuals' and couples' decisions about attempting pregnancy, undergoing preimplantation or prenatal diagnosis, and discarding embryos or terminating pregnancies when the embryo or fetus is identified as likely to be afflicted with a condition such as cystic fibrosis or Down syndrome have been criticized as leading to a new kind of eugenics through the "back door."[3] While they are far removed from coercive state programs, standard screening and testing protocols reflect a de facto policy of selecting among potential or future persons on the basis of whether they may be born with specific disabling conditions. Individual choices are made with at least some degree of freedom, but "voluntary" is a slippery term, and strongly held social values can be partially coercive of individuals.[4] The history of eugenics teaches us that even well-intentioned efforts to improve the population's health and welfare through genetic intervention are susceptible to our deepest social prejudices, and that future genetic technologies may carry eugenic threats in a more subtle guise than the Nazis' brown shirts or jackboots.[5] Even as new genetic technologies enable wonderful medical advances, we must be alert to the unintended ways in which their use may lead to grave injustice.

## GENETIC DIFFERENCE, DISEASE, AND DISABILITY

Eugenic policies and practices in the early twentieth century also suggest another difficult challenge for the contemporary use of genetic testing and screening: how to define health and illness in a way that identifies preventable or treatable disease but also respects the inherent moral value of individuals affected by such conditions. In the early 1900s, individuals and groups targeted for sterilization as "unfit" usually fell into one of several categories. Early sterilization statutes focused on the "feeble-minded." Others afflicted with serious mental illnesses—especially schizophrenia or severe bipolar affective disorder—were soon also considered "unfit," as were people with epilepsy and Huntington disease. In some cases people with physical disabilities such as visual or hearing impairments were also singled out as candidates for sterilization. The "science" that underlay such efforts viewed these conditions as clearly defined traits that were inexorably transmitted from one generation to the next. Among many eugenicists, race, class, ethnicity, and religion were also commonly held to be inheritable determinants of pathology.

## THE PROBLEM OF DEFINITION

Contemporary science gives us a much better understanding of the multifaceted genetic and environmental factors that underlie the conditions that eugenicists sought to eliminate from future populations. Nonetheless, the eugenicists' classification of and response to the "unfit" reflects a phenomenon that faces contemporary genetics as well: Definitions of disease are always bound by cultural context and influenced by the concerns of those who establish the definitions. Genetics may give us more precise ways of describing disease, but science cannot remove the social dimension in defining "normal" (and the differences and deviations from "normal" that are classified as disease). Both health care practitioners and the lay public will tend to accept the insights of genetics through their preexisting intellectual and experiential frameworks of health and illness, incorporating many of society's prevailing views of medicine and disease and the ethical tensions that they already embody. Even if we pay heed to historical tendencies to define marginalized and socially stigmatized persons as diseased, new categories of genetic diagnosis are likely to reflect contemporary views of normalcy and deviance that are not simply the conclusions of scientific observation.

The influence of cultural and societal norms on the accepted description, diagnosis, and etiology of human disease is well illustrated by the World Health Organization's (WHO's) *International Classification of Diseases*, the authoritative catalog of human maladies: only about half of its entries are considered "real" diseases in Western medicine.[6] The rest typically reflect non-Western worldviews that define human health and disease in terms of systems of social harmony, balance, or spiritual purity, and that have little to do with genetics. Conversely, even in the industrialized West, some conditions associated with a genetic mutation, such as congenital deafness or extremely short stature, which may be viewed as diseases by medical specialists, may not be interpreted or experienced as medical conditions by those who are affected by them.

## Defining Health and Disease

Because what is viewed as disease varies with culture and environment, one of the more difficult issues in diagnosis is determining which signs and symptoms define the presence of disease. In genetic diagnosis, this question is particularly difficult: Whether the presence (or absence) of a recognized genetic mutation or abnormality in itself constitutes a disease further complicates this issue. Traditionally disease has been defined in terms of particular physical or behavioral symptoms and limitations on daily function. The meaning of an abnormal gene *without* accompanying dismorphology or dysfunction is a scientific and ethical question of real significance. We know today that even the healthiest human being has genetic anomalies linked to disease. Thus interpreting the presence of a genetic mutation as the essence of any disorder, irrespective of other symptoms, would make everyone sick with something. Such a reclassification, easily and too frequently done outside the knowledgeable community, could greatly expand the role of medicine and the authority of health professionals in society and redirect a significant proportion of society's resources toward addressing these new "diseases." This shift would also likely add to the already significant health-related activities of the "worried well," a growing number of basically healthy people whose concern for disease prevention has contributed dramatically to the demand for health services.[7]

As the possibilities for testing expand to reveal even inconsequential genetic characteristics, the common desire to be healthy or to have a healthy baby may be redirected toward the goal of being free from genetic flaws or having a child without genetic flaws, a quest for an unattainable perfection. But if no one is truly free of genetic mutations, a meaningful definition of "healthy" would depend as much or more on the absence of mutations linked to serious disease or disability as to any definition of a model genotype. Still, this wildly expansive definition of health would also be misleading. Although genetic screening can rule out the presence of serious genetic anomalies, there is no way to ensure that individuals who test negative for all known, potentially harmful genetic abnormalities are truly free of genetic mutations or that they will not develop new mutations that might lead to serious disease.

Efforts to reduce the effects of genetically linked disease among individuals may also subtly foster a shift in the baseline definition of genetic health, encouraging the application of genetic techniques to address conditions once considered part of the spectrum of "healthy." While few can argue against the importance of eliminating diseases that cause terrible suffering, defining genetic health as the absence of certain genetic abnormalities may further blur the already fading distinction between therapy for disease and enhancement of characteristics that are statistically normal but less than ideal. Again, such a shift threatens to redefine the place of medicine in society and redirect social resources toward ends that we might not choose to pursue otherwise.

## Impairment, Disease, Illness, and Disability

Another way to underscore the importance of the social nature of human maladies and the potential social implications for genetic diagnosis is to examine the different meanings and implications of the notions of "disease," "impairment," "disability," and "handicap" as originally proposed by the WHO in 1980.[8] This model has subsequently been refined, and its precise terminology has been set aside, but the underlying conception remains. The model is based on the notion of a continuum comprising biological, psychological, and social/cultural components of the concept of sickness or disability. According to the early WHO model, a *disease* was the biological abnormality or dysfunction within the person's body (such as a malfunctioning optic nerve); an *impairment* was the external manifestation of the disease (such as blindness); a *disability* was the behavioral limitation associated with the impairment (such as the inability to see); and a *handicap* was defined as the socially created difficulties or disadvantages that were experienced by the individual due to a combination of biological, behavioral, and institutional or attitudinal factors (such as the difficulty a blind person encounters in a social environment full of physical barriers and a lack of auditory cues). Thus, from this perspective, a blind person always has a biological disease or disorder, as well as an impairment. That person will most likely also have a disability or behavioral limitations to some degree (depending upon the person). But that person need not have a handicap in a well-organized and accommodating social environment.

It is important to note, however, that on this account, a "disability" is not equated with an "impairment" (real or perceived) as in the language of the Americans with Disabilities Act (ADA), and it does not follow that persons with impairments who are able to minimize the extent of their disability should not be entitled to the same legal and moral rights and protections afforded to others who are less well able to compensate for the disabling aspects of their impairment. Other criticisms of the 1980 WHO model have been raised as well, and later versions of WHO documents have abandoned this terminology. Nonetheless, the underlying notion of a continuum from biology through behavior to social arrangements and cultural attitudes remains widespread in thinking about chronic illness and disability issues.[9]

Indeed, the words disease, illness, impairment, and disability are often used interchangeably in everyday discourse, and their respective meanings vary according to the social effects of the condition. For example, both medicine and the social sciences use the term "disease" to refer to an abnormal condition characterized by a recognized constellation of physical and mental symptoms, whereas "illness" is the social state that results from the disruption of normal behavior and subjective experience of suffering that may accompany the experience of disease. Sociologist Talcott Parsons described "illness" as a form of social deviance and contended that society prescribes an acceptable "sick role" as a means of establishing an acceptable range of deviance.

The words "impairment" and "disability" are more recent terms with less general agreement about their meaning and appropriate use. "Impairment" typically refers to a demonstrable biological or physical abnormality that imposes limitations on an individual's choices or activities. "Disability" is a parallel word that acquired important legal and political meaning in the ADA. The ADA defines a disability as "a physical or mental impairment that substantially limits one or more major life functions," including limitations that occur only as a result of the attitudes of others toward the impairment.[10] Thus a disability may be construed as any condition that others regard as serious enough to limit one in some major life activity, even if those assumptions are wrong.

In these terms, an individual can have a genetic abnormality or mutation without necessarily having a disease, and indeed it is estimated that each one of us carries several potentially lethal genetic abnormalities that never surface in the absence of triggering environmental factors. However, given that very few if any conditions are the result of only a genetic abnormality and that genetics is likely involved in many physical and mental ailments, the term "genetic disease" should be used cautiously, as it suggests a genetic determinism that is scientifically indefensible. The phrase "genetic impairment" is similarly misleading, although impairment may certainly result from genetically linked conditions.

The concept of genetic disability is both socially and politically difficult. While some genetic mutations can lead to serious physical and mental impairments, in such cases it may be difficult to distinguish the disabling effects of the mutation per se from the limiting physical or mental condition. The greater risk is that, even in the absence of symptoms that limit an individual's major life activities, misinformation and misunderstanding about genetic diagnosis will foster prejudice against individuals with specific genetic mutations; the resulting stigma may prevent diagnosed persons from gaining or retaining employment, housing, education, insurance, and important social relationships. Thus the disability would be the value-laden diagnostic labels and stereotypical characterizations that define the future actions and life choices of individuals with certain mutations, not the mutation or condition itself.

Debate continues about whether the identification of a genetic mutation linked to disease is somehow different from more traditional diagnosis, particularly with respect to confidentiality and the potential for discrimination. To date the protections provided under the Americans with Disabilities Act to persons diagnosed with stigmatized genetic conditions are not clearly distinguished, whether in the workplace, public accommodations, or private settings, and, of course, many forms of prejudice cannot be controlled by legal sanctions. Thus, it is extremely important to examine the motives of varying individuals, agencies, and organizations for defining disease in terms of genetic markers or combined genetic and other physical symptoms, as well as their interests in pursuing, recommending, or requiring genetic testing. Because it may not be possible to prevent the discriminatory use of genetic diagnostic information once it has become available, the reasons for seeking and providing genetic information should be well understood by all parties in advance.

### Definition and Self-Definition

Changing definitions of health and illness related to genetics may also affect the social identity of individuals and groups with identified genetic anomalies linked to disease. The diagnosis of disease, both generally and with respect to specific conditions, often implies a certain social role for the afflicted.[11] Symptom-free individuals who test positive for certain genetic mutations may find themselves suddenly cast as patients, expected to adopt new health-related behaviors, such as dietary or lifestyle changes or medication or regular screening regimes, that enforce the notion that they are sick or at serious risk of becoming so.

A further problem is the negative psychosocial effects of *anticipating* symptoms that may develop slowly or might never constitute a state of illness. On a societal level, the goal of reducing the harmful effects of genetic disease through screening and prevention strategies may promote false analogies with the control of infectious disease and its vectors, implicitly identifying carriers of specific genetic mutations as a threat to the public health.[12] And, as disability rights advocates have often pointed out, prenatal testing that identifies certain genetic conditions as warranting abortion may contribute to prejudice against individuals born with those conditions and others born healthy but who develop similar disabilities from other causes.

The social identity and roles of individuals and groups diagnosed with some genetic anomalies may also be subject to the unfortunate tendency of even educated Americans to interpret illness in moral terms and to find the afflicted "deserving" of their conditions. As we pointed out in chapter 1, the Anglican tradition rejects the idea that disease is the result of sin, spiritual impurity, or a lack of faith, and the *Book of Common Prayer* makes it clear that God does not impose illness as a punishment. Nonetheless, these beliefs recur throughout the history of Judeo-Christian thought and many people's "operational theologies" readily interpret unwanted medical diagnoses as a form of divine justice or a test of their personal faith.[13] Still others may express their belief in immanent justice in more impersonal terms, interpreting illness as "payback" for bad behavior in a system where "what goes around comes around."[14] After the original epidemiologic work that linked homosexuality with AIDS—known initially as "gay-related immunodeficiency syndrome" or GRIDS—clergy and laity from many Christian denominations were quick to pronounce God's judgment on the sick, as the sick themselves may be.[15] As the nature of the viral syndrome and the many modes of HIV transmission became clear, the name was changed, but the original medical and moral characterization had done significant harm.

The line between the moral judgment of disease as punishment for sin and the scientific view of disease as a natural consequence of unhealthy behavior is blurry. Conceptualizing a problem as a medical issue can benefit individuals and society in that it may reduce or eliminate the social judgment and shame associated with some forms of deviance that historically have been considered to be moral failings. The reclassification of alcoholism as a biological affliction with at least some genetic links is one such example. However, when the predominant biological origins of a disease are also associated with morally questionable behavior, as in the case of alcoholic cirrhosis of the liver, it can be particularly difficult to separate conclusions about biological causality from those about moral causality. Moreover, attempts to explain the relationships between genetic predisposition, personal behavior, and physical disease may also link medical ailments to groups and activities that society already condemns as immoral, making science appear to justify the condemnation of certain groups and behaviors.

## THE SOCIAL FACE OF TECHNOLOGY

The genetic information that creates these new definitional challenges and may expand the category of "patient" to include many who show no symptoms of disease is not a new *kind* of knowledge. Family medical histories and pedigrees provided insight into individuals' risks for inherited disease long before genes were even discovered: Such risk profiles have historically been a component of marital matchmaking in communities that carry devastating inherited conditions. What is new is that today's genetic diagnostic tests offer a degree of specificity and sensitivity that makes their results *seem* certain and thus their predictive ability seem higher than it actually is. Genetic testing technology also appeals to many Americans as "cutting edge" medicine that offers patients and care givers the very best benefits of science.

The role and social effects of diagnostic and screening technologies in genetics are a remarkable example of Americans' enduring love/hate relationship with technology in general and medical technology in particular. On the one hand, technology has often been seen as an engine of dangerous change and as the principal threat to settled ways of life, a kind of Old World corrupting import into the pristine beauty of the garden of the New World.[16] At the same time, technology is frequently perceived as the vehicle of progress and freedom. Every period of technological innovation has its prophets of salvation and its prophets of doom. Perhaps the opponents of technological innovation fight so hard to keep certain technologies from being introduced because they share the general American assumption that technology cannot be reversed: Once the genie is out of the bottle, the typical cliché holds, there is no putting it back. And for each technology that will ruin us, usually an alternative is proposed to save us, but the alternative is rarely to return to a pre-technological condition. Rather, the alternative is some other form of technology.[17]

### The Technological Imperative

Much of the U.S. dedication to medical research, and in particular to genetic research, stems from the belief that medical knowledge gives us power over disease and enhances our ability to control nature and forestall death. Diagnostic technology is appealing because it appears to offer resolution to medical uncertainty. However, because diagnostic information is so highly valued by both patients and health professionals, new diagnostic technology often diffuses widely before the meaning, ramifications, or appropriate use of its results are clear. Many of the genetic tests currently available today began to be used in clinical settings well before their use was understood in the research setting.

The rapid diffusion and application of genetic tests may be at least partly attributable to the "technological imperative," the perceived need to use a new medical technology simply because exists, whether or not it has been shown to work. The technological imperative is a recognized force in health care internationally, particularly in the care of the seriously ill and individuals for whom no intervention is known to be effective. When there is no obvious harm to the individual or no clearly definable cost to society, new and untested technologies appear to offer alternatives to the frustration of doing nothing for someone in need. As in the case of BRCA1 testing, genetic diagnostic tests are used prematurely in clinical settings in response to the formidable anxiety and uncertainty of individuals and families at risk for diseases linked to genetic mutations. Too often, however, the limitations of the diagnostic technology are evident only after individuals who sought genetic information have taken radical steps to respond to results with uncertain meaning.

The fallacy of the technological imperative is the presumption that technology is somehow outside the realm of human agency and choice, and that technology itself drives human behavior. No one is forced to use technology. Individuals can turn off the television or often ride a bike instead of traveling by car. Society has rejected or sharply restricted such new technologies as thermonuclear weapons, space exploration after the moon landings, and both solar and nuclear power. However, in health care, the temptations at both the individual and the social level are often too great to resist. Few individuals offered genetic testing are entirely comfortable turning down the opportunity to learn something, however inaccurate, about their medical futures. And because diagnostic information typically serves as the basis for medical intervention, the availability of test results may imply a need to take further action, irrespective of the test's appropriateness.

## Technology and Choice

An important assumption about technology, especially diagnostic technology, is that it automatically expands choice. A pregnant woman does not have to know before birth whether her fetus has trisomy 21 (Down syndrome), but she can use genetic testing to find out, giving her the options of preparing for a potentially disabled child or terminating the pregnancy. The son of a man with Huntington disease does not have to learn whether he carries the gene before he develops unmistakable symptoms, but he can, thus preparing himself for the choices of whether to plan a family, become financially secure prior to becoming disabled, etc.

This notion of choice provided by diagnostic technology has several interesting twists, however. First, it takes an unrealistic, individualistic view of the nature of choice and deliberation and underplays the social and cultural pressures at work in the chooser's mind. Ironically, assuming that technology opens up a course of action as a choice transforms the moral meaning of the outcome: the consequences of both using or not using the technology are subsequently treated by others as the results of a deliberate choice rather than as an unfortunate blow of fate. Before prenatal genetic tests were available, a couple who had a child with extreme and special needs could count upon some measure of social sympathy and support. But today the birth of a child with a genetically linked affliction may seem like a deliberate act on the part of the parents, who either decided to forgo the test that would have told them about the condition or decided to have the child despite the known diagnosis. Either way, somehow, the birth of the afflicted child is their fault, or at least their responsibility, and they are then expected to live with the consequences. In this way technology feeds upon a myth of individualism but then turns self-determination into a destructive social practice.

Moreover, while technology expands our apparent choices in some ways, it may limit choice in others. While the new genetics may give us new ways to treat, cure, control, and alleviate diseases that are now chronic, incurable, degenerative, and devastating, it may limit choice directly by forcing us to make decisions that we would not have to face if we did not have the information provided by technology. Sometimes technology limits choice by setting up social situations, expectations, and pressures that individuals and families find virtually impossible to resist. Who is really free to forgo the test for Down syndrome except those who have already made the choice to do whatever is necessary to raise a child with mental and physical impairments?[18] For those for whom the right course of action and its consequences are still open questions, the very availability of the diagnostic test offers them no choice but to undergo testing, because they—plausibly—do not want to decide in ignorance. Moreover, if diagnosis is possible but effective treatment or adequate management is not, diagnostic knowledge can create a sense of helplessness rather than offering positive options for both patients and practitioners. In some instances, patients and clinicians eager to take definitive action may feel compelled to intervene on the basis of test results even where "watchful waiting" may be safer or more effective.

Most subtly still, we often unconsciously internalize the imperatives and expectations of technology as we live in modern society. The power of the genetic technology to define who you are, what you are, what your life possibilities are, and what limits you should place on yourself is a phenomenon that is obscured by the social ideology of technology as an expander of choice and freedom. The great risk is that we will see and evaluate ourselves *only* in these terms, disregarding virtues and gifts we may have that are at least as relevant to decisions about employment, marriage, or having children as predictions about susceptibility to a genetic problem that genetic testing might reveal.

## The Nature of Technology, Genetic Information, and Social Justice

One of the most subtly dangerous aspects of technology is the common assumption that technology simply refers to equipment or a group of tools or machines. We often understand technology in terms of its surface physical instrumentation. Understood as mere tools, it is hard to see how technology could not be neutral, how it is not the gun but the gunman that kills. And it is hard to see how technology could be implicated in the disruption of our relation to God and to our fellow creatures. But a more adequate understanding views technology as a complex structure of information, scientific and engineering knowledge, instrumentation, authority, and social relations, the totality of which adds up to a structure of power over nature and over other human beings. The very power—indeed the power for goodness—of this technological capability and mind-set so easily obscures other perspectives among persons that it is not so far-fetched to ask about the moral and spiritual valance of the new genetic technology.[19] The technology can inspire an idolatrous veneration that displaces more basic commitments to seeing our lives as gifts and other persons as creatures to whom justice is due.

## Genetic Technology and Insurance

The information made available by genetic diagnostic technology, however complete or accurate, and the diagnostic labeling and medical decision making that accompany diagnosis, raise the further issue of how to use that information in a socially just way. For example, insurance companies have traditionally claimed the right to all of any insured's known health information in order to make an actuarially fair assessment of risks and rates. In an effort to rule out costly health risks from genetic disorders, insurers may place inappropriate weight on genetic diagnostic tests because they are interested in reducing uncertainty and its associated costs whenever possible. Employers, who often fund both health insurance and life insurance for their employees and who have certain duties to protect workers from potentially dangerous environmental exposures, may also seek employees' genetic diagnostic information in hopes of reducing their costs and increasing their productivity.

Defining "disease" in terms of abnormal genetic makeup would nullify the distinction between "new disease" and preexisting conditions that typically define health insurance coverage under experience rating arrangements. Any discovered but nonsymptomatic abnormality could be called a "pre-existing condition." Thus the new genetics may have the effect of making anything but community rating conceptually incoherent, and may force a radical reassessment within the insurance industry of many assumptions concerning actuarial fairness, "moral hazard," and adverse selection.

A word is in order here about the nature of insurance. There are basically two fundamental types of insurance, "social insurance" and private "indemnity insurance." Social insurance is the keystone of the modern welfare state. It protects individuals from burdensome financial loss from situations in their future that are foreseeable and likely to occur to a reasonably large number of people in a population. Social insurance works by pooling individual risk into a very large population; each individual in that population pays a small contribution to the insurance fund. A few will suffer loss (become ill or disabled) and need to draw money from the fund; most members of the fund will not. Those who stay well subsidize and support those who become sick; each is protected from the devastating loss that would occur if they had to pay the expenses associated with illness (or other misfortune) alone. In a social insurance arrangement such as this, the point is to include as many people as possible, not to exclude anyone.

By contrast, indemnity insurance is designed to protect individuals from unlikely or unforeseen misfortunes that are nonetheless probable and frequent enough to pose a real risk to individuals. Loss of one's home or business due to fire and the possibility of unexpected, premature death that would deprive one's family of financial support are two classic examples of situations that indemnity insurance is designed to protect against. Here the financial solvency of the pooled resources depends upon equal knowledge and equal uncertainty. Actuarial calculations are made to determine a member's premium contribution relative to their risk of misfortune. Those with older homes or homes in fire-prone areas will pay more into the insurance fund than those with safer homes, and that is fair in this type of arrangement. Special knowledge that the insurer does not have gives the insured an unfair advantage. Those who plan arson or suicide are to be excluded from indemnity fire or life insurance, and if these acts are committed the insurance fund is relieved of its obligation to pay. The notion of "moral hazard" in indemnity insurance refers to the fact that individuals covered by insurance are tempted to cause the covered event in order to profit financially from it. "Adverse selection" means that individuals who have special knowledge of their future may be motivated to enroll in the insurance plan because they are assured of a payout far greater than the premiums they pay into the fund. The solvency of an indemnity insurance fund depends upon "rating" or scrutinizing would-be members of the fund to make sure that they are not joining only because they know that they (or their survivors) will soon benefit from the insurance.

The notion that fairness requires a level playing field of information between the purchasers and the sellers of insurance becomes less important once we abandon the notion that insurance should be sold only to those who are very unlikely to make a claim on it. As things stand today in the United States, however, individuals and families may try to hide or deny genetic diagnostic information from their insurers and employers with good reason, lying to prevent a likely loss of employment or coverage for a condition that might leave them or a loved one disabled and destitute. Even after defining employers' and insurers' legitimate access to an individual's or family's genetic information, the use of that information remains a serious question of justice for all parties. Some health policy analysts have suggested that genetic diagnostic technology will lead to the end of risk-based insurance, and after a period of chaos in the funding of health care, will inevitably bring about the creation of a national health care system or universal health insurance coverage.

## SHARING RISKS AND BENEFITS

Also lurking in the future are some difficult issues of distributive justice concerning whose group and what part of the world will receive the benefits and burdens of genetic intervention and which will not. As importantly, differences are likely in which of the world's peoples will see themselves as being treated equitably in genetics and which will not. The risk is that, within a given culture, groups that appear to be collectively less susceptible to culturally significant diseases may be considered the healthy or superior groups, and vice versa. Racial identification as a social category may be an important marker of health-related behavioral and environmental considerations that affect genetic and other physical characteristics. In the past decade, efforts to understand the meaning of differences among ethnic groups and genetic research into human genetic variability have called the very meaning of race as a category into question. Increasingly, geneticists confirm that the genetic differences among racial groups are negligible, and epidemiologists argue that individuals are often assigned arbitrarily to racial categories that are inconsistently defined and interpreted. Replacing racial links to genetic connections, such as high blood pressure and heart disease, will require much more knowledge about the interaction of genes, behavior, and the environment. It is also likely to require a greater willingness to examine the cultural and environmental origins of health-related behaviors.

We will turn to some other issues of social justice raised by genetics in chapter 9.

# NOTES

1. William W. Lowrance, *Modern Science and Human Values* (New York: Oxford University Press, 1985).

2. Cf. Newborn Screening Task Force, "Serving the Family from Birth to the Medical Home: Newborn Screening—A Blueprint for the Future," *Pediatrics* 106 (August 2000): 2.

3. Troy Duster, *Backdoor to Eugenics* (London: Routledge, 1990).

4. Diane B. Paul, *Controlling Human Heredity, 1865 to the Present* (Atlantic Highlands, N.J.: Humanities Press International, 1995); Philip Kitcher, *The Lives to Come: The Genetic Revolution and Human Possibilities* (New York: Simon & Schuster, 1996).

5. Ruth Hubbard and Elijah Wald, *Exploding the Gene Myth* (Boston: Beacon Press, 1999).

6. J. M. Janzen, *The Quest for Therapy: Medical Pluralism in Western Zaire* (Berkeley: University of California Press, 1978).

7. T. F. Buss and W. R. Gillanders, "Worry About Health Status Among the Elderly: Patient Management and Health Policy Implications," *Journal of Health and Social Policy* 8, no. 4 (1997): 53–66.

8. World Health Organization, *International Classification of Impairments, Disabilities, and Handicaps: A Manual of Classification Relating to the Consequences of Disease* (Geneva: WHO, 1980). A revised edition of this work was published in 1993. Then a much more drastically revised version appeared as World Health Organization, *ICIDH-2: International Classification of Functioning and Disabilities* (Geneva: WHO, 1999).

9. Patrick Fougeyrollas and Line Beauregard, "Disability: An Interactive Person-Environment Social Creation," in Gary L. Albrecht, Katherine D. Seelman, and Michael Bury, *Handbook of Disability Studies* (Thousand Oaks, Calif.: Sage Publications, 2001), 171–194. See also Anita Silvers, David Wasserman, and Mary B. Mahowald, *Disability, Difference, Discrimination: On Justice in Bioethics and Public Policy* (Lanham, Md.: Rowman & Littlefield, 1998).

10. Americans with Disabilities Act of 1990, 42 U.S.C. §12112.

11. Barbara K. Rothman, *The Book of Life: A Personal and Ethical Guide to Race, Normality, and the Implications of the Human Genome Project* (Boston: Beacon Press, 2001).

12. Martin S. Pernick, "Eugenics and Public Health in American History," *American Journal of Public Health* 87 (1997): 1767–1772.

13. H. Anderson, "After the Diagnosis: An Operational Theology for the Terminally Ill," *Journal of Pastoral Care* 43 (1989): 141–150. And see chapter 2 of this volume.

14. Lakshmi Raman and Gerald A. Winer, *Children's and Adults' Understanding of Illness: Evidence in Support of a Co-existence Model," Genetic, Social, and General Psychology Monographs* 128, no. 4 (2002).

15. Loretta Kopelman, "The Punishment Concept of Disease," in C. Pierce and D. VanDeVeer, eds., *AIDS: Ethics and Public Policy* (Belmont, Calif.: Wadsworth, 1988), 49–55.

16. Leo Marx, *The Machine in the Garden: Technology and the Pastoral Ideal in America* (New York: Oxford University Press, 1964).

17. Landon Winner, *Autonomous Technology* (Cambridge: MIT Press, 1977).

18. See the various perspectives on this question represented in Erik Parens and Adrienne Asch, eds., *Prenatal Testing and Disability Rights* (Washington, D.C.: Georgetown University Press, 2000).

19. Rayna Rapp, *Testing Women, Testing the Fetus: The Social Impact of Amnio-centesis in America* (New York: Routledge, 1999). See also John Robertson, *Children of Choice: Freedom and the New Reproductive Technologies* (Princeton: Princeton University Press, 1994).

# 8

## The Economics and Politics of the New Genetics

*Mary R. Anderlik and Jan C. Heller*

As a society, we are generally optimistic about the prospects for dramatic improvements in human well-being that might result from recent genetic discoveries. We hope to use new genetic findings to cure diseases, eliminate or relieve disabilities, keep aging at bay, and even improve our features or our nature. Yet at the same time, some of us are concerned about the combination of technological and corporate power that is driving the genetic developments discussed in this book. Others are alarmed by the astonishing speed with which the products of genetic research are being brought into the clinic and the marketplace. They believe that our society has not had enough time to debate these developments or to decide how to respond to them ethically and legally.

In this chapter, we examine the economic and political forces that have shaped and will continue to shape the choices offered by the new genetics. In keeping with the rest of the book, we direct our attention primarily to the health care arena, putting aside the related but distinctive issues that arise with agricultural applications of genetic research. We begin by looking at the genesis of the Human Genome Project and the effort to speed the translation of research results into useful products through alliances with industry and patenting. The controversy surrounding the launch and progress of the Human Genome Project provides the backdrop for an examination of the oft-expressed concern that existing law and policy endanger respect for life by treating it as simply another commodity to be bought and sold.

Before addressing the substantive issues, we offer a summary of the current state of the law on patenting of genetically engineered organisms and DNA sequences and explain the concept of commodification. We then step back to consider how an understanding of stewardship might illuminate the debate over the appropriate paths for development of products and services based on genetic research. Simple but morally adequate answers remain elusive, but an approach informed by the metaphor of stewardship rules out some bad options and links the patenting debate to a larger discussion concerning the norms of science versus commerce, the relationship between public and private sector funding of research, and the adequacy of oversight of controversial areas of research.

We also consider the effects of current policies and practices on access to the benefits of genetic research. We believe it is helpful to distinguish among the various kinds of access-related concerns. Further, we acknowledge the trade-offs inherent in a system that awards time-limited monopolies to inventors before reviewing a range of positions on patenting and licensing issues. We draw on ideas about justice found in the Bible and echoed in some secular writing in evaluating those positions. In particular, we find a repeated injunction to attend to the problems experienced by vulnerable persons on the margins of society. These ideas lead us beyond questions of access to genetic testing and therapies to the broader question of what to do about the millions who lack access even to basic health care in the United States. Here we draw on the understanding of community, and related concepts of solidarity and subsidiarity, within our own Episcopal tradition.

These themes lead us to take up concerns about genetic discrimination, and we explore the case for laws limiting corporate and individual freedom to act on genetic information. More broadly, we argue for laws and public processes that increase transparency and enhance the role of the public in oversight of the developments discussed in this chapter. We conclude with some brief reflections on the church's role in providing safe places to debate these concerns, educating its members, and advocating for change in our society.

Some of these matters may seem esoteric, but they are relevant to all of us. Increasingly, the science is prompting individuals, families, and health professionals, as well as legislators, to ask questions about public policy. We hope the following vignettes will provide some insight into the issues of public policy we address in the remainder of the text, issues that pervade our decisions about use of the new genetics.

> Joan, thirty-five, has her first appointment with her new family physician. After she tells him that both her mother and her grandmother died of breast cancer in their early forties, he refers her to a geneticist to be tested for the heightened susceptibility to breast and ovarian cancer associated with certain mutations in the BRCA1 and BRCA2 genes. Waiting for the test results, she worries not only about herself, but also about the implications of her decision to undergo testing for her daughters, and about her husband's reaction if she tests positive and decides to un-

dergo bilateral prophylactic mastectomy (removal of both breasts) and prophylactic oophorectomy (removal of both ovaries). Joan worries about her prospects for promotion, or even continued employment, since her company is self-insured and may have access to her test results; indeed, she does not know how she could keep the situation confidential in any case, especially if she undergoes the surgery.

Don is the family physician who just referred Joan for the susceptibility testing at a cost of over $2,500. Joan's health insurance will cover the test, but he worries about his patients who have no insurance or minimal insurance. If they need testing, how will they pay for it? Don wonders whether he should advise Joan to pay for the test herself, giving her the option of keeping the information from her employer-insurer. He is also concerned about the biotech company that provides the test. He believes Joan is an appropriate candidate for testing, but the company has just announced that it will begin marketing this test directly to the public. Literally billions of dollars are at stake for the company, and he wonders how he will respond to the many questions his patients will raise after they see the TV ads. Why, Don wonders, doesn't the government better regulate such practices? Why is there no law protecting Joan and his other patients against possible discrimination by their employers once they have such tests? And what's going to happen to his poorer patients, who will see the ads for such tests and won't be able to afford them?

Tom is a U.S. congressman and chair of a congressional committee charged with evaluating draft legislation increasing funding for genetic research and creating incentives for the development of commercial applications based on the research, especially in health care. He worries about the wisdom of provisions that give academic scientists a financial stake in the development process, indeed, encourage them to find commercial partners and seek patents on the products of their publicly funded research. He also wonders about the unintended consequences of such legislation for citizens. If testing becomes widespread, will those who learn that they are at heightened risk for disease, especially types of disease for which no effective treatments are available, face discrimination? And what about the forty million or so uninsured in this country? Congress seems to be in no mood to address the long-standing problems of health care access. Should Tom support legislation that would pay for genetic testing and other genetic services for those who lack insurance? Or would that detract from efforts to build support for universal health insurance?

As these stories suggest, decisions at the level of public policy have far-reaching implications for individuals, and vice versa. These stories also indicate some of the complexity associated with evaluating current policies and the alternatives.

## GENETIC SCIENCE, COMMERCE, AND STEWARDSHIP

We have only to recall the public arguments over the use of recombinant DNA in the 1970s to realize that concerns about genetic research are not new. Recent controversies over the commercialization of genetic research products highlight once again what has long been a contentious, if sometimes overlooked, issue in the United States. This issue is often treated under the heading of "technology transfer," and it includes a complex mix of economic, political, and ethical issues.

Technology transfer refers to governmental practices and policies that "transfer" to the private sector the results of basic scientific research originally financed with public funds. Much of the research discussed in this book was either made possible by the Human Genome Project or made available almost unimaginably more quickly than would have been the case without the project. The funds for the Human Genome Project were initially justified (in part) by the desire of many in the U.S. Congress to increase the efficiency of the technology transfer processes in this country. The findings of such research are transferred to private groups to encourage the rapid development of technological applications that are, in turn, often sold back to the same public (and others) whose tax dollars financed the original research.

### The Human Genome Project and Technology Transfer

The Human Genome Project is the largest single biological research project ever undertaken in human history and the first "big science" project in biology. Before it was initiated, basic biological research was conducted piecemeal by independent bench scientists in private university and corporate laboratories and in a few public laboratories. Sociologists of science describe this situation in the biological sciences as a "cottage industry" approach, which they often contrast with large-scale, "big science" projects in physics. The cottage industry approach to research lacked systematic coordination between biological researchers and a publicly agreed-upon agenda. Instead, individual scientists or small teams of scientists simply pursued the research they found interesting, building on each other's findings, but not necessarily coordinating efforts.

The Human Genome Project changed this environment dramatically. It was centrally coordinated, with publicly stated goals, a defined budget, and a time line for completion. The total cost of the Human Genome Project to U.S. taxpayers was originally estimated at roughly $3 billion over fifteen years. It is by far the largest part of the worldwide Human Genome Initiative, the goal of which is to map an entire representative human genome and the genomes of a selected number of model animal organisms. The project began officially in Fiscal Year 1990 and was recently declared complete with the publication of a rough draft of the human genome several years ahead of schedule. Even as scientists work to refine the draft, attention in the research community has turned to other large-scale projects, many of which are continuing in the private sector.

Traditionally, technology transfer was accomplished through peer-reviewed scientific publication, which made the fruits of the public's investment in science broadly available. The trend over the last several decades has been to give researchers and research institutions a direct financial stake in the commercial exploitation of the results of public projects. Thus, laws passed in the mid-1980s encouraged alliances between research institutions and industry and gave researchers the right to patent the fruits of their federally funded projects. Influential congressional leaders, urged on by certain scientific and corporate leaders, had become convinced that American preeminence in basic biological research would generate significant biomedical and related economic benefits, but only if coupled with an accelerated program of technology transfer.[1]

This rapid movement from publicly funded research to private sector development has raised concerns that the new emphasis on efficiency in technology transfer is blurring boundaries between science and commerce and the public and private sectors. How is it possible to justify the public funding of scientific research when, for example, millions of citizens in this country whose taxes help to pay for it do not have access to basic health care? That justification is all the more difficult to discern in light of the increasing merging of the political and economic spheres, which leads citizens to fear that public interests are being neglected by the very representatives elected to protect them.[2]

*The critics and their concerns.* Some critics assert that in the wholesale embrace of the commercial ethos, political leaders have confused the goal of achieving benefits for the public (e.g., reasonable prices on products of biotechnology for U.S. consumers) and the goal of achieving benefits for U.S. industries (e.g., ensuring that any profits reaped from biotechnology would flow to U.S. companies). These criticisms reveal the need for greater attention to the ways in which decisions concerning the structure of research and development activities accord or conflict with fundamental social values.

*Patenting and concerns about commodification.* One of the ways governments encourage technology transfer is through their systems for protecting intellectual property, particularly the patent system. Most of us have never filed a patent application nor, we hope, infringed on someone else's patent. Yet the world of intellectual property is not as alien as we might think. Anyone who has written a paper or penciled a cartoon, or used someone else's paper or cartoon for a class or presentation, has encountered the form of intellectual property protection known as copyright. As a matter of federal law, the creators of "original works of authorship" fixed in a tangible form of expression have the exclusive right to control the reproduction and distribution of those works.[3] Yet this right is limited, because costs as well as benefits are associated with the award of a legally enforceable monopoly. Copyright protection exists for a limited period of time,[4] and ideas and familiar symbols and slogans are among the categories of things that are ineligible for federal copyright protection. Educators and scholars are likely familiar with the copyright law's "fair use" exemption, which allows reproduction without permission from the copyright holder for purposes such as teaching, criticism, and news reporting, provided certain conditions are met.

Patents operate in much the same way, protecting the rights of creators, but with limits based on considerations of public policy. In general, patents serve an important public function. They give the originator of a useful invention a right to exclude others from using, making, or marketing that invention for a limited period of time.[5] In exchange, that person discloses information about the invention to the public. This arrangement allows others to learn about the invention and benefit from it, while preventing "free riding" or the use of the invention without compensation. Those who want to use the invention to their own commercial advantage must first strike a deal with the patent holder. "Patent monopolies are granted in order to stimulate invention of useful devices, protect investments required to produce invention, and encourage the disclosure of trade secrets. . . . The social cost is higher prices for and underutilization of the patented process or product during the period of the monopoly."[6] In the United States, the foundation for patent protections, and other forms of intellectual property, is the Constitution. Article I, Section 8 gives Congress the power to "promote the Progress of Science and useful Arts, by securing for limited Times to Authors and Inventors the exclusive Right to their respective Writings and Discoveries."[7] Supporters of the current system argue that patents provide a strong incentive for investment in research and development efforts that ultimately yield great benefits for individuals and for society as a whole.

Under U.S. patent law, all machines, manufactures, compositions of matter, and processes are eligible to be patented unless they fall into one of three categories: laws of nature, natural phenomena or "products of nature," and abstract ideas.[8] Working out what these concepts mean in practice is an extremely complex matter, especially in light of developments in biotechnology. Keeping in mind that the purpose of the patent system is to spur innovation, and to a lesser extent, reward inventors for their insight and labor, one can identify some underlying themes that link the three categories. Laws of nature are fundamental truths that operate independently of human agency. Knowledge of them may provide a foundation for human powers of creation, but they themselves are not under human control. Further, a system that awarded exclusive rights in laws of physics or mathematical principles would seem not only wrong but unworkable. How would such rights be enforced? Would scientists and others have to pay a fee each time they pondered the motion of physical bodies or performed a calculation as part of their own research and development efforts? Likewise, while I may be the first to describe a natural phenomenon, that does not give me the status of its inventor. There must be some intervention or manipulation that takes the thing out of nature. And there are good policy reasons for such a rule: If others are bound to trip over the phenomenon, literally or figuratively, there is little reason to make the monopoly rights-for-publication trade-off. Finally, abstract ideas have not yet reached the stage of development where their applications are clear, and their lack of "tangibility" would create problems related to enforcement similar to those with laws of nature.

Everything else is potentially patentable if disclosure is adequate and requirements of novelty, nonobviousness, and utility are met.[9] In 1980, the Supreme Court ruled that a researcher who had developed a bacterium to devour oil spills could patent not only the process but the bacterium itself,[10] because the bacterium was not found in nature. In deciding that living organisms could be patented, the Court said that it had to accept and interpret the law that Congress had passed, even if some of its members were convinced that it was bad public policy. This ruling set a precedent for allowing the patenting of nonhuman living organisms that are created by intervening in natural processes. Decisions by the Board of Patent Appeals have affirmed that patents can be granted on higher animals altered by genetic manipulation, although not on human beings owing to the Constitution's prohibition on slavery.[11]

The Supreme Court's ruling also opened the door to patenting of genes found in humans. Some argue that the patenting of genes, sequences of DNA, or DNA sequence information is equivalent to patenting human life. In its guidelines, the U.S. Patent and Trademark Office stresses that a patent on a gene covers the "isolated and purified" gene but does not cover the gene "as it occurs in nature."[12] The guidelines also emphasize that patents "do not confer ownership of genes, genetic information, or sequences."[13] Nevertheless, many people are concerned that current law, as interpreted by the courts, undermines important values by permitting the patenting of "life," or if not that, then by treating the constituent elements of human beings and the natural world as mere commodities.

Thus, fears surrounding patents on the products of genetic research can lead to concerns about commodification. Commodification is a process in which a thing takes on more and more of the features of a commodity like grain or iron ore—a process in which we become increasingly comfortable talking about and acting toward some thing or being as if it were an object that is appropriately bought and sold on the open market versus having intrinsic value.

Commodities share at least three features. First, they are alienable, meaning they can be bought and sold. Second, they are commensurable, meaning they can be exchanged or compared using a common metric, such as dollars and cents. Third, they are fungible, meaning they can be exchanged without loss of value. Some things, like grain or iron ore, are treated as commodities across most societies. Most things are valued in more complex ways. For example, to a jeweler, a diamond ring is a commodity—the jeweler would be happy to exchange it for money or for another piece of jewelry of equal market price. The jeweler may feel differently, though, about a piece she regards as an incomparable work of art, and you will certainly feel differently about your grandmother's wedding ring. In contemporary U.S. society we treat many things as alienable, and so as at least partial commodities, that in others times and places were regarded as inalienable.

Can the concept of stewardship help us here? The notion of stewardship provides Christians with a general orientation toward creation, and while it does not necessarily yield definitive answers to particular ethical questions, it may provide guidance as we experience or seek to understand concerns about commodification. Stewardship involves an exercise of power, but it is responsible power grounded in dominion, not domination. In the Genesis narrative (2:15), the Hebrew word *shamar* is used to describe human responsibility for the garden of Eden: ". . . God took the man and put him in the garden of Eden to till it and keep it." *Shamar*, as naturalist Calvin DeWitt notes,[14] is often translated "keep," and it indicates a "loving, caring, sustaining" relationship that is dynamic rather than static. The same word is used in the blessing God gives to Moses for the Israelites: "The Lord bless you and keep you" (Num. 6:24). Genesis suggests that stewardship is central to the purposes of God for human beings. Further, the biblical tradition stands against any view that is inattentive to the full richness and variety of the created world. In the Gospels, Jesus tells us that God is concerned about individuals, not just creation in the aggregate: "Are not five sparrows sold for two pennies? Yet not one of them is forgotten by God" (Luke 12:7). This saying also reflects the assumption that market price and ultimate value are two separate things. Finally, the Gospels contain stories that warn against stagnation—burying gifts rather than using them. The parables of Jesus are, however, open to multiple interpretations, and these passages are by no means straightforward appeals for increased economic activity.

Still, throughout Scripture, we do find an emphasis on the cultivation of the natural world and our own gifts, and this orientation is in keeping with many of the goals of the patent system. At the same time, all human activity is set within a moral framework that focuses on responsibilities rather than rights and encompasses spiritual and other intangible values. We are not to use the natural world, and more particularly the beings that inhabit it, as mere tools to achieve our own purposes. Responsibilities accompany all forms of dominion or ownership. Also, our gifts are deformed rather than developed when we exercise them carelessly, without reflection on the meaning of our capacities, or without consideration of the consequences of our actions and practices for creation. Based on this understanding of stewardship and its influence on our perspective toward the natural world, we think it is important to avoid two extremes when addressing concerns about commodification: refusing to acknowledge the benefits of granting intellectual property rights in useful inventions that result from investments in genetic research, and refusing to acknowledge any grounds for concern.

It is also important to avoid sliding into the position known as "genetic reductionism";[15] we should not focus exclusively on the legal status of the genes, and we urge attention to the big picture. Gene patenting should be placed within a larger context of conflicts between scientific and commercial values and public and private interests. The debate over patenting of the products of basic scientific research is only one piece of a larger debate about whether scientific research that is funded by private industry will be biased and conducted within an atmosphere of secrecy that is at odds with the public interest, as well as traditional scientific values of objectivity and openness. Controversial experiments such as those crossing species barriers might be hidden from the public, curtailing opportunities for debate over the wisdom of this kind of intervention. It makes little sense to fight the "patenting of life" while neglecting oversight of firms engaged in the manipulation of living processes. If permitting the patenting of genes under current guidelines has the effect of opening private research to public scrutiny, benefits may outweigh the costs.

### Patenting and Concerns about Access to the Benefits of Research

The concept of stewardship also offers a guide for the goals of economic life generally, as they affect genetic research. Perhaps the most fundamental of these goals is to produce in a sustainable way the goods and services that satisfy the basic needs of God's creatures and then distribute them equitably. Are for-profit biotechnology and pharmaceutical companies engaged in genetic research doing a good job of meeting this goal under the current regulatory and policy regime? That is a matter of debate. First, some people are concerned about limitations on researchers' access to tools patented by other researchers. This access issue is distinct from the corporate secrecy issue, since once a patent application is filed, basic information about an invention is available to everyone. Second, there is concern that patients lack access to needed medical tests and treatments.

The downside of the current law that allows the researchers—and their corporate partners—to patent both tests and treatments developed on the basis of the new knowledge derived from genetic research is that it may keep others from developing competing tests and treatments. The conflict runs deep, and patenting results in trade-offs for our society.

Private investors will not invest in research and development without some assurance of reward down the road, assuming the research leads to a useful product. At the same time, examples of greed and overreaching by researchers and corporations in making and enforcing patent claims rightly arouse dissatisfaction. Genetic researchers often benefit from the contributions of affected families as well as generous public funding, and yet they or their companies may seek to tie up a whole field of research, including research into therapies for a genetic disease, on the basis of a patent for isolating and cloning a particular region of DNA. That is what some critics allege concerning the biotechnology company that holds patents for the BRCA1 and BRCA2 genes.[16] They believe that the company charges an exorbitant price for the product, the diagnostic test, especially given the use of federal research money in its development, and that the company is blocking the work of other researchers. The company's defenders respond that the private investment required to bring the product to market was considerable, that its control over testing protects consumers, and that its consolidation of testing and the information generated through testing facilitates research.

Richard Gold and other experts on patent law and policy argue that fine distinctions in this debate matter. While new drug therapies take many years and lots of money to bring to market owing to a high failure rate and the long and involved regulatory approval process, commercialization of other kinds of inventions, like tools used in research, is both less time-consuming and less costly. That is especially true for DNA sequence information that can be generated with little time or investment building on the knowledge and technology offered freely to the world by the Human Genome Project. Gold concludes: "Given that a patent allows its holder to prevent anyone else from using the invention, a patent right over a research tool affects a vast amount of research . . . and could potentially stifle further R&D [research and development]."[17] Gold's concern, then, is not so much directed toward the patent system as such, but at access to patented inventions. Access to patented inventions is controlled through licensing. Licenses can be exclusive, meaning that only one person or entity is given access, or nonexclusive. Access may be free, provided that the licensee complies with the terms of the license, or there may be an up-front fee and/or an agreement that the patent holder will share in any revenues or profits realized by the licensee through payments called royalties. In the past, some holders of patents on research tools that represented significant innovations, such as the technique for joining genetic material from two different sources, made their inventions available to all legitimate users at an affordable rate. The fear is that this practice is changing, in the absence of laws or policies requiring nonexclusive licensing at reasonable rates. In assessing concerns about access, it is helpful to distinguish among patents on research tools; patents on DNA sequences and related diagnostic, prognostic or predictive tests; and patents on therapeutic targets and related therapeutic agents (e.g., drugs) or procedures. It is also helpful to recall that licensing practices, and not the patent system alone, affect access.

The Biotechnology Industry Organization asserts that gene patenting is not an obstacle to independent research, since under U.S. patent law others are free to use the invention unless and until they seek to develop commercial products. A number of commentators have called for an expansion of this so-called experimental use or research use exemption from liability from patent infringement as a partial solution to the problem of patents as barriers to promising research.[18] It is interesting that the major pharmaceutical companies are presently collaborating on a large-scale project, known as the SNP Consortium, intended to put information about genetic variation in the public domain. (SNP stands for "single nucleotide polymorphism," and the SNP Consortium is an effort to identify points of genetic variation across individuals and populations that may have significance for health.) This approach seems to be a recognition that, at least with basic knowledge, the benefits of sharing among researchers exceed the benefits of patenting by a single researcher.

The second concern raised about access is focused on patients' access to needed tests and treatments developed on the basis of patented genetic research products. The question of patients' access—the equitable distribution of the fruits of genetic research—is really a question of basic justice. As Christians understand it, basic justice has to do with the right ordering of life in a group, community, or society. Christians are called to ensure that basic needs are met, to work for the full participation of all persons in society. Scripture has a great deal to say about such right ordering. Consider the idea of the Jubilee year: "And you shall hallow the fiftieth year and proclaim liberty throughout the land to all its inhabitants" (Lev. 25:10). Debts are to be cancelled, property is to be recovered, and slaves are to be freed. The broad purpose of the Jubilee year is clear: Society should be ordered and reordered so that an inclusive people is formed. This proclamation of the purpose of God's rule is repeated over and over again by the prophets and by Jesus himself, who identifies his teaching with Isaiah's proclamation of "the year of the Lord's favor" (Luke 4:19).[19] Particular rules for ordering life are subordinate to the greater vision of a society in which the value and dignity of all persons is recognized. Thus, in the just society, all persons are treated with respect and share in the basic goods of life. Economic and political systems are to serve persons, not the other way around.

Owing to current technology transfer policies, some claim that citizens are forced to "pay twice" in the health care arena. As taxpayers, we fund the basic research, and then we pay again when the products of the research are patented and sold to us as consumers. If that were all there is to it, this arrangement would offend the commonsense notion of justice as fair dealing, as well as more sophisticated conceptions of justice. The evidence on this point is hardly clear, however. The Human Genome Project's budgeted funding amounted to about $200 million per year, whereas private funding for biotechnology research in 1987 alone was about $2 billion[20]—in other words, in the aggregate, public investment scarcely compares to private investment and is certainly not sufficient to compensate private firms for a wholesale removal of patent protection from the results of their research and development efforts.

On the other hand, the conception of justice as distribution in accordance with need also comes into play. Current federal technology transfer policy may seem to authorize and even encourage exploitation of those most in need of testing or therapies, since companies acquiring patents for tests or therapies gain a monopoly with few strings attached. At present, they have the freedom to charge whatever the market will bear. If the benefits of genetic research are to be realized, it is important that the biotechnology industry survive and even thrive, but we should be skeptical of claims that "whatever is good for the biotechnology industry is good for America."

A few critics of the status quo emphasize that it is possible to compensate investors adequately *and* ensure that patients have access to needed genetic services. The federal law encouraging technology transfer in publicly funded research contains a "march in" provision that could be invoked given sufficient public pressure. This provision gives the federal agency that funded the research the right to require licensing upon reasonable terms, or to grant such a license itself, if it finds this action is "necessary to alleviate health or safety needs which are not reasonably satisfied" by the patent holder or its licensees.[21] Consistent with this provision, the American College of Medical Genetics has taken the position that (1) basic sequence information (i.e., research tools) should not be patented; (2) patents on genes with clinical implications should be very broadly licensed (i.e., patent owners should deal with "all comers" absent significant concerns about quality and the like); and (3) licensing agreements should provide for moderate royalties and contain reasonable terms.[22] This approach could be implemented through new laws or through a renewed commitment on the part of scientists to the philosophy toward patenting and licensing that characterized the field of genetics in years past. Finally, some commentators worry that the current system does not provide adequate incentives for investment in research that may produce great benefits for small numbers of people—or for large numbers of people in the developing world, since stewardship responsibilities do not stop at national borders.[23] These needy groups simply cannot supply the kind of financial return demanded by shareholders of for-profit corporations.

## JUSTICE, COMMUNITY, AND THE LIMITS OF MARKETS

If patent holders are reasonable in their demands and support is provided for research on conditions that are rare, mostly affect minority populations, or are prevalent in the developing world, is the problem of equitable distribution solved? Unfortunately, the answer is "no."

### From Access to Genetic Services to Access to Health Care

Resolution A095 of the 1991 General Convention affirms that the "benefits of this new [genetic] technology should be equally available to all who need these for the prevention or alleviation of serious suffering, regardless of financial status."[24] But that should be true of all basic health care services. Access to needed health care is not just an issue for genetic researchers or holders of gene patents; it is an issue for all of us as members of society. The present system for financing and delivering health care in the United States combines minimal assessment to establish the value of technologies with rationing by ability to pay. The U.S. health care system is highly decentralized, meaning that it has no gatekeeper to ensure that health services meet tests of value or even benefit before they are made widely available. At one time, the Congress relied on the Office of Technology Assessment to issue reports on significant new technologies, but that office was eliminated in 1995. As for rationing, persons who lack insurance face many barriers when they attempt to gain access to the health care system. Many choose not to seek services for fear of the bills that will follow. Health care expenses are the second most frequently cited cause of personal bankruptcy in the United States.[25] These two factors, the technological juggernaut and rationing by ability to pay, mean that the resources dedicated to health care in this country continue to grow at a rapid pace for the benefit of an ever-shrinking proportion of the population.

In addition, the ill consequences are not visited randomly across the population. Insurance products increasingly emphasize "segmenting risk" rather than "pooling risk." One idea behind insurance is that certain serious, costly accidents or events are unpredictable for individuals but predictable for groups. If people join together, they can take advantage of the predictability of costs for the group. A premium can be computed that will cover payments to members of the group who actually experience an event. Risk pooling can also be a form of solidarity among members of a community. For example, I may have a personal history of few health-related complaints, a family history relatively free of disease, and a house in one of the nicer suburbs, while you have a chronic condition, a family history of cancer, and a house next to a landfill. With community-rated health insurance, we will pay the same premium; I protect myself, but I also subsidize your health care, since there are reasons for predicting that your health care costs will be higher than mine.

Another approach to insurance is to define people as precisely as possible based on their risk factors, and then segment them, i.e., assign them to separate pools and charge those in the higher risk pools more. Some people may have such high risks, approaching certainty of a claim, that they are in effect uninsurable. If a positive result on a BRCA test meant that a woman were destined to develop breast and ovarian cancer, then she might have a very hard time obtaining health insurance. Cancer survivors who are at high risk for a recurrence and others with a record of disease or a strong family history of disease face these problems every day. Segmenting risk reflects the erosion of solidarity. Where this approach dominates, the sick are the persons who have the greatest difficulty in obtaining *secure* access to necessary health care.

Even assuming some tinkering with patent policy, we have every reason to believe that at least early genetic interventions will be expensive. The introduction of these interventions is likely to add to the inequities of a health care sector increasingly focused, ironically and tragically, on serving the well and the well-off. Although some safety net programs exist, many are now in crisis, and impoverished childless adults and the working poor have few if any options. Yet the Bible makes it clear that the community has a responsibility to provide for the basic needs of *all* people, especially those most in need, and to do so systematically rather than as a matter of occasional charity. For example, a number of passages in Deuteronomy contain instructions to deal justly with the vulnerable—the landless poor, the resident alien, the orphan, and the widow—and put aside goods for those on the margins of society. Jesus echoes the Hebrew prophets in rebuking individuals in authority for failing in their obligations to those in need. Indeed, his concern for the poor and oppressed is offered as proof of the authenticity of his ministry. As noted above, in Luke's Gospel, Jesus lays claim to the prophetic call described by Isaiah. In Luke 4:18, Jesus shows special concern for the marginalized: "The Spirit of the LORD is upon me, because [the LORD] has anointed me to bring glad tidings to the poor. He has sent me to proclaim liberty to captives and recovery of sight to the blind, to let the oppressed go free."

Persons on the margins of society, precisely because they are marked by some disability or disadvantage, are vulnerable to being exploited or denied their rights with virtual impunity. Further, benefits and rights are too often created or arrayed to serve and protect the interests of an economic or political elite. The Bible not only condemns this injustice, it suggests that society as a whole can and will be judged according to its treatment of those on the margins.

## Fears of Genetic Discrimination

Secular commentators on justice such as John Rawls align with religious writers in recognizing protection of the vulnerable, those who lack or are deprived of the means to participate fully in society, as one of the functions of government. If a democratic society is understood merely as one in which individuals and groups compete in asserting their interests in the political sphere, it would seem paradoxical or quixotic to charge government with the task of protecting those on the margins. In the biblical view, however, the assertion of various interests is constrained by the demands of justice in the economic and political spheres. Hence political leaders are obligated to pursue the cause of justice with special attention to the rights and welfare of vulnerable persons. In working through the economics and politics of the new genetics we need to be especially attentive to the needs and concerns of children, people with disabilities, the poor, those in poor health, and other groups seldom heard in the corporate boardroom or the halls of government.

As with access to genetic services and access to health care, the problem of discrimination in insurance and employment based on genetic information is a subset of a larger problem, here the problem of reconciling the "natural" outcomes of a market-based economy with a vision of a just society.

To be sure, some aspects of the problem of genetic discrimination are distinctive. As noted in chapters 2 and 3, because genetics is new and complicated, some may treat probabilistic information as if it were certain information. An employer or insurer who discriminates against a woman testing positive for a mutation in the BRCA1 gene because "she's going to get cancer" has simply interpreted the science incorrectly. Further, genetic discrimination is partly a problem of timing, arising from the gap between our rapid progress in identifying genetic factors in disease and our slower progress in overcoming them. If advances in gene therapy gave us steps to prevent or cure diseases linked to genetic mutations or malfunctions, then there would be much less concern about genetic discrimination. An employer would be unlikely to care that once upon a time a job applicant or employee had a genetic defect that was promptly remedied. However, given the knowledge–therapy gap, employers and insurers have reason to request genetic information and incorporate it in their decision making.

It is not always irrational of them to do so. We currently allow many kinds of insurers to consider prior health history or family history in setting premiums, if there is an "actuarial basis" for doing so, and to demand that applicants submit to a battery of medical tests. A positive test for a known BRCA1 mutation *does* suggest an above-average risk for breast cancer, and therefore an above-average risk of a claim, all things considered. Insurers will want access to this information, if it can be had cheaply, and so will employers to the extent that they pay for health care or worry about employees' absences. It may seem unfair for individuals to suffer for things over which they had no control, such as an inherited genetic defect, but how is that different from the plight of persons who are injured in accidents and suddenly find that they are uninsurable and unemployable?

In fact, we as a society do put additional limits on insurers and employers where important social values are at stake. We think it is important that people lead productive lives, and so we limit employment discrimination against people with disabilities under the Americans with Disabilities Act. If individuals can presently perform the essential functions of a job, on their own or if the employer provides reasonable accommodations, and they do not present a safety threat, then their disabilities cannot be used as a basis for any form of negative treatment. We think it is important that people have health insurance—although we have yet to insist that our elected leaders find some way of implementing universal health insurance—and so we limit discrimination in health insurance based on health status, including genetic information.[26] Many states have laws that restrict the ability of employers and insurers to discriminate on the basis of genetic test results that reveal a predisposition to disease or carrier status.

Proposals have been made over the years for more comprehensive laws addressing genetic discrimination in employment and health insurance. In addition to affirming the value of work and access to health insurance, these proposals are motivated by public health concerns. If people fear genetic discrimination, they may be unwilling to undergo testing for their own benefit, for the benefit of family members, or for greater good through participation in research. Yet even those who are sympathetic to these values and concerns may have reservations about an approach that focuses on "genetic" discrimination rather than irrational, unfair, or socially damaging discrimination related to health or receipt of health services generally. As the science advances, we are discovering that nearly every health condition imaginable has a genetic component. Even in the area of infectious disease, genetics may play a role by affecting susceptibility or response to the activity of the infectious agent. At the same time, many scientists believe that attention will soon shift to proteins and biomarkers that are not genetic, strictly speaking. Giving the category "genetic" a special place in antidiscrimination law will create enormous problems in interpretation and could also create a situation in which many repugnant forms of discrimination escape regulation.[27]

## WHERE DO WE GO FROM HERE?

As we have seen, the federal government has used technology transfer in genetics both to encourage the rapid development and distribution of applications and to stimulate the growth of new markets. We have also seen, however, that these benefits are not realized without the imposition of some costs, both to individuals and to our society. To mitigate these costs, the government provides oversight and regulates industry practices. In a democratic society, government oversight and regulation should incorporate elements of transparency and voice. Transparency refers to processes that open an activity or sphere of activity to public scrutiny, including open meetings and disclosure of documents. Transparency contributes to the creation of an informed citizenry and helps prevent abuses of power and other forms of corruption or mismanagement. Also, because markets depend on trust and the circulation of accurate information in order to operate efficiently, transparency increases market efficiency. The second aspect of regulation in a just society includes "voice," which refers to processes by which citizens participate in government. It allows for action on the basis of knowledge, and hence it complements transparency. Because citizens do not always speak with a single voice, however, public participation also opens the door for conflict among voices.

The church uses a related principle, the principle of subsidiarity, which tries to locate the authority for making decisions and governing relationships at the appropriate level of society. According to this principle, decision making should rest at the most local and immediate level appropriate to the particular decision; a central authority should perform only those tasks that cannot be carried out by local groups.[28] The Anglican bishops indicated at the Lambeth Conference of 1998 that within the church the principle of subsidarity provides that the various levels "are accountable to each other by openness to dialogue, by attentiveness to the particularity of people, times and places, by acceptance of interdependence on both the personal and corporate levels and by honouring plurality and diversity as gifts of God."[29] The principle of subsidiarity expresses respect for individuals as members of families and other social groups, and at the same time, for individual liberties.

Individual citizens and individual Christians have little control over the laws, regulations, and policies discussed in this chapter, although it is clear how these same laws, regulations, and policies shape individuals' choices with respect to new genetic research and applications. Yet little control is not the same as no control, and there are ways citizens, whether Christian or not, can influence their government, ways they can give "voice" to their concerns. One of those ways is exercising the right to associate in groups with others of like mind to influence the government's actions with respect to these issues. The Episcopal Church has a lobbying arm in Washington, D.C., as do many other religious bodies. Further, the local parish plays an important role in providing "public space" for debate and reflection on issues such as patenting, technology transfer, and health insurance. It can also provide opportunities for educating members about these issues and for forming possible theological and ethical responses to them.

Yet in exploring these issues, we also discover how difficult it is to bring our theologically informed ethical principles to bear on the complex processes of science, governments, and markets. The research and development "engine" in this country is made up of an interconnected web of universities, industries, and government agencies, and it is arguably the best in the world for generating basic scientific knowledge, efficiently moving research results through the development process, and then delivering products to the marketplace. Does this efficiency represent good stewardship of limited public resources, or are we diverting funds from other, more worthy concerns? Many immediate needs and short-term goals are by-passed when funding basic research—research that is funded in the hope of future, long-term benefits that are far from guaranteed. Is that just? Might it create competition for resources between generations?

Moreover, while biotechnology companies bring us important biomedical benefits, they are also exploiting this system to make a profit, sometimes the maximum profit feasible under current market conditions. But if millions of citizens cannot get access to these benefits, how can that be just? Is this system creating or leading to the kind of community we want? These are only some of the questions raised by our faith in the face of the developments described in this chapter. The church is a good place to debate them, and it is our hope that the information presented here will inform and enrich those debates.

## NOTES

1. For an in-depth discussion of technology transfer in relation to the funding of the Human Genome Project, see chapters 2 and 3 of Jan Christian Heller, *Human Genome Research and the Challenge of Contingent Future Persons* (Omaha: Creighton University Press, 1996).

2. For background on this claim, see Jurgen Habermas, *The Structural Transformation of the Public Sphere: An Inquiry Into a Category of Bourgeois Society*, translated by Thomas Berger with assistance from Frederick Lawrence (Cambridge: MIT Press, 1989).

3. See U.S. Copyright Office, *Copyright Basics* (Washington, D.C.: U.S. Copyright Office, 2002), available at http://www.copyright.gov/circs/circ1.html.

4. Interestingly, a case pending before the U.S. Supreme Court at the time of this writing involves a claim that Congress has violated the U.S. Constitution in continually expanding the period of copyright protection. According to one report, the plaintiffs argue that "progress in the arts and culture is being hampered because lawmakers have forgotten the notion that copyrights are limited." David G. Savage, "Publish, but Never Perish? Copyrights Live Too Long, Say Plaintiffs As They Take on Hollywood and Publishers," *ABA Journal* (October 2002): 23.

5. In the United States, the current period of protection is twenty years from the time a patent application is filed.

6. Donald S. Chisum, *Chisum on Patents* (New York: Matthew Bender, 2002), §3.01, available from LexisNexis.

7. Quoted in Leon Kass, *Toward a More Natural Science: Biology and Human Affairs* (New York: Free Press, 1985), 133.

8. See *Chisum on Patents*, volume 1, chapter 1. Finer points debated among patent law attorneys and scholars include whether DNA sequence information, in contrast to DNA molecules, should be eligible for patenting based on traditional concerns about tangibility. See Rebecca S. Eisenberg, "How Can You Patent Genes?" *American Journal of Bioethics* 2 (Summer 2002): 3–11. A recent issue of *Academic Medicine* is devoted to the topic of patents, with a focus on gene patenting (*Academic Medicine* 77, no. 12 (December 2000): part 2.

9. The requirements of novelty and nonobviousness serve to limit patent monopolies to innovations that "advance the state of the useful arts" (Chisum, *Chisum on Patents*, §5.01). "If an invention is not new, then the invention is not patentable. That ends the inquiry." If the novelty requirement is satisfied, "further inquiry must be made into whether it is 'new enough,' that is, not obvious to one with ordinary skill in the art." The utility requirement is met if the invention passes three additional tests. "First, it must be operable and capable of use. It must operate to perform the functions and secure the result intended. Second, it must operate to achieve some minimum human purpose. Third, it must achieve a human purpose that is not illegal, immoral or contrary to public policy" (Chisum, *Chisum on Patents*, §4.01). As described in the text, some critics contend that the utility requirement in particular, if more rigorously interpreted, would prevent patenting of genes (or sequence information) where the applicant is unable to describe the function of the gene in disease or health.

10. *Diamond v. Chakrabarty*, 447 U.S. 303 (1980). The researcher did not use the technique of recombinant DNA to engineer the bacterium, but many persons rightly saw this case as a test for patenting of the products of genetic engineering. See Daniel J. Kevles, "Patenting Life: A Historical Overview of Law, Interests, and Ethics" (paper prepared for the Legal Theory Workshop, Yale Law School, New Haven, Conn., Dec. 20, 2001, available at www.yale.edu/law/ltw/papers/ltw-kevles.pdf), 16.

11. Kevles, "Patenting Life," 19–20.

12. U.S. Patent and Trademark Office, "Utility Examination Guidelines," 66 *Federal Register* 1092, Jan. 5, 2001. What is patented is the clone or copy of the naturally occurring DNA.

13. Ibid.

14. Calvin DeWitt, *Earthwise: A Biblical Response to Environmental Issues* (Grand Rapids, Mich.: CRC Publications, 1994).

15. See chapters 1, 2, and 7.

16. See Kimberly Blanton, "Corporate Takeover," *Boston Globe Magazine*, April 18, 2002.

17. E. Richard Gold, "Finding Common Cause in the Patent Debate," *Nature Biotechnology* 18 (2000): 1217–1218. Rebecca Eisenberg reaches the same sort of conclusion. Rebecca S. Eisenberg, "The Shifting Functional Balance Of Patents And Drug Regulation," *Health Affairs* 19, no. 4 (2001): 119–135.

18. The research exemption to the general patent statute has been created by judges and is currently quite narrow. A bill introduced in Congress by Rep. Lynn Rivers would amend the statute to permit an individual or entity to use genetic sequence information for purposes of research without fear of an action for infringement. The provision would not apply to any individual or entity directly engaged in commercial manufacture or sale of a product. *Genomic Research and Diagnostic Accessibility Act of 2002*, 107th Cong., H.R. 3967. The Rivers bill would also add "genetic diagnostic, prognostic, or predictive testing" to the list of activities that are noninfringing if performed by a medical practitioner or related health care entity. Currently, this statutory exemption is confined to medical or surgical procedures that do involve use of a patented machine, manufacture, composition of matter, or process in violation of the patent. 35 U.S.C. 287(c).

19. The Episcopal Church U.S.A. has embraced the concept of Jubilee, adopting this title for a national ministry that aims to "make a direct and dynamic link between our theology and our ethics" through human rights advocacy, service, and empowerment. See Jubilee Ministry Mission Statement, Episcopal Church U.S.A., available at http://www.episcopalchurch.org/jubilee/Mission_Statement/Mission_ Statement.htm. See also Frank T. Griswold, "Reflections on Jubilee," *Episcopal Life*, Nov. 1, 1999, available at www.episcopalchurch.org/presiding-bishop/postings/ article_69asp.

20. Rebecca S. Eisenberg, "Genetics and the Law: Patenting the Human Genome," *Emory Law Journal* 39: 738–739.

21. 35 U.S.C. §203. Two commentators have interpreted this provision as a requirement of reasonable pricing. See Peter Arno and Michael Davis, "Paying Twice for the Same Drugs," *Washington Post*, March 27, 2002, A21. This argument is sharply contested by the chief sponsors of the legislation, former Senators Birch Bayh and Robert Dole. Birch Bayh and Robert Dole, "Our Law Helps Patients Get New Drugs Sooner," *Washington Post*, April 11, 2002. For a time, the National Institutes of Health included a reasonable pricing clause in licenses for inventions that the agency had patented. However, this policy was changed in 1995. See Lori Andrews and Dorothy Nelkin, *Body Bazaar: The Market for Human Tissue in the Biotechnology Age* (New York: Crown Publishers, 2001), p. 62.

22. American College of Medical Genetics, "Position Statement on Gene Patents and Accessibility of Gene Testing," August 2, 1999, available at http://www.faseb.org/ genetics/acmg/pol-34.htm.

23. For a discussion of the global impact of developments in genetics, with special attention to the implications for the developing world, see World Health Organization, *Genomics and World Health: Report of the Advisory Committee on Health Research* (Geneva: World Health Organization, 2002); Abdallah S. Daar, Halla Thorsteinsdottir, Douglas K. Martin et al., "Top Ten Biotechnologies for Improving Health in Developing Countries," *Nature Genetics* 32 (October 2002): 229–232. The potential contributions of genetic research to global health include the development of molecular technologies to create affordable, simple diagnostic tests for infectious disease and recombinant technologies to develop and produce vaccines against infectious disease. The recent publication of the genomes for the main malaria parasite and the mosquito carrier, with enormous potential for good in the areas of prevention and treatment of an illness that kills an estimated 2.7 million people a year, is a

welcome sign of progress in this area. See Nicholas Wade, "Genetic Decoding May Advance Malaria Fight," *New York Times*, October 3, 2002.

24. General Convention of the Episcopal Church U.S.A., "Resolution A095: Guidelines in the Area of Genetic Engineering," Proceedings of the Seventieth General Convention, 1991.

25. See Melissa B. Jacoby, Teresa A. Sullivan, and Elizabeth Warren, "Rethinking the Debates Over Health Care Financing: Evidence from the Bankruptcy Courts," *New York University Law Review* 76 (2001): 375–418.

26. The Health Insurance Portability and Accountability Act of 1996 (HIPAA) prohibits discrimination (based on a list of factors) in large and small group health insurance. This protection does not extend to individual policies. Also, HIPAA limits preexisting condition exclusion periods and prohibits group health insurers from treating a genetic condition as a preexisting condition in the absence of a diagnosis of disease. See General Accounting Office, *Health Insurance Standards: New Federal Law Creates Challenges for Consumers, Insurers, Regulators* (Washington, D.C., 1998).

27. For a more extensive discussion of discrimination concerns from the perspective of persons contemplating genetic testing, see Committee on Medical Ethics, Episcopal Diocese of Washington, D.C., *Wrestling with the Future: Our Genes and Our Choices* (Harrisburg, Pa.: Morehouse, 1998), 30–36. For a more extensive discussion of the difficulties surrounding drafting of laws to protect against discrimination, see M. A. Rothstein and M. Anderlik, "What is Genetic Discrimination and When and How Can it be Prevented?" *Genetics in Medicine* 3 (2001): 354–358.

28. See Cynthia B. Cohen, "Genetics, Ethics, and the Principle of Subsidiarity," *Anglican Theological Review* 81, no. 4 (Fall 1999): 621–631.

29. "The Virginia Report: The Report of the Inter-Anglican Theological and Doctrinal Commission," *The Official Report of the Lambeth Conference* 1998 (Harrisburg, Pa.: Morehouse, 1999), 16–68, 53.

# 9

# The Role of the Church in the New Genetics

*David A. Ames*

Although the era of the new genetics is upon us, its real impact is still on the horizon. What do we need to know? How will we use our new knowledge? What are some of the promises and dangers of this new and developing information? What can we do to aid the formation and education of Christians and help them make responsible and faithful decisions about genetic screening, testing, and treatment? How can the church participate in the dialogue and provide appropriate leadership while raising the necessary critical issues or questions? What is our role in advocating for the well-being of others?

In the preceding chapters, we have discussed several issues that provide resources for understanding the role of the church as we move forward in our understanding of genetics and our ability to alleviate suffering and perhaps relieve or even cure some genetically related diseases. We should now begin a conversation about these issues and the courses of action that will serve the common good. At the conclusion of this chapter are a few case studies that can be used for study and discussion.

Laura is a twenty-one-year-old college student who lives with cystic fibrosis (CF), a genetic disease that causes the lungs to become filled with mucus. It is fatal, with a median survival age in the early thirties. Laura has been in and out of the hospital so many times that she considers herself a resident. "It's like my hotel."

In a tape-recorded diary of the past two years of her life with CF, Laura says she started college "by telling everyone about it (CF) and I realized— oh, my God, they don't care. Everyone's a freshman and everyone is going through their own stuff, and they don't need to hear, in depth, about my stuff." Laura's story aired on National Public Radio on "All Things Considered."[1] A year ago she received a lung transplant, and now her body experiences mild rejection. She says, "The last year of my life has taught me not to depend on anything. When you've had a transplant, one minute you can feel fine and the next, you're in the hospital. . . . I don't really count on anything anymore, I just go with the flow. I think that's okay."

There are times when pastoral care continues for many years, for a lifetime of uncertainty, of hope, and of frustration. Laura knows the transient nature of human life and she strives, often against considerable odds, to make the most of it.

An important lesson here is that we can never know how another person really feels. Feelings about life, about health and disease, are personal. One person with a particular condition might feel quite differently than another person with the same or similar condition. What actually happens in a pastoral care setting is *listening* to others' feelings. Being with them to listen is more important than anything. In Laura's case, her parents anguished and grieved at various stages of her life. When Laura was born, life expectancy for people with cystic fibrosis was much less than it is today. Laura's parents feared she would not live through her teenage years, but they and Laura remained hopeful.

As Laura's story indicates, choices about medical treatment generated by new knowledge of genetics and genetic technologies increasingly are becoming everyday decisions. Unlike the medical treatment of traumas—a broken bone or a major infection—the genetic revolution in medicine is especially challenging because it offers interventions in the basic building blocks of life. These interventions will demand greater knowledge in making decisions, often requiring weighing consequences that may be stated only in terms of probabilities. As the chapters in this book have addressed, these decisions include providing information about genetic lineage, human reproduction, and medical treatments.

The role of the Episcopal Church with respect to the new genetics is first of all a ministry of pastoral care to those who suffer from disease and illness. The support of Laura's family and her determination "to go with the flow," as she states, is significant. They have functioned as a family unit. As the images of family and the church as one body in which all are "members one of another" suggest, the church is also a community of care. That means offering prayer and support during times of difficult and sometimes tragic decisions, bearing one another's burdens in times of crises and for the long haul.

Pastoral care is also educational. Care for others requires providing knowledge and information about genetics, treatment, and community resources for counseling and support. In this way, persons in the church offer pastoral support and guidance, including a model of how Christian faith may inform decisions. All of this requires the development of teaching material—such as this book—to provide basic knowledge about genetics, moral questions and challenges, and how they are informed by Christian faith.

In examining the ethical issues presented by the new genetics, it is important to recognize that ethics and morality are related to the prophetic task of the church, which is to bear witness to truth and justice to society at large. The prophetic task is in a sense educational. Christians must identify the outstanding issues we face as a society and offer the perspective and wisdom born of our faith and tradition. This task also encompasses advocacy. The church is called to be an advocate for basic human justice in order that all persons may have equal access to medical knowledge and treatment. This book itself seeks to offer moral teaching for the church and in that way to serve its pastoral and prophetic vocation.

Ministries of healing and pastoral care include concerns about the physical body, the mind, and the spirit. To be a whole person is to accept the limitations of life and to live healthfully through all our days. However, in order to provide effective pastoral care in specific areas of genetic screening, testing, diagnosis, and treatment, care givers, including ministers or pastors, must have a solid education about the issues and conditions Christians and others encounter, and we all must speak out for quality health care, including access and a just allocation of resources.

## EDUCATION

Adult education programs that can assist persons to grapple with questions raised by the new genetics provide a venue for teaching and learning about the issues discussed in the preceding chapters. Programs designed to inform Christians about bioethical decisions begin by teaching the Christian story and relating it to the decisions they make in their own lives. Case studies and stories about death and dying often help to address questions about decisions whether to continue or curtail life-sustaining treatment. Who has the authority to make such decisions? When and why does it make sense to stop treatment? What is the fear related to death? What does Christian care look like? How does a Christian "live ill" and die faithfully reconciled to God and to relatives and friends? Focusing on these and similar questions may provide the basic context for discussion of other bioethical issues, including some of the issues addressed in detail in this book.

An illustration of this point occurred many years ago when David was born with severe combined immunodeficiency (SCID) and "sentenced" to twelve years of life in a vacuum-sealed polyethylene bubble until he was freed following a bone marrow transplant. A few days after the transplant, David became very sick and was taken out of the sterile bubble for the final two weeks of his life.[2]

While expressing gratitude to David and his parents for their remarkable contribution to science and new discoveries in the area of treating a disease that was incompatible with a "normal" human life, we are left with a troubling question. What does it mean to maintain a life in a sterile environment, in effect a prison, for so long a time? David never had the opportunity to give voluntary or informed consent to his participation in this experiment. He had no choice; it was his birthmark. Should lives of this sort be maintained simply because we have the technology to do so? Would any of us choose such a life if we were in a similar situation? Some people may say yes to this question, but others will say no. Is ethical flexibility appropriate in decisions about life and death and the quality of life? What Christian moral values support a decision one way or the other? The problems posed by the present state of the art in science and technology do not lend themselves to easy right or wrong, yes or no decisions.

When it comes to biology and genetics, scientists seem to agree that "all forms of life, current and extinct, are interconnected through evolutionary relationships." In theological terms, "God's immanent creative action in the world generates within the created order a being, the human being, who becomes self-aware, morally responsible, and capable of . . . being creative and of responding to God's presence. Thus the natural, biological, and human worlds are not just the stage of God's action—they *are* in themselves a mode of God in action. . . . To give due weight to the evolutionary character of God's creative action requires a much stronger emphasis on God's immanent presence in, with, and under the very processes of the natural world from the 'hot, big bang' to humanity."[3]

This point is important for understanding the relationship between science and religion. For Christians, God is not only the Creator who creates in God's own image, but what is created—natural, biological, cultural—is embodied *in* God.

There is an acute need for congregational and diocesan adult education addressing bioethics in general and genetics in particular. A four- or five-week series of discussions about a particular subject led by a respected and knowledgeable person is often an effective format. Educational programs focused on issues of ethics and the new genetics should be designed so participants will (1) gain current and useful information about genetics for themselves and for those close to them; (2) understand how to relate to others who live with genetic disease or who are struggling with concerns about genetic testing and diagnosis; (3) identify resources that address issues raised by the new genetics, including referrals for family members and others who would benefit from genetics counseling and services; and (4) be encouraged to continue to participate and work with others to develop education programs for congregations, for the larger community, and for health care professionals. Congregations should be educated about the relation between the body and the self, about guilt and responsibility, and about other theological concerns that are arising with increasing frequency because of the Human Genome Project.

The knowledge we are gaining about genetics is impressive, and medicine will change profoundly as it incorporates this knowledge. Physicians, genetics counselors, and clergy all have a role in responding to these concerns. Beyond the parish level, continuing education programs for diocesan clergy should consider developing collaborative relationships with health care professionals to further knowledge about genetics, about addressing persons confronting issues raised by the new genetics, and about resources within the community. Some programs in genetic counseling at universities, for example, have offered educational events for clergy.

Episcopal seminaries could offer continuing education opportunities addressing genetics, pastoral care, and advocacy, which might be done with other groups, for example, the Assembly of Episcopal Healthcare Chaplains. Ethics, the new genetics, and the challenge of ministry should also be a part of basic courses in bioethics that should be a regular offering in degree programs at Episcopal seminaries. The provinces of the church could also sponsor convocations addressing ethics and the new genetics.

The National Coalition for Health Professional Education in Genetics (NCHPEG) has endorsed several core competencies in an "effort to promote health-professional education and access to information about advances in human genetics" that will serve "to improve the nation's health." Some of these competencies should be included in curricula for the church, its clergy, and lay leaders. Those especially applicable include:

*Understanding basic human genetics terminology.* The vocabulary of genetics is essential. One need not be a scientist to be adequately informed. It is sufficient to understand how genetic traits are expressed and transmitted from one generation to the next.

*The importance of family history (minimum three generations) in assessing predisposition to disease.* The health histories of siblings, parents, and grandparents often provide useful information about the risks for contracting a genetic disease or for having children with a particular genetic trait.

*The role of genetic factors in maintaining health and preventing disease.* Sometimes, as with PKU, cystic fibrosis, or diabetes, diet and exercise can contribute to disease management.

*The influence of ethnicity, culture, related health beliefs, and economics in the clients' ability to use genetic information and services.* Different population groups are at risk for different disease manifestations. Understanding the role of socioeconomic and ethnic backgrounds can help in responding to the needs of others.

*The resources available to assist clients seeking genetic information or services, including the types of genetics professionals available and their diverse responsibilities.* Knowing when and to whom to refer individuals and families in need of counseling or other assistance is of paramount importance.

*The ethical, legal, and social issues related to genetic testing and recording of genetic information* (e.g., privacy, the potential for genetic discrimination in health insurance and employment). These issues are addressed below in discussing advocacy for and access to just and equitable care.[4]

## PASTORAL CARE

In *Coping with Genetic Disorders*, John Fletcher reminds us that "it is never the lot of humans to be secure. . . . Beginning with the threat of death, . . . life poses a long series of terrors to individuals and their culture."[5] With a positive diagnosis of genetic disease, patients and their families are struck with "terror." What is needed most is a caring presence to listen and to walk with the person and family members as they struggle with decisions about further testing, possible treatment, and the effects and probabilities of passing the same genetic trait to the next generation. Fletcher calls this a ministry of faithful companionship. "What the faithful companion has mostly to offer is the bread of reality and the symbolic bread of the word of God that can transform even the worst terrors of reality."[6]

This ministry is not confined to clergy, but surely clergy are at its core. Clergy are to be "faithful companions" at times when religious need is great, at times of stress and crisis. Religion is a "process for making sense in ourselves when conflicts that arise from the condition of being human threaten to tear apart our basic confidence that we are worthwhile." When persons face crises of meaning and assurance, the role of the faithful companion is to provide "help to face the full meaning and impact of every terror, especially death." The companion helps me to "learn the meaning of life without resort to illusion or injustice."[7]

We are called to be stewards not only of creation, the environment, and the allocation of resources, but also of our own lives and the lives of others. Life is a dynamic process always progressing through change and transformation, always in relationship, and always subject to surprise from external and internal forces. The impact of illness and disease can alter our thinking about what it means to be human, and it can challenge us to ask about the limits of our lives. We are mortal beings, and we need to know that God does not cause sickness and suffering, but is a source of compassion and strength in times of trouble and need. Effective pastoral care works to communicate this reality of God's presence.

Ned Cassem, a psychiatrist, Jesuit priest, and the director of psychiatry at the Massachusetts General Hospital, understands his role as one of helping others to learn the meaning of life when confronted by illness and the impending end of life. He has spoken about the palliation of spiritual suffering and raises an essential faith question: "How do I live *ill?*"[8]

The question "How do I live *ill?*" is a question about the meaning of one's life. To really understand patients' medical needs, we must understand their spiritual, faith, philosophical, or theological perspective. Health is not the absence of disease or illness; health has to do with how a person copes with human limits and the inevitability of mortality.

When death occurs because of a genetic disorder, clergy, in their role as pastoral care givers, can help the surviving members of the family cope with suffering and loss. Bereavement support groups that offer spiritual guidance and the shared stories of others coping with grief are useful.

Effective pastoral care cannot be rendered without an adequate knowledge base of the particular context of the presenting and underlying issues. Hence, pastoral care assumes appropriate education about the issues as well as the ability to listen, to empathize, to enable the consideration of possible courses of action, and to support the decisions that are made. Pastoral care always requires compassion and thus it is important to know the background and perspectives of the parishioners and their family members. Also needed is a keen appreciation for the sensitivity of genetic information and concerns about privacy and confidentiality.

When an answer is not readily available, it is important to be able to say, "I don't know, but I can help by providing a referral to someone who does." The information we are learning about genetics and the human genome is developing fast, and as soon as we think we understand, it is likely that something new will come along to increase our present level of understanding. Pastoral care involves keeping abreast of developing knowledge and its application.

Being "other-centered" is the norm for helping parishioners to make informed decisions about genetic information and how to use it. If individuals are at risk for developing breast cancer or Huntington disease, for example, how will they decide whether to be tested? What are their concerns and fears? What about other family members? What impact will this new information have on future employment or health insurance policies?

The clergy generally have responsibility for pastoral care. They are the ones who provide leadership and coordination of care and outreach to parishioners and others in the community. Forming a parish committee or commission of trained lay persons for pastoral care is an effective way of involving concerned parishioners in responding to those in need. Training programs that reflect on case studies, personal experience, developing skills in listening, and formulating effective questions are important ingredients in developing this ministry.

The Episcopal Church's chief pastor, Presiding Bishop Frank Griswold, has explored the challenges facing clergy, especially in light of the terrorist attacks of September 11, 2001. In speaking about the role of prayer as an important ingredient in pastoral care he said, "The quality of our own prayer is so integral to our pastoring. It is something that we can so easily set aside in favor of the various external needs that present themselves. We can be very sort of Ignatian and apostolic and talk about finding God in all things—which is, of course, true. But, I really do think we have to, as Thomas Merton once said, 'waste time conscientiously with God.' That's a wonderful way of describing prayer because so often people think of prayer as another thing to achieve or to do—and particularly in our society."[9]

Bishop Griswold went on to quote a Benedictine monk who once observed, "'Prayer is an opening to love on every level of our being.' Our prayer is not an achievement, it is a stance of availability before the mystery of God. Prayer transforms our consciousness, working in us over time. There are times when we are profoundly free, and there are other times when we are profoundly bound. Playing with this double dynamic in terms of our own lives can help us to be discerning as we move through active ministry."[10]

With respect to genetics, pastoral care begins with premarital counseling and continues from the birth of a child throughout that person's lifetime. Although the general components of pastoral care pertain throughout the span of life, the various stages or moments of transition are important. Questions related to genetics can occur at any time across the life span, especially questions about medical treatment and whether—and if so, how—genetic information should be shared with others. Particular questions and reflection, however, may be addressed at the time of marriage, when children are desired, and during pregnancy.

Questions prior to marriage and before considering parenthood include carrier testing, prenatal care and diagnosis, including chorionic villus sampling, amniocentesis, ultrasound, and fetoscopy. Persons who are having problems with infertility should be supported in their decision making about the possible courses of action to pursue, including burdens and potential benefits. This discussion should include the issues raised regarding in vitro fertilization (IVF), preimplanation genetic diagnosis, adoption, and surrogate parenting.

Although all of us desire to live a healthy life, we should not understand the word "health" as the opposite of "illness" or "disease." The literal meaning of health is wholeness. In this sense, a person can live in health with a genetic disease or condition. Recognizing the religious and spiritual needs of individuals and families who live with genetic abnormalities is important. *Enriching Our Worship 2* offers several useful prayers, psalms, and litanies that may be used or adapted to respond to particular needs. For example, a prayer for difficult treatment choices is the following:

Jesus, at Gethsemane you toiled with terrifying choices. Be with me now as I struggle with a fearful choice of treatments which promise much discomfort and offer no guarantee of long-term good. Help me to know that you will bless my choice to me, and, good Savior, be my companion on the way. *Amen.*

Another prayer for care givers and others in support of the sick also merits quoting:

> Lover of souls, we bless your Holy Name for all who are called to mediate your grace to those who are sick or infirm. Sustain them by your Holy Spirit, that they may bring your loving-kindness to those in pain, fear, and confusion; that in bearing one another's burdens they may follow the example of our Savior Jesus Christ. *Amen.*[11]

Other prayers, including one for the loss of a pregnancy, are also found in this book.[12] These and some of the psalms and a litany for healing might be used by individuals, couples, or families when a pregnancy is terminated because of a serious abnormality, or when a person is struggling with a decision about genetic testing, or considering options for therapy following a genetic or other diagnosis.

Another important resource for understanding genetic conditions and decision making is *Wrestling with the Future,* a book by the Committee on Medical Ethics of the Episcopal Diocese of Washington, D.C.[13] The book focuses on genetic testing for adults, infants, and children and offers excellent discussion about decisions to conceive a child and prenatal testing. It includes several case studies.


## ADVOCACY

As we prepared material for this book, we heard from several people who have been living with genetic diseases. One who wrote to us said that she has several inherited genetic illnesses for which she has been discriminated against in insurance coverage. A recovering alcoholic who also has bipolar disorder, she is stable on medication. She has been hospitalized and has had repeated surgeries for a rare form of nonalcoholic pancreatitis, a structural problem within the organ that has resulted in chronic pancreatitis.

She has several relatives with a history of pancreatic disorders, and family deaths have been caused by pancreatic cancer and pancreatitis. Since she is disabled with chronic pancreatitis, she would like to have genetic testing to determine whether she carries the gene for familial pancreatic cancer. She fears that if she goes ahead with the testing she may lose her health insurance coverage. Other family members, including a daughter about to be married, would like genetic testing as well, but they also fear discrimination in their medical coverage.

Advocacy can take many forms. Support for those who suffer from genetic disease, who live with uncertainty or disability, is of primary importance. Another form of advocacy is to ensure that people are informed about screening, testing, and diagnosis for genetic disease. At another level is the need to educate and sensitize physicians and genetic counselors about the religious and spiritual issues that trouble patients. Clinicians must be able to converse with appropriate language and tools that will be helpful to patients and family members who are coping with genetic issues. It is important to be involved in establishing effective public policy to assure access and equality about screening, testing, treatment options, privacy and confidentiality, and employment and insurance discrimination. Public policy advocacy can be carried out through letter-writing campaigns, meetings with legislators at local, state, and federal levels, and building networks with a variety of organizations. Church members and other organizations can lobby for helpful legislation and necessary social and policy change. Letters to the editor, phone calls to local and state legislators, and testimony at hearings are all effective methods for supporting sound statutes and regulations.

A basic concern for health care in general, and for the new genetics in particular, is access to quality health care and public policy that ensures just and equitable distribution of resources. The basic principles of "doing good" and "doing no harm" are paramount. From these principles, others follow: treating all persons equally; allocating resources justly; being truthful; respecting self-determination; developing mutual trust; and furthering an attitude of thankfulness for the benefits gained from knowledge and treatment.

Public policy issues of justice, equality, and access to appropriate health care and insurance are necessary to ensure the safety and well-being of every person. If genetic therapy is available, it should be available to anyone in need. We are struck by the response of American citizens to individuals who manage to have national media exposure. Certainly those with similar conditions who, for whatever reason, cannot garner media coverage deserve equal consideration for treatment.

Christopher Reeve is one person who has been very active in advocating for legislation and public policy that will further quality research in genetics, which could lead to new therapies for any number of genetic diseases. Reeve suffered a spinal cord injury in an equestrian accident several years ago. Through strenuous physical therapy he has been able to regain some minimal movement in his left index finger, and with support, he can move his legs under water.

When it comes to advocacy, Reeve is hoping for a grassroots movement from state to state across the nation that will further research, especially stem cell research designed to find effective therapies to alleviate human pain and suffering. He was present when California adopted legislation to approve research that could lead to breakthroughs in treating disorders ranging from Alzheimer's disease to spinal cord injuries. The California law requires "that projects be reviewed by an approved industry review board," and that "fertility clinics . . . tell patients how they can donate unused embryos to science. The measure requires written consent for donating embryos and prohibits the sale of embryos."[14] Unused embryos from fertility clinics are the most likely candidates for stem cell research.

The allocation of limited resources is always problematic, and it is appropriate to lobby for their just allocation. Daniel Callahan suggests a six-tier structure for a shift in health care away from an approach that is centered on the individual toward one that is centered on society.[15] Callahan is concerned with a vision of the good for all of society. The first four tiers in his proposal concern societal needs for health. They include basic caring for all; public health and prevention; immunization; and emergency medicine and primary care. The last two tiers focus on individual needs and include medical cure and restoration, and advanced technological therapy. Callahan's vision merits careful and widespread discussion especially in a day of high-tech medicine pitted against concerns about cost containment and charges of malpractice for doing either too much or too little.

The church has an important role to play in advocating for parishioners who need care and treatment. By building constructive relationships and networks with health care professionals in hospitals, nursing homes, assisted living centers, and departments of health, church members can help those in need. They can also volunteer to provide support and care for those with disabilities, whether they live at home or in an institutional setting.

Finally, it is important to ensure that our church buildings are accessible. Providing access to worship spaces and having a reserved section for wheelchair use is important. All of these measures are part of our baptismal covenant to "respect the dignity of every person."

## CASE STUDIES FOR DISCUSSION

### Mass Genetic Screening

A single, inexpensive blood test for prospective parents can detect high risk for virtually all serious genetic disorders as well as a broad range of genetic susceptibilities for illnesses.[16] An initiative is afoot to provide mass genetic screening using the test. A government commission examining the feasibility of this proposal notes that the program's cost-effectiveness depends on whether a sufficient number of those tested "act on the knowledge of

positive results—that is, whether they choose to avoid conception of affected fetuses." An advocate of the mass screening program says "this is a
public health matter; people should not be free to inflict avoidable diseases
on their children, especially if we are ever to have an affordable health care
system that provides coverage for everyone." An opponent replies that "genetic services of any kind are strictly a matter of personal choice—respect for
reproductive freedom requires this. People must be free to act on the test results as they see fit; any program that will result in pressures that limit reproductive freedom would be unacceptable."

*Discussion Questions*

1. Do you tend to agree with the government official or the opponent of
   this mass genetic screening?
2. Is this proposal, from your perspective, a eugenic danger? Why? Why
   not?
3. Is this proposal, from your perspective, a positive benefit to society and
   universal health care? Why? Why not?
4. What guidelines would you propose for use in genetic screening and
   testing?
5. What, if any, are some of the theological questions or challenges in pro-
   posing genetic screening and testing?

**Alzheimer's Disease**

A woman carried a rare genetic mutation that made her almost certain to
develop Alzheimer's disease before age forty.[17] Her brother and sister, who
also had the gene, had shown signs of dementia in their mid-thirties. Their father had died at forty-two, with memory loss and psychological problems.
The woman wanted a family, but she did not want her children to inherit the
Alzheimer's gene. So at age thirty she had her embryos screened at a private
clinic in Chicago, the Reproductive Genetics Institute, and a year and a half
ago gave birth to a daughter who is free of the mutation. The type of testing
she had cannot be done for the more common forms of Alzheimer's disease,
which affect much older people.

*Discussion Questions*

1. Was the woman acting responsibly in having children "since she would
   soon be unable to take care of them and they would have to suffer
   through her deterioration and death"?
2. What concerns do you have "about using genetic tests to weed out embryos carrying a gene that might do no harm for forty years"?

3. Is "genetic testing that leads to family planning" acceptable? In all cases? For a disease that does not manifest itself for three or four decades?

## Prenatal Testing and Abortion

Two years ago this summer, my wife and I lost a baby.[18] At seventeen weeks, we went to Mount Sinai Hospital in New York City to view ultrasound pictures of our future child and have amniotic fluid drawn for testing. The ultrasound image showed that the fetus was not growing as fast as expected, and before long we had a couple of specialists puzzling over the pictures. Why was there so little fluid? Why was the placenta so large? Was there a defective chromosome? Were the kidneys missing? They rushed the tests, but the chromosomes revealed nothing more about our stunted fetus, except that he was male. This is the double-edged scalpel of reproductive science. The technology that informs you your future baby is mysteriously endangered also makes him real, a boy-like creature swimming in utero. No amount of reasoning about the status of this creature can quite counteract the portrait that begins to form in your heart with the poetry of the first heartbeats. Sentimental fools, we gave him a name, Charlie, maybe imagining it would help him put up a fight.

For the next five weeks [my wife] Emma was examined by the best minds at one of the best hospitals. She was screened for viruses, blood disorders, hereditary indicators—all normal. She had weekly sonograms by virtuosos of the machine. There were momentary highs (kidneys were functioning after all; a dissenting sonogram reader even thought the amniotic fluid was on the rise) and dispiriting lows (bad blood flow to the fetus, which meant organs were probably not developing properly), but no definite answers. Something was clearly, badly wrong. The doctors assumed that, of course, we would want to abort, as soon as possible. "We know you can get pregnant easily," Emma's obstetrician said. "Why risk an unhappy outcome?" She urged us to schedule quickly, because it would be difficult to line up a surgeon around the July 4 holiday. Appalled by the rush, Emma changed doctors, but we never quite escaped the feeling that by holding out, week after week, hoping for better odds, we were being more than a little eccentric.

As we approached twenty-four weeks, the legal deadline for abortions in New York, the most explicit prognosis we could wheedle from the experts was that chances were high (90 percent) that the baby would be born dead or in a vegetative state. And, carrying the child to term would pose some danger to Emma's health. Facing the prospect of a greater heartbreak, watching a child die or suffer inconsolably, or exhausting the emotional resources needed for two other children, we decided to end it. The last thing Emma was aware of before surrendering to the anesthetic was Charlie kicking madly.

Two years later our experience at the intersection of science and parent-hood haunts my thinking in ways I did not anticipate. Among other things it has deepened my suspicion of moral clarity, and also of disembodied rationalism, both of which seem to offer a kind of ethics without human beings. The ideologues on both sides, those who view abortion as an absolute wrong and those who view it as an inalienable right, too often treat these decisions as if they were clear-cut and pain-free.

If you'd asked me before that summer, I'd have told you reflexively that I was pro-choice. As a matter of law and politics, that is still my position, for this is not a decision I would entrust to courts and legislatures, even given that some parents will make choices I would find repugnant. But like a lot of parents who have lived through it, I have come to see "choice" as a mixed blessing. I've often wondered what we'd have done if . . . the doctor had said 50-50, or if the gamble had been on Down syndrome or one of the severe crippling diseases. Would we have had the strength to ride it out?

## Alpha 1 Antitrypsin Deficiency

My wife has a genetic condition known as Alpha 1 Antitrypsin Deficiency. This is a condition that leads to either a kidney or lung failure. The membership organization, Alpha 1 Association, has been dealing extensively with issues of confidentiality, testing, and discrimination. Alpha patients have a very hard time dealing with their children and others in the blood line who may have the condition. If children, or others, are tested, then that information, if positive, becomes part of the medical history, and all sorts of job and insurance discriminations are all but automatic. If a person is not tested, and treatment is not started, biological damage progresses, often without symptoms. It is a tough call with jobs and life on the line.

## Huntington Disease

My family is one that has faced a terrible genetic disorder known as Huntington disease. My wife's sister was diagnosed with it in 1988, but at the time, the genetics test was very expensive and required participation by family members who were already dead, including their mother and her father. The diagnosis was made on symptoms, the doctor's gut instinct, and a line in their grandfather's medical records that his gait was ungainly. My wife had her sister's blood banked until such time as a more definitive test became available. My reaction to this devastating diagnosis was clinical depression, a dark night of the soul. I lived in fear for the health of my wife and children for over ten years.

In 1997, the newly available (and inexpensive) test was conducted on my sister-in-law's blood and Huntington was confirmed. Since both our children were ready to marry and start their own families, it was time to have my wife's blood tested, too. The test was negative and removed the threat from our children so they could plan their own futures free of worry for this disease.

## NOTES

1. The audio for Laura's story, along with photos and information about cystic fibrosis, is at www.radiodiaries.org.

2. Allen J. Hamilton, "Who Shall Live and Who Shall Die," *Newsweek*, March 26, 1984, 15.

3. A. R. Peacock, "The New Biology and Nature, Man and God" in F. Kenneth Hare, ed., *The Experiment of Life* (Toronto: University of Toronto Press, 1983), 41, 46–47.

4. The full text of the National Coalition for Health Professional Education in Genetics can be found at www.NCHPEG.org.

5. John Fletcher, *Coping with Genetic Disorders: A Guide for Clergy and Parents* (New York: Harper & Row, 1982), 36.

6. Ibid., 41.

7. Ibid., 39.

8. Notes from a lecture at a symposium on spirituality and medicine, presented at Butler Hospital, Providence, Rhode Island, April 26, 1999.

9. September 12, 2002, Hobart Lecture at the Diocese of New York's Synod House.

10. Ibid.

11. The Church Pension Fund, *Enriching Our Worship 2: Ministry with the Sick or Dying; Burial of a Child* (New York: The Church Pension Fund, 2000), 79, 93.

12. Ibid., 78, 79.

13. Committee on Medical Ethics of the Episcopal Diocese of Washington, D.C., *Wrestling with the Future* (Harrisburg, Pa.; Morehouse, 1998).

14. *San Francisco Chronicle,* September 23, 2002, A-1.

15. Daniel Callahan, *What Kind of Life: The Limits of Medical Progress* (New York: Simon & Schuster, 1990).

16. From Allen Buchanan, Dan W. Brock, Norman Daniels, and Daniel Wikler, *From Chance to Choice: Genetics and Justice* (New York: Cambridge University Press, 2000), 2 and 244. Reprinted with the permission of Cambridge University Press. The discussion questions are provided by the authors.

17. This case study was published in Denise Grady, "Genes, Embryos and Ethics," *New York Times*, March 3, 2002; Copyright © 2002 by The New York Times Co. Reprinted by permission.

18. Excerpted from Bill Keller, "Charlie's Ghost," *New York Times*, June 29, 2002, A15. Copyright © 2002 by The New York Times Co. Reprinted by permission.

# Suggestions for Further Reading

## RELIGIOUS

Cole-Turner, Ronald. *The New Genesis: Theology and the Genetic Revolution*. Louisville, Ky.: Westminister/John Knox Press, 1993.

Lebacqz, Karen, ed. *Genetics, Ethics and Parenthood*. New York: Pilgrim Press, 1983.

Peters, Ted. *Playing God? Genetic Determinism and Human Freedom*. New York: Routledge, 1997.

Peters, Ted, ed. *Genetics: Issues of Social Justice*. New York: Pilgrim Press, 1998.

Ramsey, Paul. *Fabricated Man: The Ethics of Genetic Control*. New Haven: Yale University Press, 1970.

## OTHER

Andrews, Lori, and Dorothy Nelkin. *Body Bazaar: The Market for Human Tissue in the Biotechnology Age*. New York: Crown, 2001.

Cook-Degan, Robert M. *The Gene Wars: Science, Politics, and the Human Genome*. New York: Norton, 1994.

Holland, Suzanne, Laurie Zoloth, and Karen Lebacqz. *The Human Embryonic Stem Cell Debate*, edited by Suzanne Holland and Laurie Zoloth. Cambridge: MIT Press, 2001.

Kevles, Daniel J., and Leroy Hood, eds. *The Code of Codes: Scientific and Social Issues in the Human Genome Project*. Cambridge: Harvard University Press, 1992.

Lauritzen, Paul. *Pursuing Parenthood: Ethical Issues in Assisted Reproduction*. Bloomington: Indiana University Press, 1993.

Nelkin, Dorothy, and M. Susan Lindee. *The DNA Mystique: The Gene As a Cultural Icon*. New York: Freeman, 1996.

Rothstein, Mark A., ed. *Genetic Secrets: Protecting Privacy and Confidentiality in the Genetic Era*. New Haven: Yale University Press, 1999.

# Index

# About the Contributors

DAVID A. AMES is Episcopal chaplain at Brown University and clinical assistant professor of community health in the Brown Medical School. He is co-author of *Good Genes? Emerging Values for Science, Religion, and Society*. He is also senior associate minister at St. Martin's Church, Providence, Rhode Island.

MARY R. ANDERLIK is a scholar affiliated with the Institute for Bioethics, Health Policy, and Law at the University of Louisville. She is the author of *The Ethics of Managed Care: A Pragmatic Approach*.

ELLEN WRIGHT CLAYTON is Rosalind E. Franklin Professor and Director of the Center for Genetics and Health Policy, professor of pediatrics, and professor of law at Vanderbilt University. She is co-author of *Bioethics And Law*.

CYNTHIA B. COHEN is senior research fellow at the Kennedy Institute of Ethics at Georgetown University. She has authored and edited eight books including *New Ways of Making Babies* and *Casebook on The Termination of Life-Sustaining Treatment and Care of the Dying*.

LINDON EAVES is an Episcopal priest. He is currently distinguished professor of human genetics and psychiatry at the Virginia Commonwealth University where he directs the Virginia Institute for Psychiatric and Behavioral Genetics. He is author of *Genes, Culture, and Personality: An Empirical Approach*.

ELIZABETH HEITMAN is professor of medicine, surgery, and anesthesiology at the University of Mississippi Medical Center in Jackson, Mississippi. She is co-author of *The Ethical Dimensions of the Biological and Health Sciences*.

JAN C. HELLER is system director of the Office of Ethics and Theology for the Providence Health System, based in Seattle. He is a priest in the Episcopal Church and author of *Human Genome Research and the Challenge of Contingent Future Persons*.

BRUCE JENNINGS is senior research scholar at the Hastings Center in Garrison, New York, and teaches at the Yale University School of Public Health. He is co-author, with Willard Gaylin, of *The Perversion of Autonomy: The Uses of Coercion in a Liberal Society* and is working on a book on chronic illness and long-term care.

TIMOTHY SEDGWICK is the Clinton S. Quin Professor of Christian Ethics at Virginia Theological Seminary in Alexandria, Virginia. He is author of *Sacramental Ethics* and *The Christian Moral Life*.

DAVID H. SMITH is professor of religious studies and director of the Poynter Center for the Study of Ethics and American Institutions at Indiana University, Bloomington. He is the author of *Health and Medicine in the Anglican Tradition*.

LEROY WALTERS is Joseph P. Kennedy, Sr. Professor of Christian Ethics at the Kennedy Institute of Ethics and professor of philosophy at Georgetown University. He is co-author of *The Ethics Of Human Gene Therapy* and co-editor of *Contemporary Issues In Bioethics* and the annual *Bibliography Of Bioethics*.

MARY T. WHITE is director of the Division of Medical Humanities at Wright State University School of Medicine in Dayton, Ohio. Her research interests include ethical issues in genetic testing and counseling, and research ethics.